THE BOOK OF
JUDGES

COMMENTARY BY

JAMES D. MARTIN

Lecturer in Hebrew and Old Testament
University of St Andrews

CAMBRIDGE UNIVERSITY PRESS

CAMBRIDGE

LONDON · NEW YORK · MELBOURNE

Published by the Syndics of the Cambridge University Press
The Pitt Building, Trumpington Street, Cambridge CB2 1RP
Bentley House, 200 Euston Road, London NW1 2DB
32 East 57th Street, New York, NY10022, USA
296 Beaconsfield Parade, Middle Park, Melbourne 3206, Australia

First published 1975

Printed in Great Britain
at the
University Printing House, Cambridge
(Euan Phillips, University Printer)

Library of Congress Cataloguing in Publication Data

Bible. O.T. Judges. English. New English. 1975.
The book of Judges.

(The Cambridge Bible commentary, New English Bible)
Bibliography: p.227
Includes index.
1. Bible. O.T. Judges–Commentaries. I. Martin,
James D., 1935– II. Title. III. Series.

BS1305.M37 1975   222'.32'077   74–31797
ISBN 0 521 08639 6 hard covers
ISNB 0 521 09768 1 paperback

GENERAL EDITORS' PREFACE

The aim of this series is to provide the text of the New English Bible closely linked to a commentary in which the results of modern scholarship are made available to the general reader. Teachers and young people have been especially kept in mind. The commentators have been asked to assume no specialized theological knowledge, and no knowledge of Greek and Hebrew. Bare references to other literature and multiple references to other parts of the Bible have been avoided. Actual quotations have been given as often as possible.

˙ The completion of the New Testament part of the series in 1967 provides a basis upon which the production of the much larger Old Testament and Apocrypha series can be undertaken. The welcome accorded to the series has been an encouragement to the editors to follow the same general pattern, and an attempt has been made to take account of criticisms which have been offered. One necessary change is the inclusion of the translators, footnotes since in the Old Testament these are more extensive, and essential for the understanding of the text.

Within the severe limits imposed by the size and scope of the series, each commentator will attempt to set out the main findings of recent biblical scholarship and to describe the historical background to the text. The main theological issues will also be critically discussed.

Much attention has been given to the form of the volumes. The aim is to produce books each of which will be read consecutively from first to last page. The introductory material leads naturally into the text, which itself leads into the alternating sections of the commentary.

The series is accompanied by three volumes of a more general character. *Understanding the Old Testament* sets out to provide the larger historical and archaeological background, to say something about the life and thought of the people of the Old Testament, and to answer the question 'Why should we study the Old Testament?'. *The Making of the Old Testament* is concerned with the formation of the books of the Old Testament and Apocrypha in the context of the ancient near eastern world, and with the ways in which these books have come down to us in the life of the Jewish and Christian communities. *Old Testament Illustrations* contains maps, diagrams and photographs with an explanatory text. These three volumes are designed to provide material helpful to the understanding of the individual books and their commentaries, but they are also prepared so as to be of use quite independently.

P.R.A.
A.R.C.L.
J.W.P.

CONTENTS

LIST OF MAPS

THE FOOTNOTES TO THE
N.E.B. TEXT

The footnotes to the N.E.B. text are designed to help the reader either to understand particular points of detail – the meaning of a name, the presence of a play upon words – or to give information about the actual text. Where the Hebrew text appears to be erroneous, or there is doubt about its precise meaning, it may be necessary to turn to manuscripts which offer a different wording, or to ancient translations of the text which may suggest a better reading, or to offer a new explanation based upon conjecture. In such cases, the footnotes supply very briefly an indication of the evidence, and whether the solution proposed is one that is regarded as possible or as probable. Various abbreviations are used in the footnotes:

(1) Some abbreviations are simply of terms used in explaining a point: *ch(s).*, chapter(s); *cp.*, compare; *lit.*, literally; *mng.*, meaning; *MS(S).*, manuscript(s), i.e. Hebrew manuscript(s), unless otherwise stated; *om.*, omit(s); *or*, indicating an alternative interpretation; *poss.*, possible; *prob.*, probable; *rdg.*, reading; *Vs(s).*, version(s).

(2) Other abbreviations indicate sources of information from which better interpretations or readings may be obtained.

Aq. Aquila, a Greek translator of the Old Testament (perhaps about A.D. 130) characterized by great literalness.

Aram. Aramaic – may refer to the text in this language (used in parts of Ezra and Daniel), or to the meaning of an Aramaic word. Aramaic belongs to the same language family as Hebrew, and is known from about 1000 B.C. over a wide area of the Middle East, including Palestine.

Heb. Hebrew – may refer to the Hebrew text or may indicate the literal meaning of the Hebrew word.

Josephus Flavius Josephus (A.D. 37/8–about 100), author of the *Jewish Antiquities*, a survey of the whole history of his people, directed partly at least to a non-Jewish audience, and of various other works, notably one on the *Jewish War* (that of A.D. 66–73) and a defence of Judaism (*Against Apion*).

Luc. Sept. Lucian's recension of the Septuagint, an important edition made in Antioch in Syria about the end of the third century A.D.

Pesh. Peshitta or Peshitto, the Syriac version of the Old Testament. Syriac is the name given chiefly to a form of Eastern Aramaic used by the Christian community. The translation varies in quality, and is at many points influenced by the Septuagint or the Targums.

Sam. Samaritan Pentateuch – the form of the first five books of the Old Testament as used by the Samaritan community. It is written in Hebrew in a special form of the Old Hebrew script, and preserves an important form of the text, somewhat influenced by Samaritan ideas.

Scroll(s) Scroll(s), commonly called the Dead Sea Scrolls, found at or near Qumran from 1947 onwards. These important manuscripts shed light on the state of the Hebrew text as it was developing in the last centuries B.C. and the first century A.D.

Sept. Septuagint (meaning 'seventy'; often abbreviated as the Roman numeral LXX), the name given to the main Greek version of the Old Testament. According to tradition, the Pentateuch was translated in Egypt in the third century B.C. by 70 (or 72) translators, six from each tribe, but the precise nature of its origin and development is not fully known. It was intended to provide Greek-speaking Jews with a convenient translation. Subsequently it came to be much revered by the Christian community.

Symm. Symmachus, another Greek translator of the Old Testament (beginning of the third century A.D.), who tried to combine literalness with good style. Both Lucian and Jerome viewed his version with favour.

Targ. Targum, a name given to various Aramaic versions of the Old Testament, produced over a long period and eventually standardized, for the use of Aramaic-speaking Jews.

Theod. Theodotion, the author of a revision of the Septuagint (probably second century A.D.), very dependent on the Hebrew text.

Vulg. Vulgate, the most important Latin version of the Old Testament, produced by Jerome about A.D. 400, and the text most used throughout the Middle Ages in western Christianity.

[...] In the text itself square brackets are used to indicate probably late additions to the Hebrew text.

(Fuller discussion of a number of these points may be found in *The Making of the Old Testament* in this series.)

THE BOOK OF
JUDGES

✳ ✳ ✳ ✳ ✳ ✳ ✳ ✳ ✳ ✳ ✳ ✳ ✳

THE BOOK AS HISTORY

The book of Judges forms part of that second main section of
the Old Testament which we refer to as the Historical Books.
To that extent, then, the book of Judges tells part of the story
of Israel's history. But the books of the Old Testament are at
the same time theological books. They are written from a
particular point of view, namely that all history is controlled
and guided by God. They are theological interpretations of
history, and to that extent we must often go behind what the
books themselves actually say to try to discover what might
be called objective historical truth. The attempt to discern
behind the theological interpretation of the historical facts
these historical facts themselves will be one of the tasks of the
commentary that follows.

The book opens with an account of the settlement of the
Israelites in Palestine (1: 1 – 2: 5). This account is composed of
different elements of varying ages, and it presents a picture of
the settlement which is often very different from the one
presented by the book of Joshua. The main body of the book
consists of a series of stories about individual heroes called
'judges' who delivered their people from oppression by
various neighbouring foreign powers (2: 6 – 12: 15). Slightly
apart from these is the figure of Samson (chs. 13–16). He
is described as a Nazirite rather than as a judge, and his exploits
are often more in the nature of practical jokes than of heroic
acts of deliverance. The book ends with two appendices.
The first (chs. 17–18) is concerned with the migration of the
tribe of Dan from the western foothills to the far north and

I

with the establishment of a sanctuary there. The second (chs. 19–21) deals with the punishment of the tribe of Benjamin for a terrible breach of the laws of hospitality committed by the Benjamites in Gibeah and with the means whereby Benjamin is enabled to survive as an Israelite tribe. The final sentence of the book (21:25) looks forward to the institution of the monarchy as a means of bringing to an end the anarchy which was at that time prevalent in the land.

Thus the book of Judges appears to present a sweep of history from the days of the settlement until the advent of the monarchy under Saul. On closer examination, however, the book is more complex than that. One of the best examples of the theological interpretation of history is to be seen in the main body of the book which deals with the activities of the judges themselves. We shall return later to the problem that there are two different kinds of judges dealt with in the book. The first are those deliverer figures, usually referred to as the 'major judges', whose activities occupy the main part of the section. The others, the so-called 'minor judges', occur in a list which is in two parts, split by the story of Jephthah (10: 1–5 and 12: 8–15). It is with the 'major judges' that we are for the moment concerned.

Their activities are presented within a framework of a cyclical scheme of history. The scheme is expounded in 2: 11–19 and consists of the following elements: abandonment of the worship of their own God and turning to the worship of other gods; punishment by God by means of subjection to oppression by foreign neighbours; the people's cry for help; God's answer in providing a 'judge' to save them from their enemies; deliverance by the judge and peace for a period of forty years; renewed apostasy on the death of the judge. This cycle, with its emphasis on divine punishment and divine deliverance, is clearly a theological interpretation of historical facts. What actually happened was a series of confrontations between Israelite population elements and other, non-Israelite elements in the surrounding areas. There was no doubt a variety of reasons why these confrontations took place. One reason may have been a conflict of interests in the areas which were being occupied. That they were due to divine punishment is clearly a theological interpretation of the events. It is part of a commentator's task to go behind the theological interpretation and to try to discover what actually happened. This is, of course, an ideal, and at this distance in time it is not always possible to realize such an ideal.

Part of the cyclical scheme was the notion that, after the deliverance, the land was at peace for forty years. In this way a chronological scheme was imposed on the whole period of the judges. Since, however, these periods of peace are usually of forty years, it is clear that this is a stereotyped round number. The figure 'forty' is commonly used in the Old Testament to denote 'a substantial period of time'. It is, therefore, quite impossible to construct an accurate chronology for the period covered by the book. The figures given for the tenure of office of the 'minor judges' are not round figures, and some attempt has been made to draw chronological conclusions on that basis. But this question partly depends on how we conceive of the role of the judge in Israel, a point to which we shall return later, and there is, in fact, no certainty that these 'minor judges' succeeded each other quite in the way the list suggests that they did. The events described in the book of Judges are probably not even arranged in chronological order. The migration northwards of the tribe of Dan, which is described towards the end of the book (chs. 17–18), probably took place relatively early in the period covered by the book, since it seems to be presupposed not only by the Samson stories in chs. 13–16 but also in the Song of Deborah (5: 17). Indeed, it is probably true to say that there is only one episode in the whole book which can be dated with any degree of accuracy, that is the battle between Israelite forces under Deborah and Barak and a combined Canaanite coalition under Sisera (chs. 4–5). Even here there is dispute as to the precise date of the event, with views varying between 1150–1125 B.C. on the one hand and 1050 B.C. on the other. For a discussion on this see below on 5: 11*b*–18.

From a historical point of view, the book of Judges des-cribes the continuing process of settlement, the beginnings of which have already been described in the book of Joshua. We read of the attempt of the Danites to find a place of settlement in the far north of the country because they have been driven from the area of their first settlement by hostile pressures. Similar hostile pressures are felt from Canaanite coalitions in the Plain of Jezreel and are broken by the forces commanded by Deborah and Barak. So the story goes on. As the Israelites continue their attempts to settle in central Palestine, so these attempts are resisted from time to time by other racial elements who also have interests in the land. Gradually the attempts of these non-Israelites are frustrated, and the Israelites are able to strengthen their hold on Palestine and to extend their area of settlement. Late in this period particularly strong pressure is felt from the Philistines, who have settled in the south-west and are trying to extend their power into the central hill-country. The confrontation between Israelites and Philistines forms the theme of the Samson stories and may well also have been one of the main reasons for the Danite migration. This confrontation remains unresolved at the end of the book. It gradually came to be realized that the loose organization of single tribes under a judge was no match for Philistine pressure, and from this realization the idea of the monarchy arose. Not until the time of David was the Philistine threat finally broken. If we think, then, of the settlement in Palestine having begun somewhere in the region of 1250 B.C. and of Saul having become king about 1000 B.C., then the most that we can say of the book of Judges as a historical work is that it tells us something of what was happening in Palestine within these 250 years.

4

LITERARY SOURCES AND COMPOSITION

The book of Judges, then, is made up of various sections each with a different topic as its main concern. If we now approach the book from a literary rather than from a historical point of view, we must ask what the origins of these various sections were and how and by whom they were put together. As with most books of the Old Testament there can be no question here of a single author at work from beginning to end of the book. There are too many differences in style for that to be the case. Needless to say, various theories have been put forward over the centuries of scholarly study of the Bible as a solution to the question of the origins and authorship of the book of Judges. Here we can do no more than sketch which one is the most likely.

There is nowadays a fair consensus of opinion which would suggest that the book of Judges is part of a larger whole. That larger whole comprises the books of Joshua, Judges, Samuel and Kings with the book of Deuteronomy as its preface. (The book of Ruth did not originally belong where it now stands in the English Bible; see *The Making of the Old Testament* in this series, p. 119.) This is considered to be a unified work of history written from the standpoint expressed in the book of Deuteronomy, and the name usually applied to it is the Deuteronomistic History. (The adjective 'deuteronomistic' is used to refer to this historical work; the adjective 'deuteronomic' refers to the style, content, thought, etc., of the book of Deuteronomy.) It seems fairly clear that the deuteronomistic historian, who made his final compilation about the year 550 B.C., did not compose his story from beginning to end but made use of various sources and earlier compilations which he found to hand. On these he very often imposed his own point of view or his own particular theological ideas. We have already seen an example of this in the cyclical view of the history of the period which is a feature of the central section of the book (2: 6 – 12: 15).

It is in this central section of the book, too, that we can see what the deuteronomistic historian's sources were and how he went about fitting them together. We have already noted the fact that in this part of the book two different kinds of judges are referred to. There are the figures who delivered the people from the recurring experiences of foreign oppression, and there are those who are merely listed in 10: 1–5 and 12: 8–15 and of whom nothing is said beyond the fact that they 'judged' Israel. It seems probable that the Deuteronomist had in front of him, for the history of the period between the settlement and the rise of the monarchy, two blocks of material. On the one hand there was a collection of stories about tribal heroes of the past and on the other a list of people who had held some kind of office of 'judge' in pre-monarchic Israel. The fact that Jephthah appeared in both of these blocks gave the Deuteronomist the idea of combining both blocks into one. This seems likely in the first instance because, in the present form of the book, the Jephthah story (10: 6 – 12: 7) occurs half-way through what must surely have originally been a continuous list. The second reason for such an assumption is that the Jephthah story ends in 12: 7 with a note about the length of his tenure of office as judge and about his burial in a specific place. These two pieces of information are given for all of the 'minor judges' but not, generally speaking, for the 'major judges'. It is highly likely, then, that the list of 'minor judges' included a section on Jephthah in terms similar to the others. Of that section only the concluding note about length of tenure and place of burial survives. The collection of hero sagas also included material about Jephthah, all of which has been preserved in 11: 1 – 12: 6, and this was used by the deuteronomistic historian to replace more general material of the 'minor judges' type. The Deuteronomist placed these stories about past tribal heroes within his cyclical framework of apostasy, punishment and deliverance. As these stories are now told, they involve 'all Israel' on the one hand and the foreign oppressor on the other. The 'judge' becomes judge of 'all Israel'. As we shall see in the commentary, however, these stories involve usually only one or, at the most, two tribes, and their sphere of action is usually fairly local. It is not certain whether this 'all Israel' context was given to the stories by the deuteronomistic historian or whether this aspect was already part of the collection of stories as he found it. So by the fusion of two different blocks of source material the deuteronomistic historian compiled the central section of the present book of Judges and made it part of his larger work.

The Deuteronomistic History was originally a continuous narrative. Only at a later stage was it broken up into the individual books which we now know. It is probable that only the central section of the present book of Judges (2: 6 – 12: 15, possibly to 13: 1) originally formed part of this continuous narrative. Judg. 13: 1 was probably followed immediately by 1 Sam. 1: 1, the beginning of the story of the next 'judge', Samuel. When this continuous narrative was being broken up, the opportunity arose for the insertion of various blocks of material of different kinds. Although Samuel is referred to as a 'judge', he is perhaps primarily thought of as 'the kingmaker'. He is the immediate forerunner of the monarchy and the point where his story begins was felt to be an appropriate point for the insertion of those two appendices which lay so much emphasis on the idea that the anarchic state of the country is due to the absence of a monarchic form of government (17: 6; 18: 1; 19: 1, 25). The second of the two appendices is, as we shall see, the product of very late editing after the exile. There are no definite signs one way or the other which would determine the date of the first appendix, but those verses which emphasize the absence of monarchic rule link it closely with the second, and the two must be considered to be of a piece.

The Samson stories, as we shall also see in the commentary, are of a different kind from the stories about the old tribal heroes. They are strongly influenced by sun mythology, and it is doubtful if there are any historical facts of any significance behind this cycle of stories. The suggestion has also been made that the Samson cycle is an attempt to collect local folk-lore from the original area of Danite settlement before it became lost forever at the time of the northward migration of the tribe. The background of the Samson stories is that of Philistine oppression. This was the main issue of the Samuel–Saul period, so the story of the beginnings of that oppression could be conveniently fitted in at this point before the story of Samuel began.

The situation at the beginning of the book of Judges is slightly more complex. In Judg. 2: 6–9 we have a note about the death and burial-place of Joshua. An almost identical note is to be found in Josh. 24: 28–31. In a continuous narrative such as the Deuteronomistic History there would be no need for this to be noted twice, and it looks as if one is a simple repetition of the other. The question is why this repetition occurred and which of the two is the original occurrence. A reference to Joshua's death and burial-place follows naturally on the end of his final speech to the Israelites, that is, as a sequel to Josh. 24: 27. But the same note also serves naturally as an introduction to the Deuteronomist's cycle of apostasy, punishment and deliverance, that is, as a prelude to Judg. 2: 10ff. It is difficult to decide where the priority lies, but on balance it appears to be with the occurrence in Judges. The sequel in Judg. 2: 10ff. is a natural one. The cycle of apostasy, punish-ment and deliverance has its beginning after the death of Joshua, just as it recurs after the death of each successive judge. Judg. 1: 1 – 2: 5 contains two accounts of the settlement in Palestine, the first a pro-Judaean one (1: 1–21), the second orientated towards the north (1: 22 – 2: 5). The insertion of these *before* the note about the death of Joshua seems most likely. The settlement of the Israelites in Palestine took place under the leadership of Joshua and must therefore have been completed before he died. The opening words of the book are then most probably editorial, perhaps even modelled on the opening words of the book of Joshua, 'After the death of

Moses...' When the separate books were being formed, it was felt appropriate that the book of Joshua should end with a note about Joshua's death. So the notice about his death was repeated at the end of his final speech, in Josh. 24: 28–31.

Thus, it can be seen that from small beginnings the book of Judges has grown over the centuries until it has reached its present form. From the formation of two independent sources into the nucleus of 2: 6 – 13: 1 as part of the Deuteronomistic History, the process of literary accretion continued until at last we have the book in the form in which we now know it.

THE ROLE OF THE JUDGE IN EARLY ISRAEL

We have already noted how there were originally two completely independent sources dealing with 'judges' in early Israel and how the different kinds of judge are usually referred to as 'major judges' and 'minor judges'. The questions we must now try to answer are 'What exactly were these judges?' and 'What, if any, is the connection between the two different kinds?'

One fairly well-established theory about the function of the judge in early Israel is based on the notion that in the period immediately before the emergence of the monarchy the Israelite tribes formed a particular kind of association, for which the term 'amphictyony' is used. This term comes from Greek, and both in Greece and in Italy such associations are found. They were confederacies of tribes or peoples centred round a sanctuary. The principal function of these confederacies was the care and maintenance of that central sanctuary. This, it is argued, was the pattern in Israel as well. The Israelite tribes formed an amphictyony whose focus of amphictyonic activity was also a central sanctuary. It was the location of the Ark, that symbol of God's presence with his people, which determined where the central sanctuary was. The central sanctuary in ancient Israel was in different places in succession. To begin with it was located at Shechem, and then it moved to Bethel and then Gilgal before finally being established in Shiloh which is the principal sanctuary during the time of Samuel. This argument goes on to lay considerable emphasis on the list of 'minor judges' (10: 1–5; 12: 8–15) where we have an unbroken succession of the names of 'judges' with their terms of office noted in exact numbers of years. The suggestion is that these 'judges' were the principal figures in the amphictyony and that the core of the amphictyony was 'law'. The 'judges' were, so it is argued, legal functionaries whose task it was to expound the law to the assembled tribes at the central sanctuary. This, of course, refers to the so-called 'minor judges'. The transference of the title of 'judge' to the old tribal heroes is due to the occurrence of Jephthah in both blocks of material. Since Jephthah, the Gileadite tribal hero, also figured as an 'amphictynonic judge', it was assumed that the other tribal heroes must have had similar functions. In this way the title of 'judge' was extended from those to whom by right it belonged to those whose functions betray no sign of any judicial activity.

Recently, however, this idea of the existence of an amphictyony in ancient Israel has come under increasing criticism. The sanctuaries which were said to have been 'central' sanctuaries are not now regarded as such with so much confidence. Certainly in the book of Judges there is little indication that any of the places suggested was ever a central sanctuary in this period. Shechem is actually a Canaanite city according to ch. 9. Judg. 20: 27f. connects the Ark with Bethel, and Judg. 21: 12 suggests that Shiloh was a place of assembly for the tribes, but the final appendix to the book of Judges (chs. 19–21) is difficult to evaluate as a historical source, and there is much to suggest that it is a compilation of a very late date. Both the passages mentioned have all the signs of being very late glosses on the place-names in question. The main, if not the sole, function of an amphictyony was for the tribes who formed it to care in turn for the central sanctuary. Of such activity in Israel there is no sign at all. Another sign of an amphictyony was that the law which governed it was concerned mainly with the rights and duties of the tribes with regard to the central sanctuary and with the punishment of those who contravened that law. Again, of such a law there is no sign in Israel.

One might, then, say that the argument is about the use of the word 'amphictyony' and that a less weighted term such as 'tribal confederacy' might be acceptable. But even then there is really very little sign of united tribal activity. In most of the stories in the book of Judges only one or, at most, two tribes are involved. There are two exceptions to this statement. In the final appendix, the 'tribes of Israel' wage war against Benjamin, but, as we have just noted, the historical reliability of chs. 19–21 is far from certain. Again, in ch. 5 a coalition of six Israelite tribes takes the field under Barak against Sisera, but in the prose account of that same encounter in ch. 4, only two tribes are involved. All in all, it is very uncertain whether in the period of the judges one can even speak of a 'tribal confederacy' involving the majority, or even a substantial number, of those units which later come to form Israel.

In the book of Judges, there are only two places where a legal sense of the word 'judge' is clearly demanded. One of them (11: 27) has nothing to do with the 'judges' themselves. It refers the decision in the dispute between the Israelites and the Ammonites to God. The other (4: 5) refers to Deborah and seems to imply some kind of legal, consultative function on her part. There are, however, grounds for believing that the verse in question might be secondary to its context. If the Israelite 'judges' are not judges in the legal sense, what, then, was their function? Recent study has begun to look at the occurrences of the equivalent of the Hebrew word for 'judge' in other Semitic languages and in other ancient Near Eastern social and political contexts to see if any light can be shed on the function of the 'judge' in Israel. The main, though not the only, evidence has come from the ancient city of Mari on the upper Euphrates from about 1800 B.C. An official there, whose title is related to that of the Hebrew 'judge', seems to have been a kind of local governor. His duties certainly seem to have involved the administration of justice. It was also his duty, however, to muster troops, to despatch them on the missions where they were needed and eventually to disband them when their tasks had been accomplished. He also had to do with the securing of booty in war and with the protection of the countryside from plundering nomads.

In the 'minor judges' list, there is no certainty that the element of succession which was so essential to the amphictyonic theory is original. There is at least the possibility that it is modelled on the succession element in the king lists of later Israel of which 1 Kings 11: 42–3 is an example. The concept 'Israel' in the judges list may well also reflect later usage. One element which must be primary, however, is that the persons referred to 'judged'. If that element is removed, no other function is attributed to the persons figuring in the list. Another important element is that these 'minor judges' seem to have been very local functionaries. They are associated not with tribes or tribal areas but with towns, in which they are then said to have been buried. If we now apply the information gleaned from other cultures we can reach the following conclusions with regard to the 'judges' of Israel.

Two factors must be stressed at the outset. One is that the so-called 'minor judges' are a much more local phenomenon than they are usually supposed to be. The other is that their sphere of activity should not be restricted to the merely judicial. Only the title 'judge' has led to the conclusion that they were judicial officials, but such functions are nowhere unambiguously ascribed to them.

In the earlier period of the Israelite settlement what was important was the nomadic unit, the clan or the tribe. In this situation the 'judge' was the local leader, possibly along much the same lines as the Mari official. He was responsible for any necessary military action such as defending the territory claimed by his clan or tribe against similar claims by rival nomadic or semi-nomadic groups. It is clear from the narratives in which these 'judges' figure that this was the kind of function they fulfilled. Strictly speaking, the title 'judge' is not widely used of these figures except in the deuteronomistic framework (2: 16–19). But in using the title 'judge' the deuteronomistic historian is perhaps coming very close to the kind of role which they played within their particular social and political context. As the process of settlement went on, the nomadic unit became less important as the people became more settled. Now it was the town which became the significant unit, a process which can be referred to as one of urbanization. It is at this stage that the so-called 'minor judges' seem to have functioned. One can perhaps suggest that they were the local rulers in an urban situation. It is difficult to be other than tentative when speaking of their function, since we know so little about them. They no doubt participated in the judicial administration in their particular urban areas, but their duties surely covered other more general administrative spheres as well. The little information we have about them seems to suggest that they were figures of some considerable power and standing.

So the 'judges' of the pre-monarchic period in Israel were local leaders and rulers functioning against the changing social and political background of the times. In the early settlement period their functions were more of a military nature with regard to the nomadic or semi-nomadic unit from which they came. But in the on-going process of urbanization they became figures of considerable, though local, prestige whose functions may have been less military and more of a judicial kind. Thus both types of 'judge' referred to in the book of Judges, the 'major judges' and the 'minor judges', can be seen to be essentially of the same type, but operating at different periods in the process of the Israelite settlement in Palestine.

THE BOOK AS PART OF A LARGER WHOLE

We have already had occasion more than once to emphasize that the nucleus of the present book of Judges was part of a continuing narrative which is usually referred to as the Deuteronomistic History. To this nucleus, as we have seen, various elements have been added to form the book as we now have it. The continuity of the Deuteronomist's story has been broken and fragmented, and we now no longer have the sweep of history as he originally wrote it. But the present book of Judges is still part of a larger whole. We began by saying that it is one of what we call the Historical Books of the Old Testament. This second part of the Old Testament is referred to by the Jews as the Former Prophets. This title was given to the books of Joshua, Judges, Samuel and Kings because they were believed to have been written by prophetic figures, the book of Judges, for example, by Samuel. But the Jewish title also has a deeper significance. The prophets proclaimed what they believed to be God's will for his people, and, in God's name, they demanded the people's obedience to that will.

But the Jews believed, too, that God spoke to his people through their history. Time and again in the Old Testament we find someone reciting the facts of Israel's history and emphasizing that this shows God's guidance of his people in the past and that such guidance demands their faithfulness to him in the present and in the future. There is an example of such a recital in the book of Judges where the words are put into the mouth of an anonymous prophet (6: 8–10). This history is the history of salvation, and it is the history of salvation that is told not only in the Former Prophets but also in many other parts of the Old Testament. What we have, in this book and in the other historical books as well, is not history as such, but theological history. What we have is the word of God made living in the events of Israel's past.

We must remember that these events are not recorded for

an audience nearly contemporary with the events themselves, but for an audience of a much later age who were meant to see in them a moral which would be of relevance to themselves and to their own age. The word which is made living in these past events is first of all a word of judgement, judgement on an Israel which, from the earliest stages in her history, had been unfaithful to the God who had chosen her and had led her into the promised land. It is also a word of encouragement and assurance. No matter how often Israel is unfaithful to her God, he is always ready to respond to their sincere plea for mercy and forgiveness. The history of the past has been under his guidance; the course of events has been controlled by him. It is also a word of hope for the future. The years of Israel's settlement in the land which her God had given her have been difficult and troubled years, but the last words of the book in its present form look forward to more settled times, times of greater glory. The difficulties of the settlement are explained as due to the absence of a stable, central government. With a king and people both faithful to their God, Israel will be able to go from strength to strength. This idea was only partially to be realized in the years and centuries ahead, but that is taking the story beyond the confines of the present book. There is no hint in the closing words of the book of Judges of the story of unfaithfulness and failure which will unfold through the period of monarchy in both Judah and Israel. These closing words do not ring down the curtain at the end of the play, they carry us on in hopeful anticipation to the next act in God's unfolding drama of salvation.

✻   ✻   ✻   ✻   ✻   ✻   ✻   ✻   ✻   ✻   ✻   ✻   ✻

The conquest of Canaan completed

✻ As we have seen, when the Deuteronomistic History was being broken up into the separate books which we know today, Judg. 2: 6–9 was repeated in Josh. 24: 28–31 and the opening words of Judg. I ('after the death of Joshua') were added (see further above, pp. 8f. and below, pp. 33f.). Judg. I: I – 2: 5 had then to refer to events which had happened *after* the death of Joshua, that is, to the 'completion' of the conquest of Canaan which had been begun under him. But Judg. I: I – 2: 5 is a late collection of very old traditions referring to events which took place during the Israelite settlement in Palestine at very different and often widely separated times. Some of these traditions are old, but while pieces of old tradition may contain historical facts, age does not, of itself, guarantee historical accuracy. Some of them are in conflict with the facts of history as we know them, but the general picture which they present, that of a gradual settlement, is truer to these facts than the swift, wholesale conquest narrated in Joshua. The section I: I–20 deals with the southern part of Palestine, and was probably put together in Judah in the period of the divided monarchy. Verses 21–36 probably originated in the northern half of Palestine before the reign of David. ✻

THE SETTLEMENT IN SOUTHERN PALESTINE

1 AFTER THE DEATH of Joshua the Israelites inquired of the LORD which tribe should attack the Canaanites
2 first. The LORD answered, 'Judah shall attack. I hereby
3 deliver the country into his power.' Judah said to his brother Simeon, 'Go forward with me into my allotted territory, and let us do battle with the Canaanites; then I

in turn will go with you into your territory.' So Simeon 4
went with him; then Judah advanced to the attack, and
the LORD delivered the Canaanites and Perizzites into their
hands. They slaughtered ten thousand of them at Bezek.
There they came upon Adoni-bezek, engaged him in 5
battle and defeated the Canaanites and Perizzites. Adoni- 6
bezek fled, but they pursued him, took him prisoner and
cut off his thumbs and his great toes. Adoni-bezek said, 7
'I once had seventy kings whose thumbs and great toes
were cut off picking up the scraps from under my table.
What I have done God has done to me.' He was brought
to Jerusalem and died there.

The men of Judah made an assault on Jerusalem and 8
captured it, put its people to the sword and set fire to the
city. Then they turned south to fight the Canaanites of 9
the hill-country, the Negeb, and the Shephelah. Judah 10
attacked the Canaanites in Hebron, formerly called
Kiriath-arba, and defeated Sheshai, Ahiman and Talmai.
From there they marched against the inhabitants of Debir, 11
formerly called Kiriath-sepher. Caleb said, 'Whoever 12
attacks Kiriath-sepher and captures it, to him I will give
my daughter Achsah in marriage.' Othniel, son of Caleb's 13
younger brother Kenaz, captured it, and Caleb gave him
his daughter Achsah. When she came to him, he incited 14
her[a] to ask her father for a piece of land. As she sat on the
ass, she made a noise, and Caleb said, 'What did you mean
by that?' She replied, 'I want to ask a favour of you. You 15
have put me in this dry Negeb; you must give me pools
of water as well.' So Caleb gave her the upper pool and
the lower pool.

[a] *So Sept.; Heb.* she incited him.

16   The descendants of Moses' father-in-law, the Kenite,
went up with the men of Judah from the Vale of Palm
Trees to the wilderness of Judah which is in the Negeb of
17   Arad and settled among the Amalekites.[a] Judah then
accompanied his brother Simeon, attacked the Canaanites
in Zephath and destroyed it; hence the city was called
18   Hormah.[b] Judah took Gaza, Ashkelon, and Ekron, and
19   the territory of each. The LORD was with Judah and they
occupied the hill-country, but they could not drive out the
inhabitants of the Vale because they had chariots of iron.
20   Hebron was given to Caleb as Moses had directed, and
he drove out the three sons of Anak.

✳ I. *After the death of Joshua*: an editorial heading to the book,
possibly modelled on the opening phrase of the book of
Joshua, 'After the death of Moses'. *the Israelites inquired of the
LORD*: the word 'inquired' is the English rendering of a
technical term in Hebrew meaning 'to seek an oracle'. There
is no indication as to how this was done on this occasion, but
various means were used in later periods, the most important
of which was the use of the sacred lot Urim and Thummim.
The best illustration of the working of Urim and Thummim
is to be found in 1 Sam. 14: 41–2; it was probably some kind
of device which produced the answers 'yes' and 'no' to given
questions.

2. *Judah shall attack*: Judah is here given priority over the
rest of the tribes, but it is very probable that Judah, as a tribe,
did not emerge until David first established his kingdom
at Hebron. When Judah did emerge as a tribe, we discover
that it was composed of various elements, some of whom
are enumerated in this chapter: Simeonites, Calebites, Othnielites and Kenizzites. The fact that Judah is given priority

[a] *So one MS. of Sept.; Heb.* among the people.
[b] *That is* Destruction.

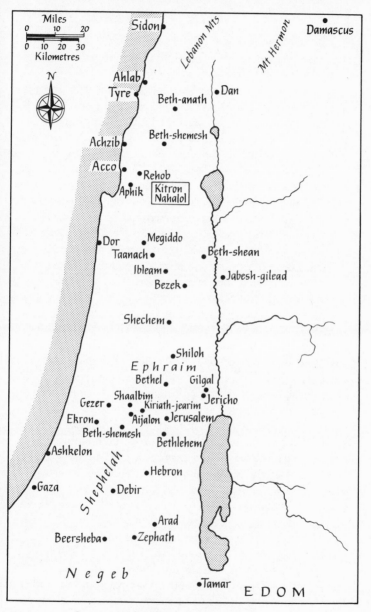

1. Conquest and settlement (1: 1–2: 5; Chs. 17–18)

throughout this first part of Judg. 1 inclines us to the view that this section of the chapter was put together to the greater glory of Judah.

3. *his brother Simeon*: the Simeonites were a tribe related to the Judahites, who eventually absorbed the smaller and weaker unit. *my allotted territory*: Josh. 13–19 contains an elaborate scheme according to which specific territories both east and west of the Jordan were allocated to specific tribes.

4. *the Canaanites and Perizzites*: 'Canaanite' is here a general term for the pre-Israelite inhabitants of Palestine. The Hebrew word *perāzōt* means 'open, unwalled settlements', and the term 'Perizzites' may be descriptive of the inhabitants of such places rather than the name of a people. *They slaughtered ten thousand of them at Bezek*: the figure 'ten thousand' is the equivalent of 'a large number'. The site of Bezek has been much debated, but it would seem likely that it was located north-east of Shechem.

5–7. The tradition preserved in Gen. 34 reminds us that, although the Simeonites eventually settled in the south, in the area around Beersheba, they probably, in their nomadic days, penetrated as far north as Shechem. The tradition here seems to preserve the memory of an encounter between the nomadic Simeonites and the city-state of Bezek, an encounter in which the Simeonites appear to have gained some kind of victory. It is probable that, in the course of the transmission of this tribal reminiscence, the details have been embroidered and the extent of the victory exaggerated. At a later stage in the history of the Simeonites, when they became virtually absorbed into the larger tribe of Judah, this tradition became associated with the tribe of Judah as well. *Adoni-bezek*: Hebrew names which have the word 'Adoni' ('lord') as their first element usually have the name of a god as the second element, e.g. Adonijah means 'Jah (i.e. Yahweh) is lord'. In this case, however, we do not know of any god called Bezek. On the other hand, no other example is known of this type of name with the name of a city as the second element, but if this were the case here, then the name of the king would be 'Lord of Bezek'. The similarity of the name Adoni-bezek to that of Adoni-zedek, the king of Jerusalem mentioned in Josh. 10, has been noted, and it has sometimes been suggested that this narrative in verses 5–7 is simply a variant of the tradition recorded in Josh. 10. However, the two narratives are so dissimilar that such a view must be regarded as highly improbable. *cut off his thumbs and his great toes*: such mutilation of prisoners of war is not unknown in the ancient world, though the sources usually cited are from the Graeco-Roman world and from a much later period than this. The reference to the *seventy kings* in the following verse is again clearly a legendary exaggeration. *He was brought to Jerusalem*: it is not clear why Adoni-bezek was taken to Jerusalem or by whom. It may be that some traditionist noted the similarity between the names Adoni-bezek and Adoni-zedek and felt that Adoni-bezek, too, had been king of Jerusalem.

8. This is a puzzling verse since it is contradicted not only by verse 21 but also by the facts of history as we know them, namely that Jerusalem remained a Jebusite city-state until it was captured by David (2 Sam. 5: 6–10). The presence of the verse here may be explained as due to the closing words of verse 7. If Adoni-bezek was taken to Jerusalem, his conquerors, the Judahites and Simeonites, were naturally thought to possess the city already.

9. *the hill-country, the Negeb, and the Shephelah*: the hill-country was the upland region lying immediately to the west of, and parallel to, the Dead Sea. The Shephelah is the term used to denote the western foothills of that upland region where it slopes down towards the Mediterranean coastal strip. The Negeb is a general term for the southern part of the country to the south of Beersheba.

10. The tradition preserved here attributes the conquest of Hebron to Judah. Verse 20, on the other hand, is in line with the main strand of Old Testament tradition, such as we find it in Num. 14: 24 and Josh. 15: 13ff., where the capture and

occupation of Hebron are associated with Caleb. Like the Adoni-bezek tradition, the Hebron tradition, too, has been appropriated by Judah.

11-15. These verses are paralleled, with only minor variations, in Josh. 15: 15-19. This tradition seems to reflect the occupation of Debir/Kiriath-sepher by the Othnielites, as well as the transference of certain water-holes from the Calebites to the Othnielites. This tribal and territorial history is expressed in the form of a personal narrative, the details of which are not all entirely clear. The word rendered here by *she made a noise* (i.e. 'broke wind' as in the first edition of N.E.B.) has also been translated as 'she alighted (from the ass)' (Revised Standard Version) or 'she clapped her hands (to attract her father's attention)'. The site of the water-holes in question cannot be located with certainty, but this tradition would suggest that Debir and Hebron shared a common water-system and that Debir is, therefore, to be located in close proximity to Hebron.

16f. *the Vale of Palm Trees*: literally and more usually rendered as 'City of Palms', it is a description sometimes applied to Jericho (cp. Deut. 34: 3; 2 Chron. 28: 15). But in view of the fact that the Kenites originated in the Sinai peninsula and are later found in the Negeb, and that the incursion described here is aimed at Arad which lies about 17 miles (27 km) due south of Hebron, it is unlikely that this attack in which the Kenites participated originated from Jericho. What is more likely is that the city Tamar, whose name was identical with the Hebrew word for 'palm-tree' and which was situated about 5 miles (8 km) south-west of the southern tip of the Dead Sea, became confused in the minds of later writers and editors with the descriptive term sometimes applied to Jericho. This confusion was made the more easily because the mainstream of Old Testament tradition associates the 'invasion' of Palestine by the Israelites as having come from east of the Jordan in the region of Jericho. This verse and the following one too, in so far as Zephath probably lies about 10 miles

(16 km) east of Beersheba, suggest the possibility, of which there are hints elsewhere in the Old Testament, that there was an invasion of Palestine from the south. It would seem likely that those smaller tribal units, some of whom make up the tribal entity we know as Judah, Calebites, Othnielites and Kenites, entered Palestine from this direction.

18. This verse is historically so unlikely that the translators of the Old Testament into Greek eased the difficulty by making the sentence negative. The Philistine cities listed here were probably not incorporated into Judah before the seventh century B.C. during the reign of Josiah, a period of territorial expansion. The present form of the text can be explained as yet another example of the tendency to exaggerate the role and the sphere of influence of Judah.

19. The word translated *Vale* in this verse is often used in the Old Testament to refer to the Valley or Plain of Jezreel. Such a geographical reference makes no sense in connection with Judah and it has been suggested that this excuse for the slow military advance of Judah has been borrowed from the Joseph traditions where it occurs correctly in a passage such as Josh. 17: 16. This is in line with the tendency which we have already noted to appropriate to Judah traditions which are more correctly to be attached elsewhere. The word occurs again in verse 34 where it seems to refer to the 'valleys' leading down towards the coastal plain from the Judaean hill country, and it may be that this is the sense intended here, too. A third possibility is to understand the word as referring to the coastal plain, but this sense is not found elsewhere in the Old Testament. The period of the Israelite settlement in Palestine (the late thirteenth century B.C.) coincided with the transition from the Bronze Age to the Iron Age. The use of *chariots of iron* (probably 'plated with iron') by the Canaanites marks the beginnings of the use of iron for weapons in this period. Only later, in the twelfth century, did the use of iron become widespread. The sophisticated armoury of the

Canaanites was easily superior to that of the incoming, semi-nomadic Israelites.

20. We have already noted, in connection with verse 10, that this is the more authentic version of the capture of Hebron, by Caleb rather than by Judah. *the three sons of Anak* were the Sheshai, Ahiman and Talmai mentioned above in verse 10. These were legendary, apparently giant-like, figures who are first mentioned in Num. 13: 22 and who are reputed to have lived in Hebron. The word 'Anak' in Hebrew means 'necklace', and the oldest form of their name refers to them as 'sons of the necklace'. The original sense of this is obscure, but it may refer in some way to their unusual height. Only later was 'Anak' thought of as a proper name.

So this first part of Judg. 1 contains a number of very ancient traditions about tribes whose home was in the southern part of Palestine and about the penetration and settlement of some of these tribes in the southern part of the country, coming either from the Negeb or from the south-east, the region around Tamar. This collection of unrelated stories gives prominence to Judah and attributes to Judah actions which other traditions more plausibly attribute to other tribes. Probably, therefore, the collection was put together in Judah. Since there is no mention of the northern tribes at all, it may have been made after the split between the kingdoms of Judah and Israel on the death of Solomon. ✳

THE SETTLEMENT IN CENTRAL AND NORTHERN PALESTINE

21 But the Benjamites did not drive out the Jebusites of Jerusalem; and the Jebusites have lived on in Jerusalem with the Benjamites till the present day.

22 The tribes[a] of Joseph attacked Bethel, and the LORD
23 was with them. They sent spies to Bethel, formerly called

[a] *Lit.* house.

Luz. These spies saw a man coming out of the city and 24
said to him, 'Show us how to enter the city, and we will
see that you come to no harm.' So he showed them how to 25
enter, and they put the city to the sword, but let the man
and his family go free. He went into Hittite country, 26
built a city and named it Luz, which is still its name today.

Manasseh did not drive out the inhabitants of Beth- 27
shean with its villages, nor of Taanach, Dor, Ibleam, and
Megiddo, with the villages of each of them; the Canaanites
held their ground in that region. Later, when Israel 28
became strong, they put them to forced labour, but they
never completely drove them out.

Ephraim did not drive out the Canaanites who 29
lived in Gezer, but the Canaanites lived among them
there.

Zebulun did not drive out the inhabitants of Kitron and 30
Nahalol, but the Canaanites lived among them and were
put to forced labour.

Asher did not drive out the inhabitants of Acco and 31
Sidon, of Ahlab,*a* Achzib, Helbah, Aphik and Rehob.
Thus the Asherites lived among the Canaanite inhabitants 32
and did not drive them out.

Naphtali did not drive out the inhabitants of Beth- 33
shemesh and of Beth-anath, but lived among the Canaanite inhabitants and put the inhabitants of Beth-shemesh
and Beth-anath to forced labour.

The Amorites pressed the Danites back into the hill- 34
country and did not allow them to come down into the
Vale. The Amorites held their ground in Mount Heres 35
and in Aijalon and Shaalbim, but the tribes of Joseph

[a] Mehalbeh *in Josh. 19: 29.*

increased their pressure on them until they reduced them to forced labour.

36   The boundary of the Edomites[a] ran from the ascent of Akrabbim, upwards from Sela.

✶ 21. This verse really belongs with what follows, though in the N.E.B. it is treated as the conclusion to the first part of the chapter. Like verses 27 and 29 and several others, it tells of the inability of the Benjamites to drive out the local inhabitants and of the continuing co-existence of the two groups. This suggests that the verse belongs with the second part of the chapter, the so-called 'negative account of the conquest'. The verse occurs again in Josh. 15: 63 with 'the men of Judah' in place of *the Benjamites*. This difference is no doubt due to the fact that at a later historical period Jerusalem became the capital of Judah. It is not clear, even from the descriptions of the tribal boundaries in Josh. 15: 6–11 and Josh. 18: 21–8, whether Jerusalem lay within the territory of Benjamin or the territory of Judah. (On this problem see the commentary on *Joshua* in this series, especially on Josh. 15: 6–11.)

22–6. These verses contain a tradition about the capture of Bethel by the Joseph tribes. *The tribes of Joseph* were Ephraim and Manasseh, but in view of the fact that separate notices about them are given in verses 27f. and verse 29, it may be that the capture of Bethel was achieved by the united tribe of Joseph before it split up. There is archaeological evidence for the destruction of Bethel by fire sometime during the thirteenth century B.C., and this may be reflected in the present tradition. The term *Hittite* is used rather loosely in the Old Testament, sometimes as a general term for the original inhabitants of Palestine. The Hittite Empire, as such, was centred in Asia Minor, and at the height of its power it extended into Syria and Mesopotamia. Apart from occasional

[a] *So one form of Sept.; Heb.* Amorites.

Old Testament references to Hittites in Palestine there is no strong evidence to suggest that there were Hittite settlements any further south than Hamath in North Syria. To this area, then, one could presume that the man from Bethel went, but there is as yet no evidence of the existence of a place called Luz in that northern area.

27f. This is the second of the series of notices which stress the limitations of the settlement of the Israelite tribes in central and northern Palestine. They occur in Judg. 1 in the form of a list; some of them have also been incorporated at various points within Josh. 15–19 where the tribal territories are being described. In this instance see Josh. 17: 11–13. The native inhabitants were able to maintain their hold on certain fortified settlements, each of which had associated with it a number of small, unwalled *villages*, the inhabitants of which would have recourse to the main settlement in times of danger. The places mentioned here curve round the southern edge of the Plain of Jezreel and include Dor which lay on the coast south of the Carmel ridge. With the exception of Dor, they guarded important approaches to the Plain. The notice further informs us that at a later stage the Israelite element in the population became sufficiently strong to enslave the Canaanite element. This no doubt reflects the circumstances of the period of the monarchy when Israel's political power and ambitions increased greatly and when the local populations were forced into slavery and to work in the king's ambitious building programmes. The main emphasis, however, both here and in the notices which follow, is on the continuing co-existence of the two elements in the population.

29. Cp. Josh. 16: 10. Here again, in Ephraimite territory, the continuing co-existence of Israelites and Canaanites is mentioned in connection with *Gezer*, an important Canaanite city which eventually became part of Israel when the Pharaoh of Egypt sacked it and gave it to Solomon as part of his daughter's dowry (1 Kings 9: 16).

30. This verse has no precise parallel in Joshua, though

Josh. 19: 10–16 describes the territory allotted to Zebulun. In verse 15 there, Nahalal and Kattath, the latter thought by some to be a variant of Kitron in the Judges verse, are listed as belonging to Zebulun. We have, however, no very strong evidence for locating the sites of these two places. Nothing more definite can be suggested than that they lay somewhere on the north-western edge of the Plain of Jezreel.

31f. The territory allotted to the tribe of Asher lay in the extreme north-west of Palestine, from Mount Carmel to north of Tyre. The places mentioned here all appear to lie in that region. Not all of them can be located with certainty, and Helbah may simply be a variant of Ahlab. Cp. Josh. 19:29f.

33. The territory of the tribe of Naphtali lay inland from that of Asher, to the west and north of the Sea of Chinnereth. Beth-shemesh and Beth-anath both lay in that area, in Galilee. Again we have a reference to the presumably eventual enslavement of the Canaanite element in the population, although there is no time-reference here as there is, e.g., in verse 28.

34f. The territory originally allotted to the tribe of Dan lay in the foothills to the west and north-west of Jerusalem, but all the evidence suggests that they never really settled there and were forced to migrate to the area of the upper reaches of the Jordan. The present passage suggests that the reason for this migration was the strong pressure exerted by the Amorites. The latter were, strictly speaking, a Semitic-speaking people who invaded Palestine and settled there at the end of the third, and the beginning of the second, millennium B.C. (i.e. about 2000 B.C.). Often in the Old Testament, however, the name 'Amorite' is simply used as an archaic term for the pre-Israelite inhabitants of Palestine. The word *Vale* here is being used to refer to the valleys leading down through the foothills to the coastal plain (see above on verse 19). Aijalon and Shaalbim were both important fortified towns in the valley of Aijalon, and Mount Heres is usually regarded as identical with Beth-shemesh (both *Heres* and *Shemesh*

mean 'sun'), which lay further south. *the tribes of Joseph* here
probably included Benjamin, whose territory lay immediately
to the east of the places referred to here, while the territory
of Ephraim lay to the north. Joseph and Benjamin were both
sons of Rachel according to the traditional Israelite genealogy
(cp. Gen. 35: 24). Note, again, the reference to the eventual
enslavement of the Amorite element in the population.

36. This final verse of the chapter may well have originally
formed part of a longer description of the boundaries between
Israel and her neighbours: cp. Josh. 15: 1–4 for the southern
boundary of the territory allotted to Judah. The Hebrew
text reads 'Amorites' at this point, but, from the places
mentioned, it seems likely that the more correct reading is
Edomites, Israel's neighbours on the south-east. *the ascent of
Akrabbim* ('scorpions') lies to the north of the road from the
Dead Sea to the gulf of Aqaba. *Sela* is unlikely to be the site
of the later Nabataean capital, Petra; it could be thought of as
lying somewhere to the south-west of the Dead Sea or it
might even be identical with Kadesh where Moses (Num.
20: 8) struck water from the 'rock' (Hebrew *sela‘*). ✶

A THEOLOGICAL POSTSCRIPT

The angel of the LORD came up from Gilgal to Bokim, **2**
and said, 'I brought[a] you up out of Egypt and into the
country which I vowed I would give to your forefathers.
I said, I will never break my covenant with you, and 2
you in turn must make no covenant with the inhabitants
of the country; you must pull down their altars. But you
did not obey me, and look what you have done! So I 3
said, I will not drive them out before you; they will decoy
you, and their gods will shut you fast in the trap.' When 4
the angel of the LORD said this to the Israelites, they all

[a] *Prob. rdg.; Heb.* I will bring.

5 wept and wailed, and so the place was called Bokim;[a] and
they offered sacrifices there to the LORD.

＊ This short section, as it now stands, seems to fulfil two
functions. On the one hand, it describes the founding of a
sanctuary at Bokim; this is expressed in terms of the move on
the part of the angel of God from Gilgal to Bokim (verse 1a);
the actual inauguration of the sanctuary is expressed in verse 5.

The middle part of the section, however, verses 1b-4,
provides a theological explanation of why the conquest of
Canaan, as described particuarly in the second part of ch. 1,
was only partial and incomplete. The Israelite tribes have
disobeyed God's commands, and verse 2 implies that they had
entered into relationships with the local population and had
adopted some of their religious practices. As a punishment for
this, God refuses to drive out the local population and promises
that both they and their gods will lead the Israelites far from
him. This attitude of the local population towards the
Israelites is expressed in verse 3 in hunting imagery, in terms
of 'decoy' and 'trap'.

1. *The angel of the LORD*: in some of the older stories in the
Old Testament, God himself is actually thought to appear on
stage, as it were (see, e.g., the story of Abraham arguing with
God about the fate of Sodom in Gen. 18: 22-33). To a later
age this appeared rather unseemly, so they thought of God
appearing to men indirectly through a 'messenger' or 'angel'
(the same Hebrew word can be rendered in both of these ways).
But we can often see that even when the text speaks of the
angel of the LORD it is God himself who is speaking, as is indeed
the case in the present passage. *from Gilgal to Bokim*: Gilgal,
about 2 miles (3 km) north-east of Jericho, was traditionally
believed to be the first holy place established by the Israelites
when they entered Palestine from east of the Jordan (see the
story in Josh. 3: 1 - 5: 12, especially 4: 19f. and 5: 9-12).
The place-name Bokim is not found elsewhere and, as can

[a] *That is* Weepers.

be seen from the N.E.B. footnote to verse 5, it simply means
'weepers', a description which is connected with the weeping
of the people when they learn of God's threatened punishment. The Septuagint has a fuller text at this point, including
the place-name Bethel, and this, taken in conjunction with the
reference in Gen. 35: 8 to the 'Oak of Weeping' (Allon-
bakuth) 'below Bethel', has led a number of scholars to
suggest that it is Bethel that is being referred to here. *I brought
you up*: the form of the Hebrew text (cp. the literal rendering
in the N.E.B. footnote) suggests that there is something
missing at the beginning of the angel's speech. This kind of
looking back over history expressed in the form of an admon-
ition is a feature of the deuteronomistic style. It occurs again
in 6: 7–10. *the country which I vowed I would give to your forefathers*: the promise of land was one of the two basic promises
(the other was the promise of descendants) made to each of
the patriarchs: see, e.g., Gen. 15: 7 (Abraham); Gen. 26: 2f.
(Isaac); Gen. 28: 13–15 (Jacob).

2f. The writer here, probably the deuteronomistic historian, is borrowing the language of the Yahwist (the author
of the oldest narrative strand in the Pentateuch, the five books
Genesis to Deuteronomy; see *The Making of the Old Testament* in this series, pp. 60–2, 65f.) who expresses similar
thoughts and ideas in Exod. 34, especially verses 10–16.
Similar phraseology is also used by other writers in Josh. 23: 13
and Num. 33: 55.

4. This verse now provides the connecting link between the
tradition which tells of the establishment of a sanctuary at
Bokim/Bethel(?) and the tradition which provides a theological explanation of the partial nature of the conquest of
Canaan. The idea of the people weeping when they hear the
divine judgement upon them may reflect some kind of ritual
mourning such as is also reflected in, e.g., Judg. 11: 40 (see
below) and possibly also in the place name 'Allon-bakuth' in
Gen. 35: 8 (see above on verse 1). *

31

Israel under the judges

✻ This section which runs from 2:6 to 12:15 forms the main, central section of the book of Judges and, indeed, is probably the original form of this part of the Deuteronomistic History. It is more than likely that the Samson stories (chs. 13–16) and the two appendices (chs. 17–18; 19–21) were added at a later stage, interrupting the original continuity between Judg. 13:1 and 1 Sam. 1:1.

This central section of the book is made up of two comparatively disparate elements, a series of deliverances of Israel from foreign oppression or domination by men usually referred to as the 'major judges' and a list of little more than the names of people usually referred to as the 'minor judges'. The latter is found in 10:1–5 and 12:8–15, split by the story of Jephthah. The 'major judges' are Othniel, Ehud, Deborah/Barak, Gideon and Jephthah, and the accounts of their heroic deeds are narrated in greater or less detail in this central section of the book (on the omission of Samson from this list of 'judges' see above, pp. 7f.).

To these stories of the old tribal rulers and heroes, the deuteronomistic historian has added a theological introduction in 2:6 – 3:6. Like so much in that historical work, this is material which has been preached to a listening congregation. Although there is no direct second-person address here, as, e.g., in Deut. 1–11, a number of parallels even within this short section recall for us the kind of preaching style which uses repetition for emphasis, and a small number of verses which look like later additions to the text suggests that this material continued to be preached by succeeding generations. ✻

FORSAKING THE LORD

JOSHUA DISMISSED the people, and the Israelites went 6
off to occupy the country, each man to his alloted portion. As long as Joshua was alive and the elders who 7
survived him – everyone, that is, who had witnessed the
whole great work which the LORD had done for Israel –
the people worshipped the LORD. At the age of a hundred 8
and ten Joshua son of Nun, the servant of the LORD, died,
and they buried him within the border of his own pro- 9
perty in Timnath-heres north of Mount Gaash in the
hill-country of Ephraim. Of that whole generation, all 10
were gathered to their forefathers, and another generation
followed who did not acknowledge the LORD and did not
know what he had done for Israel. Then the Israelites 11
did what was wrong in the eyes of the LORD, and worshipped the Baalim.[a] They forsook the LORD, their 12
fathers' God who had brought them out of Egypt, and
went after other gods, gods of the races among whom
they lived; they bowed down before them and provoked
the LORD to anger; they forsook the LORD and worshipped 13
the Baal and the Ashtaroth.[b] The LORD in his anger made 14
them the prey of bands of raiders and plunderers; he sold
them to their enemies all around them, and they could no
longer make a stand. Every time they went out to battle the 15
LORD brought disaster upon them, as he had said when he
gave them his solemn warning, and they were in dire straits.

* Verses 6–9 are paralleled, in a slightly different order, in
Josh. 24: 28–31 (the equivalent verse order is 28, 31, 29, 30),

[a] The Baalim *were Canaanite deities.*
[b] The Ashtaroth *were Canaanite deities.*

33

and both forms of the text could be entitled 'the death of Joshua'. On this see above, pp. 8f.

6. *Joshua dismissed the people*: this follows on the context of Josh. 24, that is at the conclusion of the tribal gathering at Shechem. The concept, too, that each tribe (in this context *each man*) had an *allotted portion* of land connects up with 'the division of the land among the tribes' which is the subject-matter of Josh. 13–22.

7. As long as there survived people who had had first-hand experience of God's guidance of his people's history, then the Israelites remained faithful to him. The other side of the coin is described in verses 10–13.

8. *a hundred and ten*: there is no rational explanation of the great ages attributed to personages in the early pages of the Old Testament. They are probably to be attributed to the concept that the patriarchs lived to a hoary old age, and there is a notable decrease in the ages starting from Adam (930 according to Gen. 5: 5) and eventually settling down to the Psalmist's norm of seventy to eighty (Ps. 90: 10).

9. *Timnath-heres*: literally 'portion of the sun', possibly refers to the practice of sun-worship there; the name has been deliberately altered by means of the reversal of the three consonants of the second half in Josh. 19: 50 and 24: 30, giving the form Timnath-serah. The former passage refers to Joshua's *own property*, allotted to him by the Israelites. The site of Timnath-heres is not entirely certain; it may be identical with modern Tibnah, in the south-eastern part of the Ephraimite hill-country. Mount Gaash can no longer be identified.

10. This verse is not paralleled in Joshua, but it underlines what is already implicit in verse 7. A new generation has arisen, ignorant of God's dealings with his people, and for that very reason they have no awareness of him and do not *acknowledge* him.

11–13. Their specific wrong-doing is spelled out here in terms of the worship of *Baalim* and *Ashtaroth*, both of which

the N.E.B. footnotes describe as Canaanite deities. The forms
of the words are plural, the former masculine, the latter
feminine, and the reference is to local manifestations of a
Canaanite god and goddess respectively. Baal was the god of
rain and fertility; Astarte was the goddess of fertility and the
consort of Baal. The motif of the forsaking of the God who
had guided the Israelites in their past history is again emphasized. The phrase *went after other gods* is characteristic of the
deuteronomistic literature (see, e.g., Deut. 6: 14; 8: 19; 11: 28,
not all of which have been translated in the same way in the
N.E.B.), and the fact that it recurs in verse 19 of this chapter
('give their allegiance to other gods') lends support to the
view that Judg. 2: 6 – 3: 6 is from the hand of the deuteronomistic historian. The fact that the Israelites became devotees
of the *gods of the races among whom they lived* suggests that the
situation envisaged here is that of the cultural and religious
assimilation of a people at a lower stage of development to a
people at a higher stage. The incoming Israelites were semi-
nomads, while the Canaanites were settled agriculturalists.
When the Israelites adopted a settled, agricultural life, they
naturally felt that the local fertility gods and goddesses had to
be propitiated if they, too, were to have successful harvests.
It is indicated in 3: 6 that this assimilation was not only on a
religious level but also on a broader social level.

14. This verse is almost a pattern for the contents of the
main part of the book of Judges. The Israelites are subjected
to marauding attacks on the part of the surrounding nations
and become subject to them for some years before a deliverer
is found for them. There is, perhaps, a distinction to be made
between marauding attacks by *bands of raiders and plunderers*
such as the Midianites and 'other eastern tribes' (6: 3), and
proper military subjugation such as that inflicted by the Moabites (3: 14), but too much should not be made of such a
distinction.

15. This verse expresses a much more positive aspect of
the divine punishment for the Israelites' unbelief and infidelity.

The *solemn warning* probably refers to the curses pronounced over the people if they refused to obey God's commands: Deut. 28: 15–44; see especially verse 25 there for a reference to 'going out' to battle. ✳

DELIVERANCE BY THE JUDGES

16 The LORD set judges over them, who rescued them
17 from the marauding bands. Yet they did not listen even to these judges, but turned wantonly to worship other gods and bowed down before them; all too soon they abandoned the path of obedience to the LORD's commands which their forefathers had followed. They did not obey
18 the LORD. Whenever the LORD set up a judge over them, he was with that judge, and kept them safe from their enemies so long as he lived. The LORD would relent as often as he heard them groaning under oppression and ill-
19 treatment. But as soon as the judge was dead, they would relapse into deeper corruption than their forefathers and give their allegiance to other gods, worshipping them and bowing down before them. They gave up none of their evil practices and their wilful ways.

✳ This is the first mention of the figure of the judge in the book of Judges. We have already discussed the nature and function of the judge in early Israel (see pp. 9–13), and the main point to note in this section is the setting of this whole period of Israelite history within a cyclic pattern. That pattern is as follows: apostasy on the part of the Israelites (verses 11–13); subjection to domination by a foreign power or to harassment by marauding bands (verses 14–15); appeal by the people to God for deliverance from oppression (verse 18b); appointment of a judge to rescue them from the marauding bands and to deliver them from their oppressors (verses 16 and 18a);

relapse of the people into greater apostasy on the death of the judge (verse 19).

16. *The LORD set judges over them*: the phrase emphasizes the writer's theological outlook: the office of judge is the divine response to the people's need. In technical terms, we can speak of the office of judge as being a charismatic one. What this means is that a man becomes a deliverer–judge only with the bestowal upon him of God's *charisma*, his grace, his spirit. This is made explicit in the case of several of the judges: Othniel (3: 10), Gideon (6: 34) and Jephthah (11: 29). The idea is used in a more frivolous way in the Samson stories (see, e.g., 14: 6, 19; 15: 14), and the reverse side of the coin can be observed in the Abimelech episode where God sends 'an evil spirit' to cause a breach between Abimelech and the citizens of Shechem (9: 23).

17. This verse seems to suggest that the judges had a kind of preaching function, rather like that of the later prophets, the aim of which was to warn the people of the dangers of apostasy and the desirability of remaining obedient to God's commands. To that extent it presents a picture of the judges rather at variance with the one we generally obtain from the main part of the book. With its prophet-like view of the judges, we may think of the verse as forming a later strand in this theological preface to the book. *turned wantonly to worship other gods*: this phrase is similar to the phrase 'went after other gods', discussed earlier in the context of verses 11–13. The expression *turned wantonly to worship* could be more literally translated as 'pursued like a prostitute', a translation which underlines two complementary ideas inherent in the phrase. One is the fact that the religion of Canaan was basically a fertility religion, one of whose central rites was cultic prostitution, sexual practices designed to express and assist the activities of the gods in granting fertility and increase in crops and flocks. In a real sense, then, the worship of the gods of Canaan could be described as prostitution. The other idea is that sometimes in the Old Testament

Israel is thought of as the bride of God: e.g. Hos. 2: 19–20;
Isa. 54: 6. When she turns from the worship of God to the
worship of other gods, Israel the bride becomes Israel the
prostitute. These two ideas are combined in the phrase at
present under discussion.

18. The idea that God *kept them safe from their enemies so
long as he* [the judge] *lived*, is reflected in the stereotyped phrase
which occurs at the end of several of the judges stories to the
effect that 'the land was at peace for forty years until *X* died'.
The clearest example is at the end of the Othniel story in 3: 11,
but it recurs in connection with Ehud and Shamgar combined
in 3: 30, with the Deborah–Barak episode in 5: 31 and with
Gideon in 8: 28. ✻

THE NATIONS WHICH THE LORD LEFT

20 And the LORD was angry with Israel and said, 'This
nation has broken the covenant which I laid upon their
21 forefathers and has not obeyed me, and now, of all the
nations which Joshua left at his death, I will not drive out
22 to make room for them one single man. By their means
I will test Israel, to see whether or not they will keep
strictly to the way of the LORD as their forefathers did.'
23 So the LORD left those nations alone and made no haste
to drive them out or give them into Joshua's hands.

3 These are the nations which the LORD left as a means of
testing all the Israelites who had not taken part in the
2 battles for Canaan, his purpose being to teach succeeding
generations of Israel, or those at least who had not learnt
3 in former times, how to make war. These were: the five
lords of the Philistines, all the Canaanites, the Sidonians,
and the Hivites who lived in Mount Lebanon from
4 Mount Baal-hermon as far as Lebo-hamath. His purpose

also was to test whether the Israelites would obey the
commands which the LORD had given to their forefathers
through Moses. Thus the Israelites lived among the 5
Canaanites, the Hittites, the Amorites, the Perizzites, the
Hivites, and the Jebusites. They took their daughters in 6
marriage and gave their own daughters to their sons; and
they worshipped their gods.

✻ This final section of the theological introduction to the
book of Judges provides two different answers to a difficulty
with which Israel was faced especially at the time of the settlement in Palestine, but also in later periods as well. There was,
on the one hand, her belief that God had now at last given to
her the land which he had promised to her early ancestors
(see on 2: 1 above). On the other hand, however, there was
the hard fact that the settlement had been incomplete and
partial, a fact which has been emphasized particularly in the
second half of ch. 1. One answer to this question has already
been given, namely that Israel's continuing subjection to
external pressures was a punishment for her unfaithfulness to
God. Now follow two further answers to the same question.
One is that the continuing presence of non-Israelites in
Palestine is to act as a test of Israel's faith 'to see whether or
not they will keep strictly to the way of the LORD as their
forefathers did' (2: 22) and will 'obey the commands which
the LORD had given to their forefathers through Moses' (3: 4).
The second of these two answers is given in 3: 2, namely that
these nations have been left in order to teach succeeding
generations of Israelites the art of warfare. It is interesting to
note that traditions in the Pentateuch provide yet another
answer to this same problem, namely that if these non-
Israelite nations had been wiped out all at once, the land
would have been overrun by wild beasts (see Exod. 23: 29
and Deut. 7: 22).

20. The *covenant* referred to in this verse is the Sinai

covenant, the making of which and the conditions of which
are narrated in the main part of the book of Exodus, from
ch. 19 onwards. The concept of covenant is a central one in
the Old Testament, and besides the covenant between God
and people entered upon at Sinai, God also enters into covenant relationships with Abraham (Gen. 17) and with David
(2 Sam. 7, though the word 'covenant' does not actually
occur in that chapter).

21. This verse indicates that the deuteronomistic historian
was aware that the picture of a total conquest of Palestine
under the leadership of Joshua, a picture given by the book
of Joshua, is not in accord with the more sober facts of
history.

3: 3. The *Philistines* are mentioned in Egyptian records of
the fifteenth to the thirteenth centuries B.C. as being one of
the 'Sea Peoples'. They may well have come from Crete, as
Amos 9: 7 suggests, and they settled in the Palestinian coastal
strip between the Egyptian frontier and the area to the south
of Mount Carmel. They were not a nation in the strict sense
of the word but were grouped in five city-states, Gaza,
Ashdod, Ashkelon, Ekron and Gath. Each of these cities was
ruled by a prince or lord, and together they formed a loose
federation. The term *Sidonians* may not refer strictly to the
inhabitants of Sidon but may be being used here as a general
term for the Phoenicians who lived on the coast in the
north-west. The *Hivites* were probably Hurrians, a non-
Semitic people whose most notable centre of power was the
city-state of Nuzi, east of the River Tigris. According to this
verse, the area of Hivite occupation stretched from the
southern end of the Antilebanon mountains as far as *Lebo-
hamath* on one of the sources of the River Orontes.

5. On the *Canaanites* and the *Perizzites* see on 1: 4 above;
on the *Hittites* see on 1: 22–6; on the *Amorites* see on 1: 34f.
The *Jebusites* are a people particularly associated with Jerusalem, but nothing more definite is known about them. The
names of the pre-Israelite inhabitants of Canaan often appear

like this in the form of a list. This is the standard form, consisting of six names. Occasionally a seventh name is added, that of the Girgashites, as, for example, in Josh. 3: 10. Nothing is known of this last group.

6. On this verse see on 2: 11–13. ✲

OTHNIEL

The Israelites did what was wrong in the eyes of the 7 LORD; they forgot the LORD their God and worshipped the Baalim and the Asheroth.*a* The LORD was angry with 8 Israel and he sold them to Cushan-rishathaim, king of Aram-naharaim,*b* who kept them in subjection for eight years. Then the Israelites cried to the LORD for help and he 9 raised up a man to deliver them, Othniel son of Caleb's younger brother Kenaz, and he set them free. The spirit 10 of the LORD came upon him and he became judge over Israel. He took the field, and the LORD delivered Cushan-rishathaim king of Aram into his hands; Othniel was too strong for him. Thus the land was at peace for forty years 11 until Othniel son of Kenaz died.

✲ This is the first section dealing with the activity of a specific judge, and in many respects it is a pattern for the various stories which follow. There are a number of stock phrases which will recur in more or less the same form in subsequent narratives. The Israelites, we are told, 'did what was wrong in the eyes of the LORD' (verse 7), and that, together with their abandonment of the worship of their own God and their devotion to the worship of a Canaanite god, is a frequent introduction to the various stories of the judges. The motif of God's anger and of his 'selling' of the Israelites

[a] *Plural of* Asherah, *the name of a Canaanite goddess.*
[b] *That is* Aram of Two Rivers.

into the hands of a foreign power who then keeps them
in subjection for a specific number of years will also recur
again. Other stock phrases are the cry of the people for help,
the 'raising up' of a deliverer who is then empowered for
action by the spirit of God, the defeat of the enemy and the
consequent peace for the standard period of forty years.
What we might call the framework of the story is so prominent and the specific details of this particular incident are so
scanty and so unusual, that we might be tempted to think that
the compiler of these stories has decided at the beginning to
give us a stock example and has simply filled it in with the
first names that came to his mind. It is, however, just possible
to discern some kernel of historical truth behind this unusual
story.

7. *Asheroth*: as the N.E.B. footnote indicates, the plural
here refers to local manifestations of Asherah, the Canaanite
goddess who was the consort of El, the chief god, and the
mother of the gods.

8f. In these two verses, we come to the specific details of
this particular tradition. The *Othniel* mentioned here is
certainly intended to be the same Othniel who has already
featured in 1: 13, in a passage which referred to the occupation
of Debir by Othnielites, a clan of the Kenizzites. We must
accept either that this is a very different tradition about
Othniel, one which sees him as a national hero, or else that
the real kernel of this tradition has to do with a confrontation
between Othniel in the geographical location in South Palestine in which we know him and some figure whose name and
origin have become disfigured in the present form of the text.
Aram-naharaim, 'Aram of Two Rivers', is the name usually
applied in the Old Testament to Mesopotamia, the land between the two rivers Tigris and Euphrates. The name *Cushan-
rishathaim* presents more of a problem. It means 'Cushan of
two evils' and is an obvious fabrication of a most improbable
authenticity. Attempts have been made to refer this name to
Mesopotamia (thereby regarding Othniel as a *national* hero)

by pointing out that Babylon was ruled, at roughly this period, by a Cassite dynasty (Hebrew 'Cush' = Babylonian 'Cass'). Commentators have cited a number of Babylonian personal names with greater or lesser degrees of similarity to Cushan-rishathaim. There is, however, no evidence to suggest that the Cassite dynasty of Babylon ever extended its power westwards. A more fruitful line of approach is to note that Cush is used in the Old Testament to refer to Nubia, the country lying to the south of Egypt and that Aram, in Hebrew characters, looks very like Edom and has, indeed, frequently been confused with it (e.g. 2 Sam. 8: 12; 1 Kings 11: 25; 2 Kings 16: 6; Ezek. 27: 16, all of which have been corrected in the N.E.B. and noted in the footnotes). When the original 'Edom' was wrongly written as 'Aram', the '-naharaim' element was erroneously tacked on, though only in the occurrence in verse 8, not in verse 10. The name Cushan-rishathaim may then be thought of as referring to a villainous Edomite chieftain, whose negroid features may be reflected in his being named Cushan, 'the Nubian'. This is only one theory among several, but it does seem likely that behind this tradition there lies the memory of some kind of external pressure, probably from Edom, lying to the south of the Dead Sea, on the Othnielites of Debir, a pressure which was successfully repulsed. When round numbers are found in the Old Testament, there is always the likelihood that these are artificial numbers. This is certainly true of the length of the Philistine oppression in 13: 1 ('forty years') and possibly also of the oppression referred to in 4: 3 ('twenty years'). Where a non-rounded number is given, there is a greater likelihood that we have a fragment of historical fact; so *eight years* here; cp. 'seven years' in 6: 1 and 'eighteen years' in 3: 14 and 10: 8.

10. Here Othniel becomes the charismatic leader of Israel. What we can call the 'all-Israel' aspect of these hero-sagas has been given to them by a compiler. Whether they acquired this character before the deuteronomistic historian incorporated them in his work or whether he gave it to them is a

matter for debate. Originally Othniel would be a local tribal
leader in a limited geographical area. This is in line with the
view that the major judges were such local leaders whose
functions were primarily of a military nature (see pp. 12f.). *

EHUD AND SHAMGAR

12 Once again the Israelites did what was wrong in the
eyes of the LORD, and because of this he roused Eglon king
13 of Moab against Israel. Eglon mustered the Ammonites
and the Amalekites, advanced to attack Israel and took
14 possession of the Vale of Palm Trees. The Israelites were
15 subject to Eglon king of Moab for eighteen years. When
they cried to the LORD for help, he raised up a man to
deliver them, Ehud son of Gera the Benjamite, who was
left-handed. The Israelites sent him to pay their tribute
16 to Eglon king of Moab. Ehud made himself a two-edged
sword, only fifteen inches long,[a] which he fastened on his
17 right side under his clothes, and he brought the tribute to
18 Eglon king of Moab. Eglon was a very fat man. When
Ehud had finished presenting the tribute, he sent on the
19 men who had carried it, and he himself turned back from
the Carved Stones at Gilgal. 'My lord king,' he said, 'I
have a word for you in private.' Eglon called for silence
20 and dismissed all his attendants.[b] Ehud then came up to
him as he sat in the roof-chamber of his summer palace
and said, 'I have a word from God for you.' So Eglon
21 rose from his seat, and Ehud reached with his left hand,
drew the sword from his right side and drove it into his
22 belly. The hilt went in after the blade and the fat closed

[a] only...long: *lit.* a short cubit in length.
[b] and...attendants: *so Sept.; Heb.* and all his attendants went out.

over the blade; he did not draw the sword out but left it
protruding behind.[a] Ehud went out to the porch,[b] shut 23
the doors on him and fastened them. When he had gone 24
away, Eglon's servants came and, finding the doors
fastened, they said, 'He must be relieving himself in the
closet of his summer palace.' They waited until they were 25
ashamed to delay any longer, and still he did not open
the doors of the roof-chamber. So they took the key and
opened the doors; and there was their master lying on the
floor dead. While they had been waiting, Ehud made his 26
escape; he passed the Carved Stones and escaped to
Seirah. When he arrived there, he sounded the trumpet 27
in the hill-country of Ephraim, and the Israelites came
down from the hills with him at their head. He said to 28
them, 'Follow me, for the LORD has delivered your
enemy the Moabites into your hands.' Down they came
after him, and they seized the fords of the Jordan against
the Moabites and allowed no man to cross. They killed 29
that day some ten thousand Moabites, all of them men of
substance and all fighting men; not one escaped. Thus 30
Moab on that day became subject to Israel, and the land
was at peace for eighty years.

After Ehud there was Shamgar of Beth-anath.[c] He 31
killed six hundred Philistines with an ox-goad, and he too
delivered Israel.

✷ In this section we find a recurrence of the cycle of apostasy,
subjection to foreign oppression, appeal by the people to God,
emergence of a deliverer.

[a] behind: *Heb. word of uncertain mng.*
[b] porch: *Heb. word of uncertain mng.*
[c] of Beth-anath: *or* son of Anath.

12–14. As a result of Israel's having offended God, presumably by her unfaithfulness, though this is not specifically stated, he subjects her to domination by the Moabites and their king *Eglon*. The northern boundary of the kingdom of Moab varied from time to time. Normally the River Arnon marked the northern frontier, but periodically Moab was able to extend her power northwards as far as the region which lies east of the Jordan opposite Jericho. This region was normally occupied by the *Ammonites*, but, from the fact that Moab occupied it occasionally, it is often referred to as 'Moabite country', a technical geographical term which occurs, for example, in the book of Ruth (see Ruth 1: 1 and frequently throughout the book). The situation envisaged here is that Moab has occupied this more northerly territory and has even, with the help of the conquered Ammonite inhabitants, attempted to penetrate west of the Jordan. The presence of the *Amalekites* in this alliance is more puzzling. They are normally thought of as being resident in the area to the south-west of the Dead Sea (so 1: 16). It may be that the term is here applied loosely to nomadic bedouin tribes on whose assistance the Moabites were able to call. The *Vale of Palm Trees* (literally, as in 1: 16, 'the city of palms') here certainly refers to Jericho. The subjection to Moab lasted, we are told, for the specific period of *eighteen years* (see on 3: 8f.).

15. The deliverer who emerges as a result of the people's plea to God for help, Ehud, was a Benjamite and is described as being *left-handed*. The latter expression in Hebrew could be literally rendered as 'restricted with regard to the right hand'. In 20: 16 there is a reference to 700 left-handed slingers from the tribe of Benjamin. It might be asked, therefore, whether this particular tribe, like the Scottish clan Kerr, were specifically trained to be left-handed fighters. Such an ability would give them a tactical advantage over an enemy, and in this particular instance it contributes to the element of surprise in Ehud's killing of Eglon. In addition, Ehud has easy access

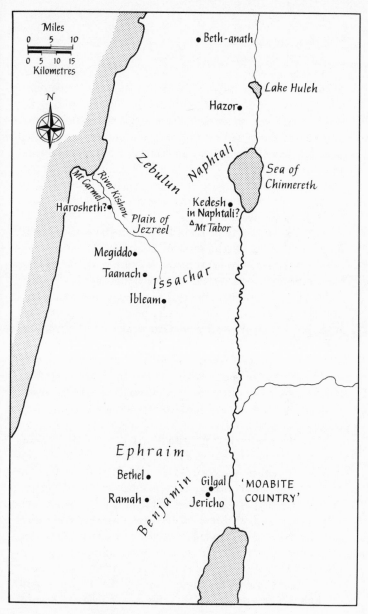

2. Ehud and Deborah/Barak (3: 12 – 5: 31)

to Eglon since he is at the head of an embassy sent with the Israelite tribute to the king of Moab.

16. *only fifteen inches long*: this is the approximate length of the so-called 'short cubit'. The normal cubit (18 inches) was usually reckoned as the measure from the elbow to the tips of the fingers. The 'short cubit' was from the elbow to the knuckles of the closed fist. *which he fastened on his right side under his clothes*: since he was left-handed, Ehud would naturally carry his sword on his right side. Eglon's guards would normally look for suspicious bulges on the left-hand side, so the presence of Ehud's sword on his person would the more easily pass unnoticed.

17. *Eglon was a very fat man*: this parenthetical statement is important for the development of the story.

18f. What seems to happen now is that Ehud accompanies his companions for a certain distance along their road home and then alone turns back in order to accomplish the assassination of Eglon. A particular difficulty here is our ignorance of what precisely is meant by *the Carved Stones at Gilgal*. The traditional site of Gilgal was east or south-east of Jericho, that is, between Jericho and the Jordan. Such a site, however, made nonsense of the idea that Gilgal in this passage was thought of as being on the way back from Jericho to Benjamite territory. More recently, Gilgal has been located 2 miles (3 km) north-east of Jericho, and such a location fits the present context more easily. It might also be that here Gilgal does not refer to a specific site but to a larger district of which Jericho was the administrative centre. It is unlikely that the Carved Stones are identical with the twelve stones set up at Gilgal in commemoration of the crossing of the Jordan by the Israelite tribes (Josh. 4: 1–8). More likely is the idea that they were some kind of inscribed boundary stones erected by the Moabites to mark the extent of their political domination. Such stones, inscribed with symbols of the gods, are known from Babylonia. Ehud's pretext for turning back is that he has *a word* for Eglon *in private*. In verse 20 this is described as 'a word from God', and this may just possibly suggest that these Carved Stones also had some kind of cultic or oracular function.

20. *the roof-chamber of his summer palace*: this structure would be built on the flat roof of the palace. Normally a roof-chamber would be a fairly simple construction whose main function was to permit the free circulation of the maximum amount of air. This one is fairly elaborate, with a porch and double doors (verse 23) and a separate lavatory (verse 24).

21. *Eglon rose from his seat* in deference to the reception of this 'word from God', and when *Ehud reached with his left hand*, Eglon had not the faintest suspicion that this was pre-paratory to a murderous attack on him. We have already noted the tactical advantage inherent in Ehud's left-handedness.

22f. The gruesome details of the inflicting of the fatal blow have been prepared for in advance by the parenthetical phrase at the end of verse 17. The words translated as *behind* in verse 22 and as *porch* in verse 23 are, as is observed in the N.E.B. footnotes, of uncertain meaning. The particular difficulty of the second of these makes it uncertain how exactly Ehud locked the doors of the roof-chamber and made his escape. It is not clear whether he locked them from inside and subsequently escaped through some exit at the rear of the building or whether he emerged through the doors, shut them behind him and walked out in full view of the guards. If the latter is the case, it is not clear how he was able to lock the doors so that they could then be opened from the outside only with a key (verse 25).

24f. The episode of Eglon's servants thinking that the king was *relieving himself* is a literary device used by the narrator to explain Ehud's long head start after the assassination (so verse 26). The locked doors were obviously a known signal, but on this occasion the delay in opening them is so great that the servants are forced to take the initiative, only to find their master lying on the floor dead.

26. Once again the *Carved Stones* seem to indicate the

limits of Moabite power. Once he has passed them, Ehud appears to be safe. No location has as yet been found for Seirah, if indeed the latter is to be regarded as an individual place-name. It may be a more general, territorial designation and have the sense of 'the wooded hills'. It does in fact have the definite article in front of it in Hebrew, 'to *the* Seirah'.

27. *he sounded the trumpet in the hill-country of Ephraim*: the sounding of the trumpet is the call to arms, as in the Gideon story in 6: 34. *the hill-country of Ephraim* is a general term for the uplands lying to the north-west of the Jericho area and occupied by the tribe of Ephraim. Immediately to the south of the Ephraimite territory lay that occupied by the tribe of Benjamin from which Ehud came. It is likely that the term *Israelites* in this verse is to be attributed to the all-Israel imprint given to these hero-sagas by the Deuteronomist and that probably only the Benjamites and their immediate neigh-bours to the north, the Ephraimites, were involved in this confrontation. It is, at any rate, the territory of these two tribes which would be most directly threatened by the establishment of Moabite domination west of the Jordan.

28. *the LORD has delivered your enemy the Moabites into your hands*: this kind of assurance was normally delivered in the form of an oracle in response to specific enquiry, as in 1: 2. *they seized the fords of the Jordan*: the strategy here was to cut off the Moabites' retreat and prevent them from fleeing back east across the Jordan to their homeland. The strategy would no doubt also effectively stop reinforcements being sent from Moabite territory, though this effect is not explicitly men-tioned.

29. The numbers and the status of the Moabites involved are no doubt attributable to the exaggeration characteristic of legend and saga.

30. The first part of this verse is probably to be attributed to the all-Israel slant given to the original hero-saga. At a later historical period Moab was often subject to the northern kingdom of Israel, particularly in the ninth century B.C., but at

this stage it is likely that the outcome of this battle was no more than the ending of Moabite domination west of the Jordan. It is unlikely that two Israelite tribes were strong enough to establish any effective control east of the Jordan. *the land was at peace for eighty years*: the usual deuteronomistic time reference is 'forty years' after the successful activity of any given judge, as in verse 11 above and in 5: 31. The doubling of the figure here is thought to be because the editor wished to include within it the judgeship of Shamgar which is briefly described in the following verse. We should note that Ehud is nowhere specifically referred to as a 'judge', and only this time reference in the deuteronomistic framework indicates that the editor regarded him as one.

31. The two short sentences of this verse present a number of peculiarities. The expression *there was* is unusual. The verse is similar in style to the minor judges list in 10: 1–5; 12: 8–15, but there the corresponding phrase is 'came' (literally 'arose') or 'was judge over'. The name *Shamgar* is not an Israelite name and various Semitic and non-Semitic parallels have been cited for it. The most likely suggestion is that it probably belongs to one of those non-Semitic elements which are found in Palestine at different periods. It can be seen from the footnote in the N.E.B. that Shamgar is described as 'son of Anath'. Anath or Anat is the sister of Baal, a warrior goddess who descends to the underworld, kills Mot, the god of the underworld, and restores Baal to life. It is unusual, though not entirely without parallel, for a human to be described as 'son of' a god or goddess, and many commentators have felt that the present Hebrew text is an error for a more original and more correct *Shamgar of Beth-anath*. The site of Beth-anath has been described in the comment on 1: 33 above. The name Shamgar occurs again in the Song of Deborah, 5: 6, a verse which links him with the non-Israelite Jael. We can deduce from this, as well as from the non-Israelite character of his name, that Shamgar himself was not an Israelite. Why, then, is he included among this list of Israel's heroes? On the

one hand, Shamgar waged war on the Philistines, and on the other the Philistines, at a later stage at any rate, were Israel's arch-enemy. The conclusion may have been drawn by some editor, or compiler, that anyone who fought against the Philistines must have been an Israelite. In this way, the non-Israelite Shamgar could have been included among the heroes of Israel's past. The reference in 5: 6, as well as his possible origin at Beth-anath, would locate Shamgar in the north, an area far removed from the usual area of Philistine pressure. But there is no reason to suppose that at some stage in their penetration of Palestine, the Philistines, or the 'Sea Peoples' in general, did not penetrate this particular area. Ch. 4 begins with the phrase 'After Ehud's death' and this would indicate that 3: 31 is a secondary addition to the text. Shamgar's exploit against the Philistines reminds us of Samson's feat with the jaw-bone of an ass (15: 14–19). This may explain why the verse has been placed, in some manuscripts of the Greek translation (the Septuagint), at the end of the Samson stories, after 16: 31. Finally, the phrase *and he too delivered Israel* is clearly an editorial addition intended to ensure that Shamgar is regarded as a judge in the sense in which that word is used of the charismatic heroes of this period in Israel's history. ✳

DEBORAH AND BARAK

✳ The account of the judgeship of Deborah and of Barak's battle with Sisera exists in two forms, one in prose in ch. 4 and the other in poetry in ch. 5. The poetic version, the so-called Song of Deborah, is often thought to stand nearer in time to the event which it describes than does the prose account. That part of it which deals with the battle is more detailed than the corresponding sections of ch. 4, but it is not easy to determine the nature of the earlier part of ch. 5, verses 2–11. Ch. 4, on the other hand, seems to be a conflation of two different stories, one concerning Jabin king of Hazor and the other concerning Sisera who alone, according to ch. 5, is Barak's enemy. Chs. 4 and 5 should be read together, but for practical purposes they are here divided into smaller units. ✶

PREPARATIONS FOR BATTLE

After Ehud's death the Israelites once again did what was **4** wrong in the eyes of the LORD, so he sold them to Jabin 2 the Canaanite king, who ruled in Hazor. The commander of his forces was Sisera, who lived in Harosheth-of-the-Gentiles. The Israelites cried to the LORD for help, because 3 Sisera had nine hundred chariots of iron and had oppressed Israel harshly for twenty years. At that time Deborah wife 4 of Lappidoth,[a] a prophetess, was judge in Israel. It was her 5 custom to sit beneath the Palm-tree of Deborah between Ramah and Bethel in the hill-country of Ephraim, and the Israelites went up to her for justice. She sent for Barak 6 son of Abinoam from Kedesh in Naphtali and said to him, 'These are the commands of the LORD the God of Israel: "Go and draw ten thousand men from Naphtali and Zebulun and bring them with you to Mount Tabor, and 7 I will draw Sisera, Jabin's commander, to the Torrent of Kishon with his chariots and all his rabble, and there I will deliver them into your hands."' Barak answered her, 8 'If you go with me, I will go; but if you will not go, neither will I.' 'Certainly I will go with you,' she said, 9 'but this venture will bring you no glory, because the LORD will leave Sisera to fall into the hands of a woman.' So Deborah rose and went with Barak to Kedesh. Barak 10 summoned Zebulun and Naphtali to Kedesh and marched up with ten thousand men, and Deborah went with him.

[a] wife of Lappidoth: *or* a spirited woman.

11   Now Heber the Kenite had parted company with the
       Kenites, the descendants of Hobab, Moses' brother-in-
       law, and he had pitched his tent at Elon-bezaanannim
       near Kedesh.

* 1. *After Ehud's death*: see on 3: 31. The remainder of verse 1
intimates the recommencement of the cycle of apostasy and
punishment which continues into verses 2 and 3.

2. *Jabin the Canaanite king, who ruled in Hazor*: the oppressor
of Israel is here said to be Jabin king of Hazor, but there is no
mention of him in ch. 5. As far as ch. 5 is concerned, Barak's
enemy and the real oppressor of Israel is Sisera. There is, in
Josh. 11, an account of a northern coalition, led by Jabin king
of Hazor, being defeated by Joshua at the waters of Merom,
with the subsequent total destruction of Hazor. It is very
unlikely, as some have suggested, that the Jabin of Josh. 11
was Jabin I, while the Jabin of Judg. 4 was his successor,
Jabin II. What is more likely is that in Judg. 4 we have the
conflation of the accounts of two major confrontations between
the indigenous population of the northern part of Palestine
and the incoming Israelites. The first, dating from the earlier
part of the settlement period, took place in upper Galilee
between the king of Hazor and Israelite elements attempting
to settle in that region. The second confrontation, probably
dating from a later stage in the process of settlement, took
place between Israelite elements already fairly firmly settled
and a number of Canaanite city-states lying along the valley
of the River Kishon. It is clear that within the context of
Judg. 4 Jabin is not a very central figure. He is mentioned
here in verse 2, and, apart from a parenthetical reference in
verse 7, he is mentioned again only at the end of the account
in verses 23 and 24 and then only in very general terms as
'(that) king of Canaan'. The central figure in ch. 4, and the
sole figure in ch. 5, is Sisera, and it is with Sisera as Israel's
enemy that these narratives are really concerned. It is only

secondarily, after the conflation with the Jabin strand of narrative, that Sisera has been described as *The commander of his* [Jabin's] *forces*. Sisera's place of origin was Harosheth-of-the-Gentiles, probably a Canaanite city-state lying north-west of Megiddo, just under the Carmel ridge.

3. *The Israelites cried to the LORD for help*: again a motif of the deuteronomistic framework, as is the harsh oppression of the Israelites by the enemy for a given number of years. The *twenty years* of the narrative here sounds like a round number (see on 3: 8f.), and the number of the *chariots of iron, nine hundred*, is certainly a saga-type exaggeration. On the chariots of iron see the note on 1: 19.

4f. *Deborah*: the name is the Hebrew word for 'bee'. She is described in three different ways: first of all as the *wife of Lappidoth*. The latter word means 'torches' and only here does it occur as a proper name. The N.E.B. footnote, 'a spirited woman', suggests the possibility of understanding this description of Deborah in a figurative sense. The fact that the name Barak means 'flash of lightning' has also been pointed out and, since this is also a possible meaning for Lappidoth, the suggestion has been made that Barak was actually Deborah's husband. This is, however, unlikely. Secondly, she is described as a *prophetess*. The term is probably slightly anachronistic here, since prophecy does not emerge till later in Israel's history. The word is used here probably to mean that Deborah was regarded as an inspired servant of God. Thirdly, we are told that she *was judge in Israel*. The title 'judge' (verse 4) is interpreted in a legal sense in verse 5 where we are told that *the Israelites went up to her for justice*, that is for legal decisions in accordance with a prescribed code of law. It is likely that verse 5 at least is secondary here. Not only does it give to the title 'judge' a legal sense which is demanded of it nowhere else in the book of Judges, but it also locates Deborah in *the hill-country of Ephraim*, whereas the main action of the Barak/Sisera episode unfolds in the Plain of Jezreel and in the area to the south-west of the Sea of

Chinnereth, with Mount Tabor as the centre of the action. This erroneous location has probably been occasioned by the confusion in the mind of some later editor between this Deborah and her *Palm-tree* and the Deborah who was Rebecca's nurse and who died and 'was buried under the oak below Bethel' (Gen. 35: 8). *Ramah*, the home of Samuel and his family, is probably to be located some 5 miles (8 km) south of Bethel.

6f. *Barak son of Abinoam from Kedesh in Naphtali*: we have already noted that Barak means 'flash of lightning', probably, as a proper name, a symbolic reference to the swiftness of the person so named. The location of Kedesh in Naphtali is disputed. It is usually taken to lie north-west of Lake Huleh, but this lies too far from Mount Tabor and the scene of the subsequent battle, and a different location has to be sought. One suggestion is that another Kedesh lay south-west of the Sea of Chinnereth. The other possible solution is that *Kedesh in Naphtali* is the traditional location in the north but that the 'Kedesh' (without the words 'in Naphtali') mentioned in verses 9 and 11 lay in the territory of Issachar, south-east of Megiddo. Verse 6 would seem to suggest that Barak belonged to the tribe of Naphtali, and this is not necessarily contradicted by 5: 15. In that context 'Issachar' could well be simply the tribe to which Deborah belonged and which supported Barak. If Deborah did belong to the tribe of Issachar, then this, too, would place her a little further north than the 'hill country of Ephraim' (see above on verses 4f.). Deborah, as 'prophetess', mediates to Barak *the commands of the LORD*, to the effect that he is to muster the two neighbouring northern tribes, *Naphtali and Zebulun*, and assemble at *Mount Tabor* on the north-eastern edge of the Plain of Jezreel, opposite Megiddo. The number *ten thousand* again sounds like the exaggeration of saga. Sisera and his chariots and infantry will be drawn up along the course of the *Torrent of Kishon*. A torrent was a stream which in summer contained little or no water but in winter, or after heavy rain, could suddenly swell to a swift-

Kishon

flowing, dangerous river. It is there that God *will deliver them* into Barak's hands.

8f. Barak's response could be taken simply as the expression of his feeling that for complete success he and his troops will need the continuing presence of the inspired and inspiring Deborah. But it is difficult to see verse 9 as anything other than a rebuke directed at Barak for his timidity. The punishment implicit in verse 9 looks forward to the dénouement of the story and Sisera's death at the hands of Jael (verses 17–21).

10. There is confusion in the tradition as it now stands as to whether the muster takes place at Mount Tabor (so verse 6) or at Kedesh (so here). This also raises the problem, already discussed in connection with verse 6, of the location of Kedesh. In view of the phrase 'had gone up to Mount Tabor' in verse 12, it would seem likely that the expression *marched up* here implies 'to Mount Tabor' as a sequel.

11. The connection between this parenthetic verse and the rest of the narrative of ch. 4 is that Jael, the heroine of the latter part of the chapter, is decribed as the 'wife of Heber the Kenite' (verse 17; cp. also verse 21 and 5: 24). The *Kenites* were usually resident to the south of Hebron (cp. 1: 16), but certain elements, such as this one mentioned here, must have been more nomadic. The location of Elon-bezaanannim is unknown, but it must have been reasonably close to the site of the battle. The Kenites were a clan of metal workers, and their presence near a large military encampment and battle is not surprising. Verse 17 very definitely links Heber the Kenite with the 'Jabin-king-of-Hazor' strand in this narrative. We have already noted that this is secondary with regard to the Barak/Sisera strand, and, in that case, the references to Jael as 'Heber's wife' will also be secondary. Jael can thus be regarded as a figure in her own right, who lives in a tent of her own, as opposed to being part of her supposed husband's household, and who is of sufficient importance to be remembered as the characteristic figure of a certain period in the past (5: 6). Cain, not *Hobab*, is usually regarded as the ancestor

of the Kenites; cp. Gen. 4: 17–24. *brother-in-law* is probably
not a correct translation of the Hebrew here; more correctly
it should be 'father-in-law', though there are conflicting
traditions about the name of Moses' father-in-law. One
tradition refers to him as Reuel (Exod. 2: 18), while another
calls him Jethro (Exod. 3: 1); both of these traditions agree in
calling him a Midianite. *

VICTORY FOR ISRAEL

12 Word was brought to Sisera that Barak son of Abi-
13 noam had gone up to Mount Tabor; so he summoned
all his chariots, nine hundred chariots of iron, and his
troops, from Harosheth-of-the-Gentiles to the Torrent of
14 Kishon. Then Deborah said to Barak, 'Up! This day the
LORD gives Sisera into your hands. Already the LORD has
gone out to battle before you.' So Barak came charging
down from Mount Tabor with ten thousand men at his
15 back. The LORD put Sisera to rout with all his chariots
and his army before Barak's onslaught; but Sisera himself
16 dismounted from his chariot and fled on foot. Barak
pursued the chariots and the army as far as Harosheth,
and the whole army was put to the sword and perished;
17 not a man was left alive. Meanwhile Sisera fled on foot
to the tent of Jael wife of Heber the Kenite, because Jabin
king of Hazor and the household of Heber the Kenite
18 were at peace. Jael came out to meet Sisera and said to
him, 'Come in here, my lord, come in; do not be afraid.'
So he went into the tent, and she covered him with a rug.
19 He said to her, 'Give me some water to drink; I am thirsty.'
She opened a skin full of milk, gave him a drink and
20 covered him up again. He said to her, 'Stand at the tent

door, and if anybody comes and asks if someone is here, say No.' But Jael, Heber's wife, took a tent-peg, picked 21 up a hammer, crept up to him, and drove the peg into his skull as he lay sound asleep. His brains oozed out on the ground, his limbs twitched, and he died. When Barak 22 came up in pursuit of Sisera, Jael went out to meet him and said to him, 'Come, I will show you the man you are looking for.' He went in with her, and there was Sisera lying dead with the tent-peg in his skull. That day 23 God gave victory to the Israelites over Jabin king of Canaan, and they pressed home their attacks upon that 24 king of Canaan until they had made an end of him.

✲ 12f. What was attributed to the direct instigation of God in verse 7 is here presented as the reaction of Sisera to the news that Barak had gathered his forces on Mount Tabor. Sisera's army consists of both a chariot force and infantry. If the location suggested above (commentary on verse 2) for Harosheth-of-the-Gentiles is correct, then he moved his troops south-eastwards, to the neighbourhood of Taanach and Megiddo according to 5: 19.

14. Deborah again mediates the divine intention regarding the outcome of the battle. It is *the LORD* who will bring about the defeat of Sisera and give Barak the victory. *the LORD has gone out to battle before you*: this idea is connected with the idea of the Ark as the symbol of God's presence with the armies of Israel. Whenever the Ark went into battle, the Israelites were generally victorious (the one great exception is in 1 Sam. 4 : 1–11, where the Philistines are victorious and the Ark is captured); if the Ark was not present, then defeat was almost certain. Barak and his forces, inspired by Deborah's promise of divinely given victory, launch their attack.

15. *The LORD put Sisera to rout*: again the emphasis is on God's initiative in achieving victory for the Israelite forces.

The description of the battle in ch. 4 is totally lacking in detail. The account in 5: 19–21 is more circumstantial. *Sisera himself dismounted from his chariot and fled on foot*: the possibilities here are either that the chariot became stuck in the mud in the vicinity of the River Kishon swollen by sudden storm (see on 5: 20f.), or else that the royal chariot would be instantly recognizable, and he abandoned it in order to escape undetected.

16. Barak pursues Sisera's army back to its base at Harosheth, and there he subjects it to the total destruction or 'ban' which is one of the characteristic motifs of the holy war. In such a war God was believed to fight alongside his people. Israel's enemies are God's enemies and as such must be totally destroyed. The 'ban' usually involved the wholesale slaughter of all the inhabitants of the city in question, together with the complete destruction of the city itself. One example among many, with the fatal consequences of disobedience, may be seen in 1 Sam. 15. Here the technical term is not used, but, although the destruction is confined to the army and does not include either the city or the civilian population, the idea is present nevertheless.

17. Sisera's flight brings him *to the tent of Jael* where the final act of the drama is played out. We have already observed, on verse 11 above, how Jael is to be thought of as a figure completely independent of Heber the Kenite. There seems to have been some kind of treaty relationship between Jabin of Hazor and this group of Kenites, and this observation would seem to link this Kenite clan with the Jabin element in the tradition. Again, the fact that Sisera arrives on foot would suggest the close proximity of Jael's tent to the scene of the battle.

18–20. Jael takes the initiative in offering shelter and sanctuary to Sisera. The word rendered as *rug* is of uncertain meaning; it might refer to some kind of 'tent curtain'. Sisera's request for refreshment will cement the obligation of hospitality incumbent upon Jael. He asks for the very minimum, *some water to drink*, but it would be churlish of Jael

not to offer him more than he asks. Having received the gift
of hospitality, Sisera can now happily demand sanctuary and
protection, secure in the knowledge that the laws of hospitality
cannot be violated.

21. Inviolable as these laws of hospitality were, God's
overriding plan for his people takes precedence. The early
Israelite reader would not feel that Jael was morally in the
wrong in killing her guest. The actual details of the killing
are spelled out in the N.E.B. translation, but the Hebrew text
is far from clear, and other renderings of the second part of
the verse are possible; cp., e.g., the Revised Standard Version,
'Jael...drove the peg into his temple, till it went down into the
ground, as he was lying fast asleep from weariness. So he died.'

22. There is no indication of the time which elapsed
between the arrival of Sisera at Jael's tent and the arrival of
Barak in pursuit of him. In view of our lack of certainty about
the geographical relationships between the various places
mentioned in the narrative, it is impossible to hazard a guess
at the answer to such a question. In any case, the narrative
may have telescoped the chronology of the events. We notice,
too, that Jael appears to have known who both Sisera and
Barak were.

23f. The final two verses are editorial. They re-introduce
the Jabin element in the narrative and they simply round off
the story in terms of a victory on the part of 'all Israel' over
the Canaanites. There was no such political entity as *Canaan*,
and the title *king of Canaan* is an impossible one. The usual
deuteronomistic ending for this particular judgeship is delayed
till 5: 31, 'the land was at peace for forty years'. In this way
the Song of Deborah is included as part of the account of
Deborah's tenure of office. ✶

THE SONG OF DEBORAH

✶ Ch. 5 is usually known as the Song of Deborah and is
generally regarded as one of the oldest pieces of Hebrew

literature. It is often thought to be practically contemporary with the events which it describes, but there are perhaps no very strong grounds for such a confident assertion. The text of this poem in Hebrew is very difficult and obscure, and some of these difficulties and obscurities can be seen from the N.E.B. footnotes. Different scholars have made different suggestions in their attempts to clarify the problems presented by the poem, and they have often produced translations which differ quite markedly from each other. Sometimes their different suggestions have been pre-determined by their ideas of what the poem is about. The commentary which follows is essentially a commentary on the translation which is offered by the N.E.B., but it should be remembered that this translation and these comments are only one line among several which are well represented in scholarly circles. Although the poem is known as the Song of Deborah, it is unlikely that Deborah herself composed it. In the poem itself, she is referred to in the second or third person. The only apparent exception, in verse 7, is of uncertain value, as can be seen from the N.E.B. footnote. Only verse 1, which is clearly an editorial heading to the poem, attributes it to Deborah. *

THE PLIGHT OF ISRAEL

5 That day Deborah and Barak son of Abinoam sang this song:

2   For the leaders, the leaders*a* in Israel,
      for the people who answered the call,
      bless ye the LORD.

3   Hear me, you kings; princes, give ear;
      I will sing, I will sing to the LORD.
      I will raise a psalm to the LORD the God of
        Israel.

[a] *Or* For those who had flowing locks.

O Lord, at thy setting forth from Seir,   4
when thou camest marching out of the plains of
    Edom,
earth trembled; heaven quaked;
the clouds streamed down in torrents.
Mountains shook in fear before the Lord, the lord of   5
    Sinai,
before the Lord, the God of Israel.
In the days of Shamgar of Beth-anath,*a*   6
in the days of Jael, caravans plied no longer;
men who had followed the high roads
went round by devious paths.
Champions there were none,   7
none left in Israel,
until I,*b* Deborah, arose,
arose, a mother in Israel.
They chose new gods,   8
they consorted with demons.*c*
Not a shield, not a lance was to be seen
in the forty thousand of Israel.
Be proud at heart, you marshals of Israel;   9
you among the people that answered the call,
bless ye the Lord.
You that ride your tawny she-asses,   10
that sit on saddle-cloths,
and you that take the road afoot,
    ponder this well.
Hark, the sound of the players striking up   11*a*
in the places where the women draw water!

[*a*] of Beth-anath: *or* son of Anath.
[*b*] *Or* you.   [*c*] *Or* satyrs.

63

It is the victories of the LORD that they commemo-
    rate there,
his triumphs as the champion of Israel.

✶ 1. This verse, as we have already noted, is simply an
editorial heading to the poem which follows. Certain elements
in the poem are of a cultic or liturgical nature, but it is probably going too far to suggest that the whole poem is a liturgical complex forming part of a supposed annual festival of
the renewal of the covenant.

2. *bless ye the LORD*: the addressees of the command are
not specified; they may be the 'kings' and 'princes' of verse 3.
The command is to praise God for those who rallied to Israel's
support and who led her in the days of her trouble and
affliction. The N.E.B. footnote 'for those who had flowing
locks' is a more literal rendering of the Hebrew than *leaders*.
The reference is to the idea that those who were preparing
for battle would consecrate themselves to God by means of
certain vows, one of which was to refrain from cutting their
hair. There is a possible reference to such a practice in the last
line of Deut. 32: 42, though this is not clear in the N.E.B.
translation; cp. also perhaps Ps. 68: 21.

3. *kings* and *princes* are summoned to hear the praises of
God sung. Such an audience of non-Israelites is a common
motif in the Psalms and in the prophets when particular stress
is being laid on the universal power of Israel's God; cp., e.g.,
Isa. 41: 1–5 where 'coasts and islands' and 'peoples' are
summoned as witnesses to God's power. The first person
singular in this verse need not refer to Deborah. The 'I' can
be thought of either, as in many of the Psalms, as the leader
in the cult who voices the thoughts of the congregation or
else simply as the anonymous author of this particular poem.

4f. In spite of the praise offered to the 'leaders' and 'people'
in verse 1, the real glory for the victory must go to God. It
was he who intervened and saved his people from the oppression under which they were suffering. God's intervention is

here described in terms which remind us of his appearing to
Moses on Mount Sinai; cp. Exod. 19: 18f.; 20: 18–21. We
are reminded also of his appearance to Elijah in 1 Kings 19
and of the elements of earthquake, wind and fire which occur
in the narrative there. The elements present here are those of
earthquake and of thunderstorm (*heaven quaked; the clouds
streamed down in torrents*). It is also possible that the latter
phrase looks forward to the actual battle where, as would
appear from verses 20 and 21, the natural phenomenon of a
sudden and violent storm was a decisive factor in giving
victory to Barak's forces. God is described as *the lord of Sinai*,
and the latter mountain, called Horeb in some traditions of the
Old Testament, was traditionally regarded as his dwelling-
place. Sinai has traditionally been identified with *Jebel Musa*
('the mountain of Moses') in the Sinai peninsula, but various
alternative sites have been proposed. The idea suggested in
verse 4 here, that God arrives directly *from Seir* and from *the
plains of Edom*, might, though not necessarily, seem to favour
a site much nearer to Kadesh.

6. Verses 6 to 8 are descriptive of the plight in which Israel
found herself prior to the advent of Deborah. It might appear
at first sight as if *Shamgar of Beth-anath* and *Jael* were foreign
oppressors who had brought about the state of desolation
and near anarchy described in these verses. But we have
already encountered Shamgar in 3: 31 where he is ranked
with the heroes of Israel, and Jael can be none other than the
heroine who is mentioned later in the poem. The sense must
be that there *were* heroes, but that none of them was Israelite
(laying emphasis on the 'Israel' in verse 7) or else that it
needed the inspiration of a Deborah to rouse them to the
necessary action. *caravans* refers to commercial trading, while
the last two lines of the verse refer to individual travellers.
Journeys of any kind are a hazardous venture. This is not,
here, specifically ascribed to the oppression inflicted on Israel
by Sisera which is described in 4: 3. That reference belongs
of course to the deuteronomistic framework of the book. The

state of anarchy described here may well have been due to the weakening of Egypt's hold on Syria–Palestine and to the invasions of the Sea Peoples, such as the Philistines.

7. The form of the verb in this verse is ambiguous. The N.E.B. renders it as a first person singular, *I...arose*, but it could equally well be read as an archaic form of the second person feminine singular, 'you arose' (see the N.E.B. foot-note). The description of Deborah as *a mother in Israel* is probably a title of respect accorded to her. The expression 'a watchful mother in Israel' is used in 2 Sam. 20: 19 as a simile for a city. The thought is that of the city as the protector of its surrounding 'daughter' villages and settlements. There may be something of this idea, too, in the application of the phrase to Deborah.

8. The first part of verse 8 is one of the most difficult parts of the poem, and a glance at other translations will reveal how varied the possibilities are. The Revised Standard Version, to cite but one, reads, 'When new gods were chosen, then war was in the gates.' The N.E.B. translation indicates that apostasy is one of the causes of the desolation which has fallen upon Israel. In addition, reference is made, in the second half of the verse, to the lack of fighting men in Israel. This is to be interpreted probably not as a reference to a total lack of able-bodied men, but rather as indicating that they were totally unorganized due to the lack of leaders referred to in verse 7.

9. Verses 9 to 11 are an anticipatory summons to all the members of the community to praise God for his deliverance of his people from their plight. Verse 9 itself takes up the language of verse 2. There, the cultic community was called upon to praise God for the leaders of Israel and for those who volunteered to fight. Here, the leaders and the people are called upon to praise God for the victory that has been won.

10f. These two verses are a poetic version of what we read in Deut. 6: 7 with regard to the commandments of God, 'you shall...speak of them indoors and out of doors, when you lie down and when you rise'. In every activity of life, God's commands are to be on his people's lips. Here, all members of the community in their varied activities are to ponder God's mighty acts. The differences in verse 10 may be differences of activity or differences of social class. Whether they are travelling, either riding, as befits the wealthier members of society, or *afoot*, or sitting in their tents on their *saddle-cloths*, they are bidden to *ponder...well* what God has done for his people. *the places where the women draw water* are thought of as social centres where ballads of the country's heroic past would be sung. These folk-songs, too, *commemorate...the victories of the LORD*. In the 'holy war', it is God who fights alongside and for his people; it is he who is the true *champion of Israel*.

This first part of the poem is not easy to evaluate. It looks as if it belongs within a context of worship. The congregation are called upon to give thanks for the faithfulness of leaders and people at this time, for those who responded to the call of Deborah to deliver the land, with God's help and direct intervention, from the state of desolation and anarchy in which it lay. Some of the language, especially in the earlier verses, is very like the kind of language used in the Psalms, and God's direct intervention in the affairs of life is often prayed for in the Psalms in terms very similar to those used in verses 4 and 5. The language of the poem in its present form may have been influenced by the language of worship, but the core of the poem, particularly the sections which follow, is much too vividly descriptive of this particular heroic event and its background for it to have originated in a context of worship. ✳

SUMMONS TO BATTLE

Down to the gates came the LORD's people: 11*b*
'Rouse, rouse yourself, Deborah,   12
rouse yourself, lead out the host.

Up, Barak! Take prisoners in plenty,
son of Abinoam.'

13   Then down marched the column*a* and its chieftains,
the people of the Lord marched down*b* like
warriors.

14   The men of Ephraim showed a brave front in the
vale,*c*
crying, 'With you, Benjamin! Your clansmen
are here!'
From Machir down came the marshals,
from Zebulun the bearers of the musterer's staff.

15   Issachar joined with Deborah in the uprising,*d*
Issacher stood by Barak;
down into the valley they rushed.
But Reuben, he was split into factions,
great were their heart-searchings.*e*

16   What made you linger by the cattle-pens
to listen to the shrill calling of the shepherds?*f*

17   Gilead stayed beyond Jordan;
and Dan, why did he tarry by the ships?
Asher lingered by the sea-shore,
by its creeks he stayed.

18   The people of Zebulun risked their very lives,
so did Naphtali on the heights of the battlefield.

✶ The main problem within this section of the Song of
Deborah is the inconsistency between the number of Israelite

[a] *Prob. rdg.; Heb.* survivor.   [b] *Prob. rdg.; Heb. adds* to me.
[c] *So Sept.; Heb.* in Amalek.
[d] in the uprising: *prob. rdg.; Heb.* my officers.
[e] *So some MSS.; others have an unknown word.*
[f] *Prob. rdg.; Heb. adds* Reuben was split into factions, great were their
heart-searchings.

tribes listed in ch. 5 as having participated in the battle against
Sisera and the number listed in ch. 4. According to ch. 4 only
Zebulun and Naphtali took part (verse 10), while according
to ch. 5 Ephraim, Benjamin, Machir (i.e. Manasseh), Zebulun,
Issachar and Naphtali all participated, with Reuben, Gilead,
Dan and Asher being rebuked for their failure to join the
other tribes. In recent study there has been increasing criticism
of the idea that, in the period before the monarchy, ancient
Israel formed an amphictyony or confederacy of twelve
tribes grouped around a central sanctuary (see above, pp. 10f.).
We have already noticed in the book of Judges that the idea
of 'Israel' acting as a unit is the imprint of later editors of
the book and that incidents have involved one or, at most, two
tribes. It has been argued that the beginnings of national
consciousness are to be found in this battle against Sisera where
six tribes participated in concerted action and where four
others failed to respond to what was felt by the others to be
an obligation. It is difficult, however, to base any firm
conclusions on this evidence since, as we have noted, the
account of this engagement in the prose version of ch. 4
involves only the tribes of Zebulun and Naphtali. If one were
to lay emphasis on the ch. 5 version, then this would suggest
a fairly late date for this battle against Sisera for the following
reason. There are no strong arguments for the existence of
inter-tribal action and national consciousness on any large
scale in the period of the judges, but the emergence of the
monarchy under Saul presupposes such a national consciousness. Therefore, this consciousness must have emerged late in
the period of the judges, just before the rise of the monarchy.
The incident recorded in the Song of Deborah must therefore
have taken place towards the end of the period of the judges,
and a date somewhere after 1050 B.C. has been suggested. If,
however, one is cautious about laying too much weight on
the evidence of ch. 5 over against that of ch. 4, then there are
perhaps no very strong arguments for deviating from the date
which is generally assigned to the battle, about 1150–1125 B.C.

If one accepts that originally only Zebulun and Naphtali participated in the battle, one would have to assume that the so-called 'roll-call of the tribes' in verses 14–18 emerged at a later stage in the transmission of the poem when the awareness of some kind of northern kinship had arisen. The absence of Judah and Simeon from the tribes enumerated is explicable on the grounds either that this was a northern action in which Judah and Simeon would have had no interest or else that this part of the poem reached its present form either before Judah was felt to be part of the tribal kinship or after the northern tribes had split from Judah at the death of Solomon.

11*b* f. *Down to the gates came the LORD's people*: the reference, at this point, can hardly be to the gates of the enemy cities of Taanach and Megiddo, since Deborah is only now being exhorted to lead the army. The gates are probably those of the individual Israelite cities from which the troops came. The city gate was the usual place of commercial and legal activity; here it seems also to be the place of local muster. Deborah is here exhorted to *lead out the host*, a role which is not actually attributed to her elsewhere. The translation of this particular phrase is far from certain, and the more usual renderings are along the lines of 'strike up the song'.

13. *down marched the column*: the idea of marching down here does not refer to coming down from Mount Tabor which is mentioned as the place of muster in ch. 4 (verses 7, 12, 14) but which has no place in ch. 5. The reference is, rather, to the descent of the Israelite warriors from the hill-country of Galilee to the plain of Jezreel, the 'vale' of the following verse.

14f. *Ephraim...Benjamin...Machir*: the three tribes of the hill-country of central Palestine. Machir was Manasseh's eldest son according to Josh. 17: 1. Gen. 50: 23 and Num. 26: 29 might suggest that he was his only son. The reference here is obviously to that part of the tribe of Manasseh which was settled west of the Jordan. *Zebulun* and *Issachar* are two Galilaean tribes, the latter apparently Deborah's tribe. Barak's

tribe was Naphtali, and one would have expected a reference
to Naphtali at this point. Some scholars suggest that the
second *Issachar* in verse 15 is an erroneous repetition of the
first and that 'Naphtali' should be read in its place. *Reuben*,
whose territory lay east of the Jordan, at the north-east
corner of the Dead Sea, is the first of the tribes reproached for
not participating in the battle. There appears to have been a
lack of unanimity about Reuben's absence.

16f. The reasons for Reuben's 'heart-searchings' have to do
with sheep-breeding, an important feature of the economy
east of the Jordan. The tradition in Num. 32 records that the
tribes of Reuben and Gad laid special claim to the particularly
fine pasture-land east of the Jordan precisely because they had
'large and very numerous flocks'. No reason is given for
Gilead's non-participation. Gilead is, strictly speaking, a
geographical term, not the name of a tribe, though it does
seem to have tribal significance in a passage such as Judg.
11: 1–2. The region of Gilead lay east of the Jordan opposite
Ephraim and was occupied by the tribe of Gad. The reasons
for the non-participation of *Dan* and *Asher* both have to do
with the sea. This is understandable with regard to Asher,
whose territory lay between that of Naphtali and the Mediterranean; it is less so with regard to Dan. The reference to Dan
tarrying *by the ships* makes no sense if we suppose Dan to be
still settled in its original territory west of Benjamin and Judah.
We must assume that the reference is to Dan settled in the
area to the north of Lake Huleh. There, of course, the Danites
were far inland from the sea, but we could assume that they,
like the Asherites, provided a labour force for the coastal
inhabitants, the Sidonians and the citizens of Tyre. Judg. 18: 7
seems to suggest some kind of relationship between the
Sidonians and the inhabitants of the region subsequently
occupied by the Danites.

18. The final verse of this section of the poem emphasizes
the particularly courageous conduct in battle of *Zebulun* and
Naphtali. Here, of course, are the two tribes which, according

to ch. 4, alone participated in the battle against Sisera. This reference may well be the kernel of which the earlier verses with their references to the other northern tribes are a secondary expansion of a later date. Otherwise there seems to be no very strong reason why these two tribes should be singled out. *the heights of the battlefield*: unless this is a general term for the warlike activity of Naphtali in the hills of Galilee, the reference might be to the belt of basalt which crosses the Kishon marshes 4 miles (nearly 6½ km) south-east of Megiddo or to an eventual flight of the defeated Canaanites into the hills. ✻

DEFEAT AND DEATH OF SISERA

19   Kings came, they fought;
       then fought the kings of Canaan
       at Taanach by the waters of Megiddo;
       no plunder of silver did they take.

20   The stars fought from heaven,
       the stars in their courses fought against Sisera.

21   The Torrent of Kishon swept him away,
       the Torrent barred his flight, the Torrent of
           Kishon;
         march on in might, my soul!

22   Then hammered the hooves of his horses,
       his chargers galloped, galloped away.

23   A curse on Meroz, said the angel of the LORD;
       a curse, a curse on its inhabitants,
       because they brought no help to the LORD,
       no help to the LORD and the fighting men.

24   Blest above women be Jael,
       the wife of Heber the Kenite;
       blest above all women in the tents.

25   He asked for water: she gave him milk,

she offered him curds in a bowl fit for a chieftain.

She stretched out her hand for the tent-peg,   26
her right hand to hammer the weary.

With the hammer she struck Sisera, she crushed
  his head;
she struck and his brains ebbed out.

At her feet he sank down, he fell, he lay;   27
at her feet he sank down and fell.

Where he sank down, there he fell, done to death. Death –
recurring theme
too.

* This third section of the poem contains an account of the
battle between the forces of Sisera and those of Barak 'at
Taanach by the waters of Megiddo'. The account in the
poem, for all its brevity, provides details of the actual battle
which are lacking in the prose account in ch. 4.

19. *Kings came...the kings of Canaan*: from this it would
seem clear that Barak's opponents were really a Canaanite
coalition headed, presumably, by Sisera. The most likely
supposition is that this was a coalition of Canaanite city-states
stretching in a north-west/south-east direction along the
southern edge of the Plain of Jezreel. They may have included
at least some of the city-states listed in 1: 27f. *at Taanach by
the waters of Megiddo*: much has been made of the fact that the
place mentioned here is the less important Taanach. It has been
concluded that Megiddo itself had already been destroyed,
and attempts have been made to date this battle to a period
when the archaeological evidence from Megiddo suggests
that the site was unoccupied. This archaeological evidence is,
however, difficult to evaluate, and too much weight should
not be placed on what is, after all, a poetic style and context.
no plunder of silver did they take: the reference here must be to
the fact that the Canaanites were prevented from securing the
normal spoils of war. Such, at any rate, is the sense demanded
by the N.E.B. translation. It would be possible to render the

Hebrew as 'they received no financial gain', and the sense would then be that the forces of the Canaanite coalition were not mercenaries but men who fought with heart and soul in defence of their own interests.

20. *The stars fought from heaven*: taken in conjunction with verse 21, this phrase must refer to a sudden and violent rain-storm. The actual wording may be thought of either as a poetical reference to the direct intervention of God in the battle or else as a reference to the primitive belief in the stars as a source of rain.

21. The strategic significance of the River Kishon is brought out in two different ways here. There is, in the first line of the verse, the reference to the flooded stream sweeping away Sisera's forces, while the second line states that they were unable to flee because their retreat was cut off. This second aspect suggests that the battle was fought to the north of the Kishon and that Sisera's forces were unable to flee in a southerly (south-westerly) direction. *march on in might, my soul!* this can be understood only as some kind of cry on the part of the poet rousing himself to participate in the battle, as it were. But this is not easy, and many scholars have emended the text to try to find a more likely sense. The most probable suggestion is perhaps 'Bless, O my soul, the might of the LORD.'

22. *his horses, his chargers*: these must be the horses of Sisera and his forces. The verse in Hebrew tries to reproduce the sound of the hoof-beats, and a similar attempt has been made in the English translation with the alliteration in the first line of the verse.

23. Meroz does not figure in the prose narrative at all and there is no certain location for it. The most that can be suggested is that Meroz was probably a Canaanite settlement which had some kind of treaty relationship with one of the Israelite tribes involved in the battle. At any rate, it was expected that Meroz would have helped the Israelites in some such way as cutting off the flight of Sisera's forces or

providing sustenance for the pursuers. Such help did not materialize, so Meroz and its inhabitants were ritually cursed. The *angel of the LORD* may be simply his 'messenger' and suggest a prophet-like figure, or else the line may have originally read, 'Curse Meroz with the curse of the LORD.' It would seem probable that as a result of the curse Meroz was totally destroyed without trace. Notice again how this identifies the war as the LORD's war.

24-7. The account of the dénouement of the story in Jael's tent here is substantially in agreement with that in the prose narrative, 4: 17-22. Here, too, the phrase *the wife of Heber the Kenite* (verse 24) is probably secondary. *curds* here (verse 25) is butter-milk, and this was probably what was intended by the 'milk' of 4: 19. While verse 26 is in agreement with ch. 4 as to the method whereby Sisera was killed, verse 27 seems to suggest a slightly different method. With its emphasis on the fact that *At her feet he sank down, he fell*, it seems to suggest that Jael felled him with a blow while he was standing up drinking from the bowl. Verses 26 and 27 may, therefore, reflect two variant traditions regarding the death of Sisera, only one of which is reproduced in the prose narrative. ✻

WAITING IN VAIN

The mother of Sisera peered through the lattice, 28
through the window she peered and shrilly cried,
'Why are his chariots so long coming?
Why is the clatter of his chariots so long delayed?'
The wisest of her princesses answered her, 29
yes, she found her own answer:
'They must be finding spoil, taking their shares, 30
a wench to each man, two wenches,
booty of dyed stuffs for Sisera,
booty of dyed stuffs,

dyed stuff, and striped, two lengths of striped stuff –
to grace the victor's neck.'

31　　So perish all thine enemies, O Lord;
　　　but let all who love thee[a] be like the sun rising in
　　　　strength.

The land was at peace for forty years.

---

* The poet, in this final section of his poem, parodies the old
custom whereby the women went out to greet the returning
victors with songs and dances. The custom is reflected in
1 Sam. 18: 6–7; Exod. 15: 20–2 and in Judg. 11: 34 where
Jephthah's daughter goes out to meet her father.

28. *The mother of Sisera*: in the royal family in Judah the
'first lady' was the queen mother, not one of the king's wives.
In the introductions to the reigns of the kings of Judah, as
these are recorded in the books of Kings (e.g. 1 Kings 14: 21),
we find that the name of the king's mother is always included
because the 'great lady', as her official title was, had a special
position at court. Here, too, among the Canaanite city-states a
similar practice would seem to have been in force, though it is
equally possible that the poem simply reflects later practice in
Judah and tells us nothing about the Canaanite city-states of
the twelfth century B.C. *lattice* is simply a poetic variant for
window, but it does reveal the type of window used. The slatted
lattice would admit the air while cutting out the harsh light.

29. *The wisest of her princesses*: the queen mother would be
in charge of the royal harem. The fact that Sisera's harem are
referred to as *princesses* indicates Sisera's independence as a king.
He is not, as the Jabin/Hazor element in the prose narrative
would have us believe, merely Jabin's army commander.

30. The princess's explanation for the prolonged absence of
Sisera is that the troops are still searching for booty. She is
confident of their imminent return. The poem breaks off at

[a] *So Pesh.; Heb.* him.

this point and the supreme artistry of the poet is revealed by his reticence here. He does not show us the women's reaction to the news of Sisera's defeat and death. The women are in ignorance, but the reader knows Sisera's real fate. It is left to our imagination to supply the ending.

31. This final verse stands apart. It does not belong with the central block of the poem (verses 12–30) but, with its address to the LORD in the second person, with the more liturgically orientated part in verses 2–11. The LORD's *enemies* are cursed and condemned to oblivion, while all who love him are compared with the unquenchable power of the sun. The final sentence of the verse is, as we have already noted, the concluding element in the deuteronomistic chronology. It would normally have come at the end of ch. 4; its displacement to the end of ch. 5 serves to include the latter chapter within the account of the activities of Deborah and Barak.   *

GIDEON

* The narrative of Gideon's judgeship is contained within chs. 6–8 and is, in its present form, closely linked with the Abimelech story in ch. 9. The various elements which go to make up the joint story of Gideon and Abimelech did not always form the connected narrative which they now do, and there is a long history of amalgamation and fusion and harmonization behind the present form of the narrative. This history is not only long but also complex, and it is not always easy or, indeed, even possible, to trace the various stages through which it has passed. The following fairly general points can, however, be made. The equation of Gideon with Jerubbaal is a secondary element in the narrative; originally these were two quite separate individuals. Gideon, son of Joash, was a member of the clan of Abiezer, a clan which was part of the tribe of Manasseh, and he distinguished himself in what was basically only clan warfare against Midianite invaders and oppressors coming from east of the Jordan.

Jerubbaal, on the other hand, was the father of Abimelech who eventually exercised a purely local kingship in the mixed Canaanite–Israelite city-state of Shechem. The name 'Jerubbaal' belongs in the context of the destruction of the altar of Baal (6: 25–31). Because of certain similarities, this story was joined with the story of the founding of the altar called 'Jehovah-shalom' (6: 19–24). Gideon was the hero of the 'Jehovah-shalom' story, and he subsequently appears as the hero of the 'Baal' story too. In this way he became identified with Jerubbaal, and verse 32 was added to indicate the change of name 'Gideon' to 'Jerubbaal'. All the other passages where the identification of Gideon with Jerubbaal is made are simply attempts to harmonize two originally independent stories. Some of the reasons for the statements which have just been made will become clear on an examination of the individual parts of the story. ✳

MIDIANITE OPPRESSION

6 The Israelites did what was wrong in the eyes of the LORD and he delivered them into the hands of Midian for seven
2 years. The Midianites were too strong for Israel, and the Israelites were forced to find themselves hollow places in
3 the mountains, and caves and strongholds. If the Israelites had sown their seed, the Midianites and the Amalekites and other eastern tribes would come up and attack Israel.
4 They then pitched their camps in the country and destroyed the crops as far as the outskirts of Gaza, leaving nothing to
5 support life in Israel, sheep or ox or ass. They came up with their herds and their tents, like a swarm of locusts; they and their camels were past counting. They had come
6 into the land for its growing crop,[a] and so the Israelites were brought to destitution by the Midianites, and they

[a] for its growing crop: *or* and laid it waste.

78

cried to the LORD for help. When the Israelites cried to 7
the LORD because of what they had suffered from the
Midianites, he sent them a prophet who said to them, 8
'These are the words of the LORD the God of Israel: I
brought you up from Egypt, that land of slavery. I 9
delivered you from the Egyptians and from all your
oppressors. I drove them out before you and gave you
their lands. I said to you, "I am the LORD your God: do 10
not stand in awe of the gods of the Amorites in whose
country you are settling." But you did not listen to me.'

* 1. The section begins, as usual, with a note on the Israelites'
relapse into apostasy with the consequent punishment of being
subjected to foreign domination, in this case the Midianites,
for the specific period of *seven years*. *Midian* was the name
given to that region in the north-west of the Arabian peninsula which lay to the east of the Gulf of Aqabah. The
Midianites, however, were a nomadic race and are frequently
found in Moabite territory. In this story they are depicted as
making invasions into the fertile area west of the Jordan.

2. In this verse and in the verses which follow, the description of the foreign oppression of the Israelites is much more
graphic than usual. The Israelites have to resort to hiding in
the wilder parts of the countryside, just as they are forced to
do at a later stage under Philistine pressure (1 Sam. 13: 6).

3–5. The conflict here is that between the settled farmer
and the invading nomad or semi-nomad. Here the Midianites
are associated with others in a general invasion from the
desert. On *the Amalekites* see above on 3: 12–14. The expression
other eastern tribes is a general designation for the bedouin of
the Arabian desert. We are told the specific reason for this
bedouin invasion, namely that *They had come into the land for
its growing crop*. As can be seen from the footnote, the translation of the final phrase is not entirely certain. The alternative

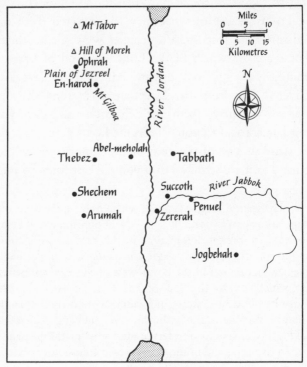

3. Gideon and Abimelech (chs. 6–9)

translation certainly corresponds to the facts, for not only did the invaders leave *nothing to support life in Israel*, but their coming is likened to *a swarm of locusts*, a figure of speech which refers both to the completeness of their devastation and to their numbers. *their camels*: this may well be the first historical reference to camel nomadism on any large scale. Individuals and families may have possessed the odd camel in earlier periods, but it was probably not until the end of the second millennium B.C. that camels were fully domesticated and widely used. The type of camel referred to here would be the single-humped Arabian camel or dromedary. The expression *as far as the outskirts of Gaza* seems to take these bedouin incursions very far to the south. The literal rendering of the Hebrew at this point, 'till you come to Gaza', may suggest that the reference is rather to 'the Gaza road' which passed along the western foothills of the central highlands.

6. *they cried to the LORD for help*: the usual response of the Israelites to their state of oppression.

8–10. The divine response to the Israelites' cry is to send them *a prophet*. This is clearly a reading back into this period of history of an office and function which belongs to a much later stage of Israel's religion. Into his mouth is put a typical deuteronomistic sermon such as we find, for example, in 1 Sam. 8: 7–9; 10: 17–19. That this is secondary is clear from the fact that Gideon's question in verse 13 is unaware of the words of the prophet. The origins of this kind of sermon are probably cultic. The content is partly credal and bears some relationship to the Israelite creed as we find it in Deut. 26: 5–10. But there is also a connection with the idea of God arguing with his people and calling them to judgement. We find this idea not only in the Psalms (Ps. 50), but also in the prophets (Isa. 1: 10–20). The point of the sermon is that the Midianite oppression is the people's punishment for refusing to *listen to* or 'obey' God. ✳

THE CALL OF GIDEON

Now the angel of the LORD came and sat under the 11 terebinth at Ophrah which belonged to Joash the Abiez-rite. His son Gideon was threshing wheat in the winepress, so that he might get it away quickly from the Midianites. The angel of the LORD showed himself to Gideon and 12 said, 'You are a brave man, and the LORD is with you.' Gideon said, 'But pray, my lord, if the LORD really is 13 with us, why has all this happened to us? What has become of all those wonderful deeds of his, of which we

have heard from our fathers, when they told us how the LORD brought us out of Egypt? But now the LORD has cast us off and delivered us into the power of the Midian-
14 ites.' The LORD turned to him and said, 'Go and use this strength of yours to free Israel from the power of the
15 Midianites. It is I that send you.' Gideon said, 'Pray, my lord, how can I save Israel? Look at my clan: it is the weakest in Manasseh, and I am the least in my father's
16 family.' The LORD answered, 'I will be with you, and
17 you shall lay low all Midian as one man.' He replied, 'If I stand so well with you, give me a sign that it is you who
18 speak to me. Please do not leave this place until I come with my gift and lay it before you.' He answered, 'I will
19 stay until you come back.' So Gideon went in, prepared a kid and made an ephah of flour into unleavened cakes. He put the meat in a basket, poured the broth into a pot and brought it out to him under the terebinth. As he
20 approached, the angel of God said to him, 'Take the meat and the cakes, and put them here on the rock and pour
21 out the broth', and he did so. Then the angel of the LORD reached out the staff in his hand and touched the meat and the cakes with the tip of it. Fire sprang up from the rock and consumed the meat and the cakes; and the angel
22 of the LORD was no more to be seen. Then Gideon knew that it was the angel of the LORD and said, 'Alas, Lord GOD! Then it is true: I have seen the angel of the LORD
23 face to face.' But the LORD said to him, 'Peace be with
24 you; do not be afraid, you shall not die.' So Gideon built an altar there to the LORD and named it Jehovah-shalom.[a] It stands to this day at Ophrah-of-the-Abiezrites.

[a] *That is* the LORD is peace.

Obedient
Gideon offer
sacrifice

✣ This section, which, in its present form, can be entitled 'The Call of Gideon', is nevertheless made up of two distinct elements. The first, verses 11*b*–18, is indeed concerned with God's call to Gideon to be the deliverer of his people from Midianite oppression; the second, verses 11*a* and 19–24, is concerned with the foundation of an altar at Ophrah and with the reason for considering Ophrah a sanctuary, namely the appearance of God to Gideon at Ophrah. There is no specific location for the story of Gideon's call, and the attribution to Gideon of the building of the altar at Ophrah may be secondary. Ophrah is a sanctuary within the tribal territory of Manasseh. Gideon was a hero of the tribe of Manasseh; he belonged to a family in the Manassite clan Abiezer. The founding of sanctuaries was often attributed to famous men, as, for example, in the patriarchal stories; it was natural, therefore, that the founding of the sanctuary at Ophrah should be associated with the hero Gideon.

11. On *the angel of the LORD* see above on 2: 1. Here, too, there is confusion of identity between the angel and God himself; see, e.g., verses 14, 16 and 18 in the call narrative and verse 23 in the altar narrative. *the terebinth at Ophrah*: trees were usually associated with Canaanite sanctuaries, usually as symbols of the fertility goddess. The presence of the terebinth at Ophrah shows that it is already a Canaanite sanctuary. The purpose of the narrative in verses 19–24 is to indicate its conversion to being a sanctuary of 'the LORD'. In this respect the story is paralleled with that in verses 25–31, although, as we shall see, there are important differences between the two stories. The site of Ophrah is uncertain. The following words, *which belonged to Joash the Abiezrite*, are secondary with regard to the place-name Ophrah. They belong within the context of the story of the call of Gideon, who was the son of Joash, who was a member of the Abiezer clan of the tribe of Manasseh. *Gideon was threshing wheat in the winepress*: wheat was normally threshed on an open hill-top where the wind could blow away the chaff and leave the wheat grains. In the present

adverse circumstances, however, the threshing had to be done as unobtrusively as possible. A winepress was usually some kind of hollowed-out cistern which in turn led into a still lower container where the grape-juice would collect. If Gideon were *in* the winepress he would be effectively concealed from view. There would also be a limit to the amount he could thresh at any one time in the winepress, and this would make it easier for him to *get it away quickly* and conceal it from any suspicious Midianites.

12. The words of the angel to Gideon are similar to those with which David is described by one of Saul's attendants in 1 Sam. 16: 18, 'he is a brave man and a good fighter, wise in speech and handsome, and the LORD is with him'. Not only is Gideon, like David, *brave*, but his activity as a warrior will be characterized by God's presence with him.

13. We have already noted that Gideon's reply in this verse reveals no knowledge of the words of the anonymous 'prophet' in verses 8–10. This indicates that the call narrative was originally independent of the present introduction to the Gideon story as a whole.

14–17. These verses contain the actual commissioning of Gideon, and, as such, they follow a specific pattern which can be found elsewhere in the Old Testament. First of all, God specifically commissions Gideon to free his people from the Midianite oppression: '*It is I that send you*' (verse 14). The second element in the pattern is the objection on the part of the person chosen to the effect that he is unfit for the task: '*how can I save Israel?...I am the least in my father's family*' (verse 15). Thirdly, God rejects the objection by means of a promise of personal assistance: '*I will be with you*' (verse 16). The final element in the pattern is the giving of a sign to the person who is being commissioned which will prove that it is really God who has given the commission. In this instance the sign is requested: '*give me a sign that it is you who speak to me*' (verse 17). This 'call pattern' can be found also in the case of Moses (Exod. 3: 10–12) and of Jeremiah (Jer. 1: 5–10) and, though in a less complete form, in the story of the anointing of Saul in 1 Sam. 10: 1–7 in conjunction with 1 Sam. 9: 27.

18. In the present form of the call narrative, no sign is given at this point. The continuation of the call narrative is in verses 36–40, and there the sign has to do with a fleece of wool. But at this point in the present form of the narrative, the place of the sign has been taken by the phenomenon which is described in verse 21 and which was the means of God's revelation of himself. Verse 18 is a transitional verse between the story of Gideon's call and the story of the building of the altar at Ophrah. It flows more smoothly on from verse 11*a*, after the words 'under the terebinth at Ophrah', but it does also, within its present context, provide a continuation of verse 17. The word rendered *gift* is, probably intentionally, ambiguous in this context; it could equally well be translated as 'offering'.

19. The attitude of Gideon to the visitor and the preparations which he makes recall the attitude of Abraham to his three visitors in Gen. 18: 1–8. The mention of *unleavened cakes* gives to the 'gift' the connotation of a sacrifice, as does the large quantity of flour used. An *ephah* was approximately a bushel, about 45 lb (20 kg) of flour.

20. *the rock*: rock-altars with cup-shaped hollows for receiving libations (cp. *pour out the broth*) are known from several sites in Palestine. See *Old Testament Illustrations* in this series, p. 152 (no. 169) and p. 158 (no. 176).

21. *Fire sprang up from the rock*: sacrifices were normally burned, either in whole or in part, and the fire here is a symbol of the divine acceptance of the offering. *the angel of the LORD was no more to be seen*: the theophany or appearance of God to man is at an end.

22. By the divine acceptance of his offering in this way, Gideon became aware that it had been God revealing himself to him; he *knew*. The idea that man was unable to see God *face to face* and survive is common in the Old Testament; cp. Judg. 13: 22; Exod. 33: 20.

23. *you shall not die*: the expected punishment for having seen God 'face to face' will not be inflicted. *Peace be with you*: this is the conventional everyday greeting of one man to another, and it provides the name for the altar which is to be built on the site.

24. *So Gideon built an altar there to the LORD*: the building of an altar on a site where God appeared to man is a common motif in the patriarchal stories; cp., e.g., Gen. 12: 7. *and named it Jehovah-shalom*: the name of the altar, as can be seen from the N.E.B. footnote, means 'the LORD is peace'; the altar is built in honour of the God who promises peace or well-being to those who obey him. The proper name of the God who is worshipped in the Old Testament was probably originally pronounced 'Yahweh'. This was too sacred a name for the Jews ever to pronounce, so every time they came across it they said 'my Lord' instead, and it is this custom which is reproduced in the N.E.B. by the use of the word LORD. The word *Jehovah* consists of the consonants of the original proper name together with the vowels of the Hebrew word meaning 'my Lord'. For a more detailed discussion of this point see *The Making of the Old Testament* in this series, pp. 143 and 160. *to this day*: the phrase is frequently found in contexts which claim to tell the story behind a particular phenomenon or place or name. ✻

THE OVERTHROW OF THE ALTAR OF BAAL

25 That night the LORD said to Gideon, 'Take a young bull of your father's, the yearling bull,*a* tear down the altar of Baal which belongs to your father and cut down the

26 sacred pole*b* which stands beside*c* it. Then build an altar of the proper pattern*d* to the LORD your God on the top

[a] the yearling bull: *prob. rdg.; Heb.* the second bull, seven years old.
[b] sacred pole: *Heb.* asherah.   [c] *Or* on.
[d] of...pattern: *or* with the stones in rows.

of this earthwork;[a] take the yearling bull and offer it as
a whole-offering with the wood of the sacred pole that
you cut down.' So Gideon took ten of his servants and 27
did as the LORD had told him. He was afraid of his father's
family and his fellow-citizens, and so he did it by night,
and not by day. When the citizens rose early in the 28
morning, they found the altar of Baal overturned and the
sacred pole which had stood beside it cut down and the
yearling bull offered up as a whole-offering on the altar
which he had built. They asked each other who had done 29
it, and, after searching inquiries, were told that it was
Gideon son of Joash. So the citizens said to Joash, 'Bring 30
out your son. He has overturned the altar of Baal and
cut down the sacred pole beside it, and he must die.'
But as they crowded round him Joash retorted, 'Are you 31
pleading Baal's cause then? Do you think that it is for
you to save him? Whoever pleads his cause shall be put
to death at dawn. If Baal is a god, and someone has torn
down his altar, let him take up his own cause.' That day 32
Joash named Gideon Jerubbaal,[b] saying, 'Let Baal plead
his cause against this man, for he has torn down his altar.'

* This story of the overthrow of the altar of the Baal and
the conversion of an original Baal-sanctuary into a sanctuary
dedicated to the God of Israel has sometimes been thought to
be a variant of the story of the founding of the altar of
'Jehovah-shalom' at Ophrah in verses 19–24. While there are
similarities between the two stories, there are too many
differences for such an explanation to be a satisfactory one.
What we have is an originally independent story about a
change in the kind of worship offered at a sanctuary which is

[a] *Or* stronghold *or* refuge.   [b] *That is* Let Baal plead.

not named. Only the present position of verses 25–32, following immediately on verse 24, makes us assume that the Baal altar was at Ophrah. In view of the fact that Gideon and his father Joash appear to be loyal and faithful worshippers of the God of Israel, we are forced to wonder whether it is likely that Joash would be the owner of an altar dedicated to the Canaanite god Baal. The names 'Gideon' and 'Joash' are now fairly well embedded in the narrative, but it may have been the slight similarities between this story and the immediately preceding one which caused this destruction of the Baal altar to be attributed to Gideon too. The 'popular etymology' at the end of the story might make us think that the original hero of the story was Jerubbaal. The identification of Gideon with Jerubbaal is, as we have already noted, secondary.

25. *That night the LORD said to Gideon*: two of the differences between this narrative and the preceding one can be noted in these words. In this narrative it is *the LORD* who speaks by *night*; in the preceding one, the protagonist is 'the angel of the LORD' who appears by day. *the yearling bull*: the translation problems apparent from the N.E.B. footnote are not of very great importance. *the altar of Baal which belongs to your father*: we have already noted the unlikelihood of Joash being the owner of a Baal altar. The possibility cannot be discounted that this narrative belongs within the Jerubbaal–Abimelech context, particularly when we remember that the setting of the Jerubbaal–Abimelech story is Shechem, whose particular god is Baal-berith (see below on 8: 33). *the sacred pole*: Canaanite sanctuaries were usually furnished with two cultic objects besides an altar. One was a standing stone (Hebrew *mazzēbāh*) which was the symbol of the male deity; the other was a sacred pole (Hebrew *'ashērāh*), the symbol of the female deity. The latter was probably a symbolic survival of the sacred grove or tree (see above on 'the terebinth at Ophrah', verse 11). Asherah was also the name of a Canaanite goddess, as, e.g., in 1 Kings 18: 19.

26. *an altar of the proper pattern*: the reference, both of the

text of the N.E.B. and of the footnote, is probably to the specific way in which the altar was to be built. There are instructions for making an altar in Exod. 20: 24-6. *on the top of this earthwork*: again, there is uncertainty as to the exact meaning of the word translated 'earthwork'. The main point to note, however, is that here the altar is on top of some kind of structure, whereas in the preceding narrative it was a rock under the terebinth (verses 19f. and 24). There were different types of offering in the fully developed system of sacrifices in ancient Israel. In the *whole-offering* the entire animal was consumed by fire; in other types of offering only certain parts of the animal were burnt, while the meat was eaten at a communal meal.

30. *he must die*: death would be the inevitable punishment for Gideon's sacrilegious act against the god.

31f. There is considerable play with the phrase *pleading Baal's cause* in verse 31, and it is clearly intended that this should indicate the meaning of the name Jerubbaal. The verb 'to plead a case' in Hebrew is *rīb* and the form for 'let X plead a case' would be *yārīb*. It can be seen that this bears some similarity to the first part of the proper name Jerubbaal, but not enough for this to be the correct interpretation of the name. The name probably means 'may Baal show himself great', but the sense suggested in this verse is close enough to pass as 'popular etymology'. There is some similarity, too, between the words of Joash in this situation and those of Elijah in his contest with the prophets of Baal on Mount Carmel in 1 Kings 18: 27. Verse 32, as we have already noted, is probably a secondary attempt to harmonize a story, which originally concerned Jerubbaal in a Shechem context, with the larger Gideon narrative. ✷

THE SIGN OF THE FLEECE

All the Midianites, the Amalekites, and the eastern tribes 33 joined forces, crossed the river and camped in the Vale

34 of Jezreel. Then the spirit of the LORD took possession of[a]
Gideon; he sounded the trumpet and the Abiezrites were
called out to follow him. He sent messengers all through
35 Manasseh; and they too were called out. He sent messengers to Asher, Zebulun, and Naphtali, and they came
36 up to meet the others. Gideon said to God, 'If thou wilt
37 deliver Israel through me as thou hast promised – now,
look, I am putting a fleece of wool on the threshing-floor.
If there is dew only on the fleece and all the ground is dry,
then I shall be sure that thou wilt deliver Israel through
38 me, as thou hast promised.' And that is what happened.
He rose early next day and wrung out the fleece, and he
squeezed enough dew from it to fill a bowl with water.
39 Gideon then said to God, 'Do not be angry with me, but
give me leave to speak once again. Let me, I pray thee,
make one more test with the fleece. This time let the
fleece alone be dry, and all the ground be covered with
40 dew.' God let it be so that night: the fleece alone was
dry, and on all the ground there was dew.

✻ This short section contains two distinct elements. The first,
verses 33–5, is Gideon's muster of troops to fight the assembled
Midianites. The second, verses 36–40, is the continuation of
the story of Gideon's call and is the description of the sign
which Gideon requested in verse 17. It should be noted that
there are differences between verses 11*b*–17 on the one hand
and verses 36–40 on the other. In the former the deity is
referred to as 'the LORD' while in the latter he is 'God'; in
the former the scene is 'the winepress', in the latter it is 'the
threshing-floor'. It might, therefore, be more accurate to
refer to this section as a fragment of an account of Gideon's
call parallel to, or as a variant of, the narrative in verses 11*b*–17.

[a] took possession of: *lit.* clothed itself with…

In their present context, verses 36–40 serve to dispel Gideon's last-minute doubts as to his fitness for the task laid upon him.

33. The scene for the ensuing battle is set in the great central plain of Palestine, *the Vale of Jezreel*. The *river* which the Midianites and their allies crossed was, of course, the Jordan.

34f. *the spirit of the LORD took possession of Gideon*: on the charismatic aspect of the office of judge, see above on 2: 16. The expression used here is, as can be seen from the N.E.B. footnote, picturesque, though 'the spirit of the LORD clothed Gideon' might be a more accurate literal rendering of the Hebrew than the one suggested in the note. *he sounded the trumpet*: as in 3: 27, the call to arms. In verse 34 the muster is confined to Gideon's own clan of Abiezer. This is in line with what we have already observed, that the encounters recorded in the book of Judges between 'Israel' on the one hand and a foreign invader or oppressor on the other are largely confined to one or, at most, two tribes. The idea that they involved an entity known as 'Israel' is a later concept, and it is likely that the idea expressed in verse 35, that the muster also involved *Manasseh*, *Asher*, *Zebulun* and *Naphtali*, is also secondary.

36–8. Gideon, resuming from verse 17, asks for a sign. God had *promised* in verses 14 and 16 to free Israel from Midianite oppression by the hand of Gideon. It is confirmation of this promise that Gideon is now seeking. To have *dew only on the fleece* was only to be expected; wool would absorb and retain moisture much more readily than the hard, beaten earth of the *threshing-floor*.

39f. Much more miraculous is the reverse process of leaving *the fleece alone...dry*, and this is what, according to the saga, happens. Gideon's words in verse 39 are strongly reminiscent of those of Abraham to God as he argues for the sparing of Sodom in Gen. 18: 23–33; see especially verses 30 and 32 there for the verbal similarity with verse 39 here. *

GIDEON'S THREE HUNDRED MEN

7 Jerubbaal, that is Gideon, and all the people with him rose early and pitched camp at En-harod;[a] the Midianite camp was in the vale to the north of the hill of Moreh.

2 The LORD said to Gideon, 'The people with you are more than I need to deliver Midian into their hands: Israel will claim the glory for themselves and say that it is

3 their own strength that has given them the victory. Now make a proclamation for all the people to hear, that anyone who is scared or frightened is to leave Mount Galud[b] at once and go back home.' Twenty-two thousand of

4 them went, and ten thousand were left. The LORD then said to Gideon, 'There are still too many. Bring them down to the water, and I will separate them for you there. When I say to you, "This man shall go with you", he shall go; and if I say, "This man shall not go with

5 you", he shall not go.' So Gideon brought the people down to the water and the LORD said to him, 'Make every man who laps the water with his tongue like a dog stand on one side, and on the other[c] every man who goes

6 down on his knees and drinks.' The number of those who lapped was three hundred, and all the rest went down on their knees to drink, putting their hands to their mouths.[d]

7 The LORD said to Gideon, 'With the three hundred men who lapped I will save you and deliver Midian into your

8 hands, and all the rest may go home.' So Gideon sent all

[a] *That is* Spring of Fright.
[b] *Prob. rdg.; Heb.* Mount Gilead.
[c] on the other: *so Sept.; Heb. om.*
[d] putting...mouths: *prob. rdg.; Heb. has this phrase after those who lapped.*

these Israelites home, but he kept the three hundred, and
they took with them the jars[a] and the trumpets which the
people had. The Midianite camp was below him in the vale.

✻ The aim of this section, in which, by a process of elimina-
tion, Gideon's army of 32,000 is reduced to a small force of
300, is to emphasize that it is God who wins the victory over
the Midianites. This is an important element in the idea of
the holy war. Israel must not be allowed to think that in her
own strength she has fought the battles and won the victory.
Only in 8: 10 is any numerical strength given for the Midianite
forces, a total of 135,000 men. Previously what was said was
that they were as numerous as a swarm of locusts or as the
grains of sand on the sea-shore (6: 5; 7: 12). One cannot, of
course, place any reliance on the figures given either for the
Midianite troops or for Gideon's own original force, but the
emphasis is clear. With such a vast discrepancy between the
two armies, God alone could have brought about the Israelite
victory.

1. The occurrence of the name *Jerubbaal* here is a secondary
harmonization of the two stories, that of Jerubbaal and that of
Gideon. It is Gideon who is the hero of the war against the
Midianites. *En-harod*: a spring on the northern edge of the
mountain area known as Mount Gilboa. It overlooked the
Plain of Jezreel, *the vale*, facing *the hill of Moreh*, behind (*to the
north of*) which the Midianites were encamped. The name of
the spring, the Spring of Fright (see the N.E.B. footnote), is
clearly connected with the word 'frightened' in verse 3. The
etymology is not made explicit, but the suggestion would be
obvious to a Hebrew reader.

2f. The dangers of an over-large army are stressed; Israel
could *claim the glory for themselves* once the victory had been
won. The process of reducing the numbers of Gideon's
forces begins with a preliminary *proclamation* suggesting that

[a] *Prob. rdg.; Heb.* provisions.

any who are *scared or frightened* should return *home* at once. Deut. 20: 8 makes provision for this kind of proclamation. The army, says Deuteronomy, is better without the man who 'has lost heart' in case 'his comrades will be discouraged as he is'. *Mount Galud*: the Hebrew text has 'Mount Gilead' at this point. This is obviously wrong since the place-name 'Gilead' is, as far as we know, confined to the area of that name east of the Jordan. There is a spring called Galud at the foot of the Mount Gilboa range, just east of the town of Jezreel; Mount Galud would then be a part of the larger area known as Mount Gilboa. It is possible to interpret the meaning of the place-name as 'Coward's Hill'; it would thus be a variant name for En-harod.

4–7. In order to reduce the numbers still further, another method is employed. As can be seen from the N.E.B. footnotes, the Hebrew text at this point is not entirely clear, but the difference between the two styles of drinking seems to be as follows. One group appear to throw themselves flat on the ground and to lick up the water with their tongues; the other group crouch or kneel and lift the water to their mouths with their hands. The selection of which group is to remain with Gideon is made on purely numerical grounds. Those who threw themselves flat on the ground are, from the military point of view, less astute than the others, but they are the smaller in number and so are chosen. In this way, Gideon's forces are reduced to 300. This story of the reduction in numbers may be partly a literary device intended to reconcile the sober facts of history, namely that Gideon defeated the Midianites with a small force of men from his own clan, with the later tradition that this was one of the great battles of the embryo Israelite nation in which several of the tribes were involved.

8. *they took with them the jars and the trumpets which the people had*: jars here is only a probable reading. There is no further mention of 'provisions' (so Hebrew; see the N.E.B. footnote), only of empty jars (verse 16); it could be that the

'provisions' of verse 8 were contained in the jars of verse 16. The reason for the retention of *the jars and the trumpets* becomes clear from the section immediately following. ✳

DEFEAT OF THE MIDIANITES

That night the LORD said to him, 'Go down at once 9 and attack the camp, for I have delivered it into your hands. If you are afraid to do so, then go down first with 10 your servant Purah and listen to what they are saying. 11 That will give you courage to go down and attack the camp.' So he and his servant Purah went down to the part of the camp where the fighting men lay. Now the 12 Midianites, the Amalekites, and the eastern tribes were so many that they lay there in the valley like a swarm of locusts; there was no counting their camels; in number they were like grains of sand on the sea-shore. When 13 Gideon came close, there was a man telling his companion a dream. He said, 'I dreamt that I saw a hard, stale barley-cake rolling over and over through the Midianite camp; it came to a tent, hit it[a] and turned it upside down, and the tent collapsed.' The other answered, 'Depend 14 upon it, this is the sword of Gideon son of Joash the Israel-ite. God has delivered Midian and the whole army into his hands.' When Gideon heard the story of the dream 15 and its interpretation, he prostrated himself. Then he went back to the Israelite camp and said, 'Up! The LORD has delivered the camp of the Midianites into your hands.' He divided the three hundred men into three companies, 16 and gave every man a trumpet and an empty jar with a torch inside it. Then he said to them, 'Watch me: when 17

[a] *Prob. rdg.; Heb. adds* and it fell.

18 I come to the edge of the camp, do exactly as I do. When I and my men blow our trumpets, you too all round the camp will blow your trumpets, and shout, "For the LORD and for Gideon!"'

19   Gideon and the hundred men who were with him reached the outskirts of the camp at the beginning of the middle watch; the sentries had just been posted. They

20 blew their trumpets and smashed their jars. The three companies all blew their trumpets and smashed their jars, then grasped the torches in their left hands and the trumpets in their right, and shouted, 'A sword for the LORD

21 and for Gideon!' Every man stood where he was, all round the camp, and the whole camp leapt up in a panic

22 and fled. The three hundred blew their trumpets, and throughout the camp the LORD set every man against his neighbour. The army fled as far as Beth-shittah in Zererah,

23 as far as the ridge of Abel-meholah by Tabbath. The Israelites from Naphtali and Asher and all Manasseh were

24 called out and they pursued the Midianites. Gideon sent men through all the hill-country of Ephraim with this message: 'Come down and cut off the Midianites. Hold the fords of the Jordan against them as far as Beth-barah.' So all the Ephraimites were called out and they held the

25 fords of the Jordan as far as Beth-barah. They captured the two Midianite princes, Oreb and Zeeb. Oreb they killed at the Rock of Oreb, and Zeeb by the Winepress of Zeeb, and they kept up the pursuit of[a] the Midianites; afterwards they brought the heads of Oreb and Zeeb across the Jordan to Gideon.

8   The men of Ephraim said to Gideon, 'Why have you

[a] *So Sept.; Heb.* to.

treated us like this? Why did you not summon us when
you went to fight Midian?'; and they reproached him
violently. But he said to them, 'What have I done com- 2
pared with you? Are not Ephraim's gleanings better than
the whole vintage of Abiezer? God has delivered Oreb 3
and Zeeb, the princes of Midian, into your hands. What
have I done compared with you?' At these words of his,
their anger died down.

* This section contains various elements within it. First of all
there is the story of Gideon's reconnaissance and his decision
to make a night attack on the Midianite camp. In view of the
fact that there are two different, though similar, war cries
(verse 18 and verse 20), the second of which would seem to
imply that 'swords' were an important element in the attack,
and that the sounding of the trumpets and the breaking of the
jars scarcely seem to be part of the same account, it is highly
likely that in the part of the narrative which concerns the
attack we have the conflation of at least two different strategies.
There follows the story of the pursuit and slaying of two
Midianite princes whose names seem to be associated with two
particular places. The final element in the section is the story
of a complaint which is levelled against Gideon by the
Ephraimites and which serves to explain the popular proverb
'Are not Ephraim's gleanings better than the whole vintage
of Abiezer?' (8: 2).

9. Verse 9 is in the form of a divine oracle commanding
Gideon to attack the Midianite camp by night and contains
the divine assurance that victory will be his.

10–12. The repetition, in verse 12, of the details of the
numerical strength of the Midianite forces (cp. 6: 5 above)
serves to explain Gideon's fear (*If you are afraid to do so*: verse
10) and his lack of *courage* (verse 11). The words *listen to what
they are saying* (verse 11) already indicate that Gideon's
reconnaissance is concerned less with the tactical disposition

of the Midianite forces than with their morale. It is their morale which finds expression in the dream (verses 13f.). *the part of the camp where the fighting men lay*: literally 'the edge of the armed men in the camp'. This may refer to an armed guard lying at the front of the camp to protect it from attack. If this is so, then this is probably a tactical aspect of Gideon's reconnaissance which is attempting to find out how best to deploy his own small forces.

13–15. The *barley-cake* of the dream is symbolic of the settled agricultural life, while the *tent* is symbolic of the nomadic way of life. The dream represents the conflict between the settled Israelites and the nomadic Midianites and their allies and the defeat of the latter. *this is the sword of Gideon*: *this* could refer either to the *barley-cake* which would thus be equated with *the sword of Gideon* or else to the operation as a whole seen from a military point of view. The *sword* motif returns in the second of the two war-cries in verse 20. *he prostrated himself*: in homage to God who has given him this further sign of divinely assisted victory. Gideon can now return to *the Israelite camp* with renewed courage and confidence that the victory will be theirs.

16–18. The purpose of the *empty jar* is to conceal the *torch inside it*. It is not quite clear, however, how the men managed to carry trumpet, torch and jar (cp. verse 20). Verse 18 refers only to the blowing of the *trumpets*, and the possibility is that the trumpets on the one hand and the concealed torches on the other may form part of two originally different methods of surprise attack.

19–21. *the beginning of the middle watch*: the night was divided into three watches, each of four hours. The night began somewhere in the region of 6 p.m., so the attack would be launched some time shortly after 10 p.m. The *sentries* were changed at the beginning of each watch. First of all, *Gideon and the hundred men who were with him . . . blew their trumpets and smashed their jars*. Then, presumably, the other two groups did the same. The *three companies* of verse 20 must, therefore,

include Gideon's company; it seems, at first sight, to imply
that there were four companies, but this conflicts with what is
said in verse 16. The war-cry on this occasion seems to suggest
that an attack with swords took place. Again, we must assume
the conflation of different traditions since it would be impossible to carry and wield a *sword* as well as having *torches in their
left hands and...trumpets in their right*. However we envisage
the attack having taken place, the sudden noise and light and
shouting would clearly instil *panic* into the hearts of the
Midianites and their allies. *Every man stood where he was*: the
phrase emphasizes the non-activity of the human agents in
the drama; God alone is active in bringing about the panic
and flight of the enemy. The motif of panic is again characteristic of the idea of the holy war (cp., e.g., 1 Sam. 14: 15).

22. The first part of the verse is resumptive of the attack and
of the fact that it was *the LORD* who was the chief combatant.
Again, only the *trumpets* are mentioned here, not the jars and
the torches. The second part of the verse gives details of the
flight mentioned in verse 21. Unfortunately, the geography
of the flight is extremely unclear, since none of the places
mentioned can be located with any certainty. It may even be
that *as far as Beth-shittah in Zererah* and *as far as the ridge of
Abel-meholah by Tabbath* refer to two different flight routes
by two different parts of the Midianite army. This would
link up with the suggestion made above that the whole
narrative of the battle consists, in its present form, of a conflation of two originally separate accounts. *Zererah* is probably
a corruption of 'Zarethan' (1 Kings 7: 46) which lay in the
Jordan valley, and *in*, here, should probably be taken as 'in the
direction of'. *Tabbath* is probably to be located east of the
Jordan, and *by* really has the sense of 'opposite' or 'over-
looking'. The goal of the flight(s) is, undoubtedly, the territory east of the Jordan, and this is confirmed by verse 25.

23. This verse is, again, probably a secondary expansion of
an originally more local narrative along the same lines as 6: 35.

24. The summons to the Ephraimites is probably more

99

historically accurate, especially in view of the specifically
Ephraimite tradition concerning the killing of Oreb and Zeeb
and of the following tradition preserving the folk-proverb
in 8: 2. The Ephraimites were requested by the Manassite
clan of Abiezer to assist them and to cut off the Midianite
retreat by preventing them from using the Jordan crossings.
This, at any rate, seems to be the general sense of the verse,
though the Hebrew text is uncertain at this point, and the site
of *Beth-barah* is completely unknown.

25. The names *Oreb* and *Zeeb* are common nouns in
Hebrew; the former means 'raven' and the latter 'wolf'.
They are extremely improbable names for *Midianite princes*,
and the whole story seems to be intended to explain the origin
of the names given to a particular rock and a particular winepress. One suspects that even such an explanation is rather
fanciful. A much more likely explanation of a rock called
'Raven Rock' is that it was shaped like a raven or had some
other association with a raven. The case of 'Wolf's Winepress'
is similar. The phrase *across the Jordan* means that Gideon was
'beyond the Jordan', that is, east of the Jordan, presumably
also in *pursuit of the Midianites*. This is clearly a separate
tradition from that of Gideon's pursuit of Zebah and Zalmunna, where he crosses the Jordan only in 8: 4.

8: 1–3. The point of this little section is the preservation of,
and the giving of a context to, the popular proverb *Are not
Ephraim's gleanings better than the whole vintage of Abiezer?*
The fact that Ephraim appears to be involved in a controversy
with the small clan of Abiezer lends support to two suggestions
which have already been made above. One is that basically
only Gideon's clan of Abiezer was involved in this confrontation with the Midianites and the other bedouin tribes from
east of the Jordan. To Abiezer belonged *the whole vintage*,
the main defeat of, and victory over, the Midianites. The
tribe of Ephraim was involved, but only in a secondary
capacity; to them belonged the *gleanings*, in military terms
the mopping-up operations. This also supports the second

suggestion, that the inclusion of the other tribes derives from a secondary stage in the transmission of this whole tradition but that the inclusion of Ephraim at a late stage in the hostilities is historically authentic. The grievance of the Ephraimites was that they were not included in the conflict from the beginning. One detects, perhaps, a note of jealousy that the clan of Abiezer was able to operate so successfully on its own. With the rise of Samuel to power, Ephraim became the principal tribe in Israel and, perhaps even now, resented the success and achievement of any other tribe or clan. An exactly parallel situation is reflected at the end of the Jephthah story in 12: 1–6, where the Ephraimites resent Jephthah's claims to leadership, to their own discomfiture. On this occasion Gideon's playing down of the part played by his own clan mollifies the Ephraimites and appeases their anger. ✳

GIDEON AND THE MEN OF SUCCOTH

Gideon came to the Jordan, and he and his three hundred 4 men crossed over to continue the pursuit, weary though they were. He said to the men of Succoth, 'Will you give 5 these men of mine some bread, for they are weary, and I am pursuing Zebah and Zalmunna, the kings of Midian?' But the chief men of Succoth replied, 'Are Zebah and 6 Zalmunna already in your hands, that we should give your army bread?' Gideon said, 'For that, when the 7 LORD delivers Zebah and Zalmunna into my hands, I will thresh your bodies with desert thorns and briars.' He 8 went on from there to Penuel and made the same request; the men of Penuel answered like the men of Succoth. He said to the men of Penuel, 'When I return safely, I 9 will pull down your castle.'

Zebah and Zalmunna were in Karkor with their army 10 of fifteen thousand men. These were all that remained

of the whole host of the eastern tribes; a hundred and
11 twenty thousand armed men had fallen in battle. Gideon
advanced along the track used by the tent-dwellers east
of Nobah and Jogbehah, and his attack caught the army
12 when they were off their guard. Zebah and Zalmunna
fled; but he went in pursuit of these Midianite kings and
captured them both; and their whole army melted away.

13   As Gideon son of Joash was returning from the battle
14 by the Ascent of Heres, he caught a young man from
Succoth. He questioned him, and one by one he numbered off the names of the rulers of Succoth and its elders,
15 seventy-seven in all. Gideon then came to the men of
Succoth and said, 'Here are Zebah and Zalmunna, about
whom you taunted me. "Are Zebah and Zalmunna",
you said, "already in your hands, that we should give
16 your weary men bread?"' Then he took the elders of the
city and he disciplined those men of Succoth with desert
17 thorns and briars. He also pulled down the castle of
18 Penuel and put the men of the city to death. Then he said
to Zebah and Zalmunna, 'What of the men you killed
in Tabor?' They answered, 'They were like you, every
19 one had the look of a king's son.' 'They were my brothers,' he said, 'my mother's sons. I swear by the LORD,
20 if you had let them live I would not have killed you'; and
he said to his eldest son Jether, 'Up with you, and kill
them.' But he was still only a lad, and did not draw his
21 sword, because he was afraid. So Zebah and Zalmunna
said, 'Rise up yourself and dispatch us, for you have[a] a
man's strength.' So Gideon rose and killed them both,
and he took the crescents from the necks of their camels.

[a] *So Sept.; Heb.* he has.

✽ It has sometimes been suggested that this section is little more than a variant of the narrative of the pursuit and killing of Oreb and Zeeb in 7: 24 – 8: 3, but there are too many differences between the two stories for this to be a satisfactory comment on 8: 4–21. First of all, the names of the Midianite leaders are different, and in this section they are described as 'the kings of Midian', as opposed to 'Midianite princes' (8: 5; cp. 7: 25). The present names Zebah and Zalmunna are, however, no less artificial than Oreb and Zeeb. Zebah means 'sacrifice', and Zalmunna means 'shelter refused'. These are obviously fabricated names given to otherwise anonymous Midianite leaders. Secondly, the present narrative is closely connected with a dispute between Gideon on the one hand and, on the other, the citizens of the two Israelite settlements east of the Jordan, Succoth and Penuel. This dispute is much more involved than, and is of a different nature from, that with the Ephraimites in the earlier narrative. Thirdly, the description of the killing of the two Midianite kings is much more circumstantial than that of the killing of Oreb and Zeeb (see 8: 20–1; cp. 7: 25). Lastly, the reason for Gideon's pursuit of Zebah and Zalmunna is seen to be a personal feud (8: 18–19). They are not the leaders of the Midianite forces whom Gideon has just defeated and routed, but men who have actually slain members of Gideon's own family at a place (Tabor, verse 18) which has not hitherto figured in the narrative. All in all, this section of the Gideon story has a fairly complicated pre-history behind it. In its present context, however, it serves to introduce the theme of kingship (cp. 'They were like you, every one had the look of a king's son', verse 18) which will recur in the Gideon story itself (see below, verses 22–3) and, in stronger terms, in the Abimelech story in ch. 9.

4. The verse connects up with the story of the battle and the subsequent flight and pursuit. As already noted, Gideon only now crosses the Jordan. This indicates the independence of this tradition from the immediately preceding one (see on 7: 25).

5. Gideon appeals for help to *the men of Succoth*. The motif of appealing for help has occurred previously. Such an appeal has usually had a successful outcome; the one earlier exception was the case of Meroz in 5: 23. *the men of Succoth* were probably the citizens as a whole. The reply is given on behalf of the citizens by 'the chief men of Succoth' (verse 6; the same word is translated by 'rulers' in verse 14), with whom the 'elders' (also verse 14) were associated in the governing of the city. The word 'Succoth' means 'booths', and the reference may, at least originally, be to a fairly temporary settlement. According to 1 Kings 7: 46, the region was noted, at least at a later date, as a centre of the metal industry. Both Succoth and Penuel (verse 8) were probably Israelite settlements; they lay about 5 miles (8 km) apart on the River Jabbok, east of the Jordan.

6. The response of *the chief men of Succoth* is a fairly defiant one. Neither its tone nor its content suggests that Gideon and his troops have already defeated a large Midianite force, the weary remnant of which they are now pursuing to an expected final defeat. Here again, the tradition seems to differ from the earlier one. The Midianites are returning from a marauding attack west of the Jordan in which they have been successful and in which they have killed some of Gideon's family. They are fairly confident and are not expecting determined pursuit (cp. 'they were off their guard', verse 11). The chief men of Succoth do not expect Gideon to be victorious either.

7. The punishment with which Gideon threatens the men of Succoth upon his successful return is obscure. The sense may be that he will trample them underfoot with as little concern as he would thorns and briars.

9. *your castle*: some kind of structure is intended, most probably a tower. Penuel may have been a more permanent settlement than Succoth; there is, at any rate, no mention of the destruction of Succoth itself.

10f. The site and location of Karkor are unknown, but it seems to have been located on *the track used by the tent-dwellers*, presumably a fairly well-defined road used by the semi-nomads and lying *east of Nobah and Jogbehah*. The last-named place lies north-west of Amman, while Nobah must be presumed to be in the same general area to the south of the Jabbok. On the expression *when they were off their guard*, see above on verse 6.

13. *by the Ascent of Heres*: the locality of this place is also unknown. The Hebrew text is uncertain at this point, and the reference may not be to a place-name at all; it is possible that it is a variant of the closing words of verse 12 and that it should be omitted.

14. *he numbered off the names*: literally 'he wrote down the names' or 'one (i.e. Gideon's scribe?) wrote down the names'. The N.E.B. translation may be an attempt to avoid the difficulty supposedly caused by the idea of this unknown *young man from Succoth* being able to write. But the Semitic alphabetic script had already been invented by this time, and the fact that some of our earliest evidence for alphabetic writing was scratched on cave walls by slaves in the mines in Sinai should make it possible for us to accept the idea that this young man might well have been able to write. Whether there was any need for the names to be written down is, of course, another question. *seventy-seven in all*: this may simply be a figure intended to mean 'a large number'. The figure 'seventy' is particularly frequently used in this way.

16f. The punishment of the *men of Succoth* (see above on verse 7) was presumably inflicted on the citizens as a whole. It is not clear whether any special punishment was reserved for *the elders of the city* or why Gideon had to have a special list of their names (verse 14). In the case of Penuel, not only were *the men of the city* punished, but *the castle* (see above on verse 9) was also destroyed.

18. *Tabor*: if the Hebrew text is correct here, then Tabor can only be the well-known Mount Tabor which was the scene of the muster by Barak in 4: 6. The incident referred to

cannot be identical with the confrontation between Gideon
and the Midianites at the hill of Moreh as recorded in ch. 7.
This must be an entirely separate incident. *every one had the
look of a king's son*: the motif of kingship is introduced here.
The likening of Gideon and his brothers to king's sons has
been used as evidence to decide whether or not Gideon refused
the kingship which is proffered to him by the Israelites
(verses 22-3).

19. *if you had let them live I would not have killed you*: the
motive for Gideon's pursuit of Zebah and Zalmunna is here
represented as one of personal vengeance.

20. *his eldest son Jether*: the name is an abbreviated form of
Jethro, the name of Moses' father-in-law according to Exod.
4: 18. As Gideon's *eldest son*, the duty of blood vengeance
would fall upon Jether. The fact that Gideon orders Jether to
do the killing will be partly a kind of initiation for the boy
and partly an attempt to humiliate the Midianite leaders.

21. *for you have a man's strength*: as can be seen from the
footnote, the Hebrew is not entirely clear at this point. The
general sense seems to be that Gideon would be able to kill
them more quickly and more efficiently than his son would be
able to do. It is just possible, however, that the sense is rather
that it is more fitting that they, as leaders, should be executed
by someone who is their equal. *and he took the crescents from
the necks of their camels*: this final part of the verse really
belongs in the context of the story of the making of the ephod
in verses 24-7. ✻

THE DEATH OF GIDEON

22 After this the Israelites said to Gideon, 'You have saved
   us from the Midianites; now you be our ruler, you and
23 your son and your grandson.' Gideon replied, 'I will not
   rule over you, nor shall my son; the LORD will rule over
24 you.' Then he said, 'I have a request to make: will every

one of you give me the earrings from his booty?' – for
the enemy wore golden earrings, being Ishmaelites. They 25
said, 'Of course, we will give them.' So a cloak was
spread out and every man threw on to it the golden
earrings from his booty. The earrings for which he asked 26
weighed seventeen hundred shekels of gold; this was in
addition to the crescents and pendants and the purple
cloaks worn by the Midianite kings, not counting the
chains on the necks of their camels. Gideon made it into 27
an ephod and he set it up in his own city of Ophrah. All
the Israelites turned wantonly to its worship, and it became a trap to catch Gideon and his household.

Thus the Midianites were subdued by the Israelites; 28
they could no longer hold up their heads. For forty years
the land was at peace, all the lifetime of Gideon, that is 29
Jerubbaal son of Joash; and he retired to his own home.
Gideon had seventy sons, his own offspring, for he had 30
many wives. He had a concubine who lived in Shechem, 31
and she also bore him a son, whom he named Abimelech.
Gideon son of Joash died at a ripe old age and was buried 32
in his father's grave at Ophrah-of-the-Abiezrites. After 33
his death, the Israelites again went wantonly to the worship of the Baalim and made Baal-berith their god. They 34
forgot the LORD their God who had delivered them
from their enemies on every side, and did not show to the 35
family of Jerubbaal, that is Gideon, the loyalty that was
due to them for all the good he had done for Israel.

✻ The death of Gideon is only one of the topics which are
dealt with in this final section of the Gideon story. Verses 22–3
are concerned with the question of kingship, an important one

within the context of the Deuteronomistic History as a whole. Verses 24–7 deal with the question of religious apostasy; this is also important within the context of the larger work. Verses 28–35 serve both as the end of the Gideon story and as the introduction to the Abimelech one. The end of the one story and the beginning of the other have been so fused together, that it is difficult to disentangle them.

22f. It is difficult to know in what sense *the Israelites* were *saved* by Gideon *from the Midianites*. We have already noted two separate traditions regarding Gideon and the Midianites, 7: 9 – 8: 3 and 8: 4–21. In both traditions probably only Gideon's own clan of Abiezer was involved, with, in the first of them, some help from the Ephraimites towards the end. The idea of *Israelites* offering kingship to Gideon is very likely a later amplification of an originally much more restricted tradition. What he is offered is undoubtedly a hereditary kingship (*you and your son and your grandson*) even though the noun 'king' itself or the verb 'reign' are not used. It has sometimes been argued that verse 23 constitutes not a rejection of the kingship but an implicit acceptance on Gideon's part. His words, so it is said, are a pious refusal and imply that he will in fact exercise a personal and hereditary kingship within the overall kingship of God. But if we regard the connection between Gideon and Abimelech as artificial and secondary, then it is clear that many of the arguments usually advanced for Gideon's having been king are no longer valid. Clearly Abimelech was a king of a hereditary type, but he exercised a limited rule over the city of Shechem and its immediate neighbourhood. Abimelech overreached himself and his exercise of kingship was a failure. What we have in 8: 23 is intended to be read in sharp contrast to Abimelech's failure. Gideon rejects the kingship which he is offered because the real ruler of the people is God himself. It is doubtful whether this offer and rejection of the kingship corresponds to any historical reality. It looks very like a secondary theological reflection on the part of the deuteronomistic historian by way of contrast to the Abimelech situation. Gideon is implicitly praised for having rejected the offer and for having given to God his proper place. A similar kind of comment on Israel's later request for a king is made in 1 Sam. 8: 7.

24. This verse returns to the theme which was already intimated in the closing words of verse 21. The *golden earrings* of the enemy are to be made into 'an ephod' (verse 27). The enemy, rather surprisingly, are here called *Ishmaelites*. A similar confusion between Midianites and Ishmaelites occurs in the Joseph story in Gen. 37 (see especially verses 25–8) where the confusion is usually explained by reference to different sources. The second part of verse 24 here certainly looks like an afterthought. The Ishmaelites, like the Midianites, were a nomadic group of tribes inhabiting the north-west part of the Arabian peninsula and the Sinai desert.

26. The second part of this verse, beginning with the words *this was in addition*, is sometimes thought to betray an interest on Gideon's part in royal vestments and jewellery and to suggest that he was in fact a king. But the words may well be a secondary addition to the text at this point, and it is hazardous to build too much on them.

27. *Gideon made it into an ephod*: sometimes an ephod seems to be a kind of garment (e.g. 1 Sam. 2: 18), at other times it is clearly an object used in the cult. Here it is made of gold obtained by melting down the earrings of the enemy. The object appears to have been used in order to ascertain the divine will on a given matter; cp. 1 Sam. 23: 9–12. Both Saul (e.g. 1 Sam. 14: 3, 18) and David (e.g. 1 Sam. 23: 9–12) had access to an ephod, and this desire for an ephod on Gideon's part has also been seen as a sign of Gideon's royal position. The main interest of the narrative in its present form, however, is the way in which this object became an object of *worship* for the Israelites and led to the inevitable apostasy.

28f. Here we come to the closing deuteronomistic framework of the judges stories. The Midianites have been *subdued*, and *the land* is *at peace* for *forty years*. The time factor indicates that Gideon, too, is included as one of the so-called 'major judges'. At least one colourful element is additional here, the idea that the Midianites *could no longer hold up their heads*; the sense is no doubt that their defeat was particularly crushing and decisive. The N.E.B. translation has telescoped the end of verse 28 and the beginning of verse 29. Verse 28 ends with the phrase *all the lifetime of Gideon*. Verse 29 reads: *Jerubbaal son of Joash…retired to his own home*. This clearly belongs to the Jerubbaal/Abimelech story and the words *son of Joash* are again a sign of the harmonizing of the two narrative complexes.

30. Verse 30 takes us back to the Gideon story again. The size of Gideon's harem and the number of his children have also sometimes been taken as an indication that he accepted the kingship, but information of a similar kind is given with regard to some of the 'minor judges' where there is no question of kingship (cp. 10: 4 of Jair the Gileadite; 12: 9 of Ibzan of Bethlehem; 12: 14 of Abdon the Pirathonite).

31. Verse 31 again belongs to the Jerubbaal/Abimelech story. In the present context the subject of the sentence must be Gideon, but it was 'Abimelech son of Jerubbaal' whose mother was the concubine from Shechem (see 9: 1). The present form of verse 31 is again to be attributed to the harmonizing of the two stories.

32. The notice about Gideon's death is very similar to the kind of information which is recorded about the 'minor judges' in 10: 1–5 and 12: 7–15. This was also true of verse 30, and this may be an indication that there is not such a great difference of kind as has sometimes been thought between the 'minor judges' and the 'major judges'.

33–5. These verses really comprise the introduction to the Abimelech story. Some elements here, such as the description of the renewed apostasy and the forgetting of what Gideon had done for these people, would seem to indicate that Abimelech, too, is to be regarded as a judge. This might seem to be borne out by the fact that the chronology is continued in

10: 1 with the expression 'After Abimelech'. But there are also arguments in favour of the opposite point of view. In ch. 9 Abimelech is not presented in any kind of heroic way, nor is he said to have delivered Israel from any enemy. There is no reference to the land being at peace for the usual forty-year period, and, indeed, the whole chapter is a fairly devastating criticism of a personally motivated kingship. There may also be significance in the fact that in 10: 1 the 'judge' who follows Abimelech is said to have come 'to deliver Israel'; in other words the whole Abimelech episode is regarded as a time of evil from which the people needed to be delivered. It may well be that Abimelech was originally a 'judge', but in the present context it is clear that the deuteronomistic historian has used his story to provide a critique of kingship. If Abimelech is not a judge, then 8: 33-5 have to be read in a slightly different way. Verses 33-4 refer not to apostasy in general but to the tendency of the Israelite element within Shechem to become absorbed into the Canaanite element by worshipping the Canaanite god of Shechem, Baal-berith ('Lord of the Covenant'). The 'covenant' referred to in the god's name may be some kind of agreement between the two elements of the population of Shechem. Verse 35, on the other hand, is yet another element of the Gideon story which is, here again, harmonized with that of Jerubbaal. ∗

ABIMELECH

∗ Ch. 9 is devoted to the Abimelech episode. We have already discussed within the context of the Gideon story in chs. 6–8 the relationship between these two stories (see pp. 77f., 107–11). Abimelech, the son of Jerubbaal, originally had no connection with Gideon, and we have noted how these two narrative complexes have been combined and interwoven. Elements of the Jerubbaal–Abimelech story are found in the earlier section, notably perhaps the story of the Baal altar in 6: 25–32, and the introduction to the Abimelech episode is to be found within 8: 33–5. Ch. 9 itself falls into several clearly defined sections. The first part of the chapter, verses 1–6, tells how Abimelech succeeded in becoming the ruler of Shechem. The second part, verses 7–21, contains Jotham's fable on kings and kingship, together with an interpretation of that fable in terms of the Abimelech–Shechem situation. The third section, verses 22–49, probably contains two distinct accounts of revolt against Abimelech's rule from within Shechem itself, one of these being stirred up by a rival claimant to the rulership. Finally, in verses 50–7, we have an account of the death of Abimelech together with the Deuteronomist's theological judgement on the whole episode (verses 56–7). *

ABIMELECH BECOMES KING

9 Abimelech son of Jerubbaal went to Shechem to his mother's brothers, and spoke with them and with all the
2 clan of his mother's family. 'I beg you,' he said, 'whisper a word in the ears of the chief citizens of Shechem. Ask them which is better for them: that seventy men, all the sons of Jerubbaal, should rule over them, or one man. Tell them to remember that I am their own flesh and
3 blood.' So his mother's brothers repeated all this to each of them on his behalf; and they were moved to come over to Abimelech's side, because, as they said, he was
4 their brother. They gave him seventy pieces of silver from the temple of Baal-berith, and with these he hired
5 idle and reckless men, who followed him. He came to his father's house in Ophrah and butchered his seventy brothers, the sons of Jerubbaal, on a single stone block, all but Jotham the youngest, who survived because he had
6 hidden himself. Then all the citizens of Shechem and all

Beth-millo came together and made Abimelech king
beside the old propped-up terebinth at Shechem.

✻ 1. It is clear from this verse that it was Jerubbaal who had
the Shechemite concubine, and this confirms the suggestion
made above that 8: 31 refers originally to Jerubbaal. It is
because of his kinship with a Shechemite family that Abimelech is able to acquire the position which he eventually does
within Shechemite society. It is usually assumed that Abimelech was 'king' in Shechem on the model of the Canaanite
city-state system where each city was an independent political
unit, the ruler of which was generally given the title of 'king'.
Certainly in this narrative, Abimelech is said to have been
made 'king' (verse 6 and throughout verses 7–21), but there
are some unusual features about his rule. It appears from the
narrative that Abimelech does not in fact reside in Shechem,
but in Arumah (verse 41); he is represented in Shechem by
Zebul who is described by a rival claimant to the power as
'his lieutenant' (verse 28) and by the narrator as 'the governor
of the city' (verse 30); he appears to have had a body of
followers who were 'Israelites' (verse 55), though he is also
said to have had a band of mercenary troops who are described
as 'idle and reckless men' (verse 4). An examination of the
governmental system at Shechem in the fourteenth century
B.C. is possible through the Amarna letters. The latter are a
collection of diplomatic dispatches sent by local Canaanite
rulers to their overlord, the Egyptian Pharaoh, complaining
that they are being attacked by brigands and asking for help.
(See further *The Making of the Old Testament* in this series,
pp. 20–5.) An analysis of the government of Shechem in the
Amarna period and in the period of Abimelech seems to lead
to the following conclusions. In periods of particular crisis
such as attack from marauding bands (Amarna period) or
from nomads seeking permanent settlement (Abimelech
period), 'the chief citizens of Shechem' (verse 2) would
invite an outsider to act as 'ruler' of the city. The day-to-day

administration of the city remained in the hands of the chief citizens; the task of the ruler was to defend the city against attack from outside and to conduct its relations with other neighbouring states. This the ruler was able to do with the help of a band of mercenary troops usually selected from the very forces which were threatening Shechem's existence, in this case the Israelites (cp. verse 55). A prominent citizen of Shechem, one acceptable to both sides, acts as liaison officer between the citizens and their ruler, especially since it was not essential that the ruler should actually reside in Shechem itself. In the present context, Zebul, 'the governor of the city', holds that position. In the Amarna period, a hereditary factor was operative in so far as the two sons of Lab'ayu, the ruler of Shechem in that period, jointly succeeded their father. In the Abimelech context the situation has been obscured by the fusion with the Gideon story, but the removal of rivals, with apparently greater claims to the position, seems to have been a necessary prerequisite of Abimelech's installation in office.

2. It is now no longer clear whether the rival claimants were really Abimelech's brothers or not. The choice presented to *the chief citizens of Shechem* may simply have been between government by a group and government by an individual. Part of Abimelech's case, however, is that he is *their own flesh and blood* on his mother's side.

3f. Abimelech's proposition is accepted by 'the chief citizens of Shechem', particularly in view of his claim to be one of themselves. They give him money from their *temple* funds to enable him to hire mercenary troops with whose assistance he will be able to consolidate his position and effectively exercise his rule. The *idle and reckless men* hired by Abimelech are doubtless of the same type as the 'idle men' who followed Jephthah (11: 3). In this context they seem to have been Israelites (cp. verse 55), but both groups may well have belonged to that class of people described by the term 'Habiru'. The Habiru were a social group who could be of any race and who seem to have been available as hired soldiers

or slaves or who even at times organized themselves as gangs
of robbers, as in the Jephthah context perhaps. (On the
'Habiru' see further *The Making of the Old Testament* in this
series, pp. 23–4.) On the name of the god *Baal-berith* see above
on 8: 33–5. The archaeological evidence from Shechem would
seem to suggest that *the temple of Baal-berith* was more or less
identical with 'Beth-millo' (verse 6) and with 'the castle of
Shechem' (verse 46). The word 'millo', which, in Hebrew,
has some connection with the verb 'to fill', probably refers
to the practice of 'filling' a stone-walled enclosure with earth
and rubble to form a platform on which buildings could then
be erected. It was a practice often used to make terraces on
sloping ground. The 'Beth-millo' ('house of filling') would
then be a temple built on such a filling, and this is exactly
how the temple at Shechem was built. For the possibility of a
similar structure at Jerusalem see 2 Sam. 5: 9. The term 'castle
of Shechem' indicates the dual purpose of the building; it
served both as temple and as fortification. It was most probably
a tower-like structure.

5. This verse again reflects the fusion with the Gideon story.
All that we can now say for certain is that Abimelech owed
his position, partly at least, to the liquidation of a number of
rival contenders and that one such contender survived as a
potential threat to Abimelech's position. *on a single stone
block*: this may have been an attempt to channel the blood of
the victims and so prevent its disastrous effect on the soil.
Cp. Gen. 4: 10 with its reference to the blood of the murdered
Abel 'crying out...from the ground' and Gen. 4: 12 with its
reference to the resultant infertility of the soil.

6. The two classes of people referred to here may be the
inhabitants in general (*all the citizens of Shechem*) and an upper
class (*all Beth-millo*). *Beth-millo* probably refers to the wider
temple area rather than to the building itself, and we might
suppose that a particularly important class of people lived in
that area. *the old propped-up terebinth*: if the text is correct here,
then this is probably the best translation of it. The narrator is

poking fun at the Shechem sanctuary where the sacred tree is so old and decrepit that it has to be held up by some kind of support to prevent it from falling. The Revised Standard Version's 'by the oak of the pillar at Shechem' depends upon an emended Hebrew text. So Abimelech is officially installed as ruler of Shechem. ✳

JOTHAM'S FABLE

7 When this was reported to Jotham, he went and stood on the summit of Mount Gerizim. He cried at the top of his voice: 'Listen to me, you citizens of Shechem, and may God listen to you:

8 'Once upon a time the trees came to anoint a king, and
9 they said to the olive-tree: Be king over us. But the olive-tree answered: What, leave my rich oil by which gods and men are honoured, to come and hold sway over the trees?

10 'So the trees said to the fig-tree: Then will you come
11 and be king over us? But the fig-tree answered: What, leave my good fruit and all its sweetness, to come and hold sway over the trees?

12 'So the trees said to the vine: Then will you come and
13 be king over us? But the vine answered: What, leave my new wine which gladdens gods and men, to come and hold sway over the trees?

14 'Then all the trees said to the thorn-bush: Will you
15 then be king over us? And the thorn said to the trees: If you really mean to anoint me as your king, then come under the protection of my shadow; if not, fire shall come out of the thorn and burn up the cedars of Lebanon.'

16 Then Jotham said, 'Now, have you acted fairly and

honestly in making Abimelech king? Have you done the
right thing by Jerubbaal and his household? Have you
given my father his due – who fought for you, and threw 17
himself into the forefront of the battle and delivered you
from the Midianites? Today you have risen against my 18
father's family, butchered his seventy sons on a single
stone block, and made Abimelech, the son of his slave-girl,
king over the citizens of Shechem because he is your
brother. In this day's work have you acted fairly and 19
honestly by Jerubbaal and his family? If so, I wish you joy
in Abimelech and wish him joy in you! If not, may fire 20
come out of Abimelech and burn up the citizens of
Shechem and all Beth-millo; may fire also come out
from the citizens of Shechem and Beth-millo and burn
up Abimelech.' After which Jotham slipped away and 21
made his escape; he came to Beer, and there he settled
out of reach of his brother Abimelech.

* Plant and animal fables are common in the literatures of
the ancient Near East, and they are generally used in order to
teach a specific truth or to present a reality of life. Jotham's
fable of the trees choosing a king (verses 8–15) is by far the
most developed in the Old Testament. Generally speaking
fables are folk-literature and were not composed specifically
for the situations into which they are later made to fit. For
this reason, as here, they are often followed by an interpretation which explains their significance for their present context
(verses 16–20). This whole section, verses 7–21, was probably
not originally part of the Abimelech material. The Deuteronomist is using this plant fable to pass a comment on the
institution of kingship.

7. The Deuteronomist's reflections are put in the mouth of
Jotham, Abimelech's remaining rival according to verse 5.

Israel under the judges

Some commentators have debated how Jotham could have *stood on the summit of Mount Gerizim* and still have been heard in Shechem, but if the delivery of the fable is correctly seen as a literary device, then the question of topography is irrelevant.

8f. The *olive-tree*, like the other two trees in the fable, the fig-tree and the vine, is one of the most common trees in Palestine and one of those most vital to the economy of the country. *by which gods and men are honoured*: the reference is to the use of oil in the ritual of the grain-offering (cp., e.g., Lev. 6: 14f.) and in the entertaining of guests (cp. Ps. 23: 5). *hold sway*: there is a note of contempt in this expression as opposed to that used in the invitation, *Be king*.

13. *which gladdens gods and men*: the human side of this reference is clear, but wine was also used as a 'drink-offering' (cp., e.g., Lev. 23: 13).

14f. The *thorn-bush* is clearly the least significant, least useful of plants, and there is considerable irony in its invitation to the others to *come under the protection of my shadow*. The meagre foliage of the thorn-bush would afford no protection whatever from the heat of the sun. The thorn-bush's threat of destruction is clearly intended to emphasize the considerable danger which could result from having someone inept in a position of power and authority. The *cedars of Lebanon* represent those of real worth and stature in the community; cp. the parable of the 'thistle in Lebanon' and the 'cedar in Lebanon' in 2 Kings 14: 9.

16f. The interpretation of the fable which now follows directs the criticism not against the king himself nor even against the institution of kingship but against those who have made Abimelech king. The fable itself is mainly satirical against the figure who eventually becomes king; there is no adverse comment directed against 'the trees' in general. The fact that the intepretation is along slightly different lines from the fable is an indication that the fable was not composed specifically for the context in which it is now set. The first criticism directed against the citizens of Shechem is that they have not *acted fairly and honestly*. The rhetorical question of the N.E.B. implies a negative response; the construction of the Hebrew is different, with a series of 'if' clauses culminating in a principal clause in the second part of verse 19, '...I wish you joy in Abimelech...' The sense of the section as a whole is summed up in the 'If not...' of verse 20. The second point of criticism is that the Shechemites have been guilty of ingratitude towards *Jerubbaal and his household* and of failing to give him *his due*. The interpretation of the parable presupposes that the fusion of the Abimelech story and the Gideon story has already taken place.

18. The third point of criticism is that the citizens of Shechem are guilty of complicity in the murder of Abimelech's rivals, and the fourth point is that they have chosen as ruler someone who is the son of a slave. Only here does the Deuteronomist reflect upon the unworthiness of the ruler himself, but even here the emphasis is perhaps less on the unworthiness of Abimelech's origins than on the unworthy reason for his having been chosen (*because he is your brother*).

19f. The N.E.B.'s rhetorical question in verse 19 again corresponds to an 'if' clause in the Hebrew text. The clause is resumptive of, and virtually identical with, the corresponding clause in verse 16. If the answer to the series of rhetorical questions is 'yes' (*If so*), then Jotham wishes the relationship between ruler and people well. If the answer is 'No' (*If not*), then he wishes that they might destroy each other. The curse is expressed in the language of the fable (*may fire come out*; cp. verse 15), but again, the interpretation goes beyond the fable which says nothing of the destruction operating also in the reverse direction (*may fire also come out from the citizens of Shechem*).

21. The final verse of the section resumes the supposed setting of both fable and interpretation, a setting which, as we have already noted, is probably a literary fiction. *Beer* ('well') is not otherwise mentioned in the Old Testament. A place

whose modern Arabic name closely resembles its Hebrew name and which lies about 8 miles (roughly 13 km) north of Beth-shean is a possible location. ✻

REVOLT AGAINST ABIMELECH

22 After Abimelech had been prince over Israel for three
23 years, God sent an evil spirit to make a breach between Abimelech and the citizens of Shechem, and they played
24 him false. This was done on purpose, so that the violent murder of the seventy sons of Jerubbaal might recoil on their brother Abimelech who did the murder and on the
25 citizens of Shechem who encouraged him to do it. The citizens of Shechem set men to lie in wait for him on the hill-tops, but they robbed all who passed that way, and so the news reached Abimelech.

26 Now Gaal son of Ebed came with his kinsmen to Shechem, and the citizens of Shechem transferred their
27 allegiance to him. They went out into the country-side, picked the early grapes in their vineyards, trod them in the winepress and held festival. They went into the temple of their god, where they ate and drank and reviled
28 Abimelech. 'Who is Abimelech,' said Gaal son of Ebed, 'and who are the Shechemites, that we should be his subjects? Have not this son of Jerubbaal and his lieutenant Zebul been subjects of the men of Hamor the father of Shechem? Why indeed should we be subject
29 to him? If only this people were in my charge I should know how to get rid of Abimelech! I would say[a] to him, "Get your men together, and come out and fight."'
30 When Zebul the governor of the city heard what Gaal

[a] *So Sept.; Heb.* And he said.

120

son of Ebed said, he was very angry. He resorted to a ruse [31]
and sent messengers to Abimelech to say, 'Gaal son of
Ebed and his kinsmen have come to Shechem and are
turning the city against you. Get up now in the night, [32]
you and the people with you, and lie in wait in the open
country. Then be up in the morning at sunrise, and [33]
advance rapidly against the city. When he and his people
come out, do to him what the situation demands.' So [34]
Abimelech and his people rose in the night, and lay in
wait to attack Shechem, in four companies. Gaal son of [35]
Ebed came out and stood in the entrance of the city gate,
and Abimelech and his people rose from their hiding-
place. Gaal saw them and said to Zebul, 'There are people [36]
coming down from the tops of the hills', but Zebul
replied, 'What you see is the shadow of the hills, looking
like men.' Once more Gaal said, 'There are people [37]
coming down from the central ridge[a] of the hills, and
one company is coming along the road of the Soothsayers' Terebinth.' Then Zebul said to him, 'Where are [38]
your brave words now? You said, "Who is Abimelech
that we should be subject to him?" Are not these the
people you despised? Go out and fight him.' Gaal led the [39]
citizens of Shechem out and attacked Abimelech, but [40]
Abimelech routed him and he fled. The ground was
strewn with corpses all the way to the entrance of the
gate. Abimelech established himself in Arumah, and [41]
Zebul drove away Gaal and his kinsmen and allowed
them no place in Shechem.

Next day the people came out into the open, and this [42]
was reported to Abimelech. He on his side took his [43]

[a] central ridge: *lit.* navel.

supporters, divided them into three companies and lay
in wait in the open country; and when he saw the people
coming out of the city, he rose and attacked them.
44 Abimelech and the company[a] with him advanced rapidly
and took up position at the entrance of the city gate, while
the other two companies advanced against all those who
45 were in the open and struck them down. Abimelech kept
up the attack on the city all that day and captured it;
he killed the people in it, pulled the city down and sowed
46 the site with salt. When the occupants of the castle of
Shechem heard of this, they went into the great hall[b] of
47 the temple of El-berith. It was reported to Abimelech
that all the occupants of the castle of Shechem had col-
48 lected together. So he and his people went up Mount
Zalmon carrying axes; there he cut brushwood, and took
it and hoisted it on his shoulder. He said to his men, 'You
49 see what I am doing; be quick and do the same.' So each
man cut brushwood; then they followed Abimelech and
laid the brushwood against the hall, and burnt it over
their heads. Thus all the occupants of the castle of
Shechem died, about a thousand men and women.

* Within the larger section, verses 22–49, it is possible to
discern accounts of two different revolts within Shechem
against Abimelech. One, verses 26–41, concerns an attempt
on the part of Gaal, an incomer to Shechem, to persuade the
citizens to accept him as ruler of the city in place of Abimelech. The other, verses 22–5 together with verses 43–9, is
more in the nature of a general movement of disaffection
against Abimelech, the practical expression of which (verse
25) is not entirely clear. Both of these accounts, indeed the

[a] *So Vulg.; Heb.* companies.   [b] *Or* vault.

whole of the rest of ch. 9, are set within a theological frame-work, verses 23–4 and verses 56–7. Verse 42 is an editorial linking verse, joining the accounts of the two revolts into a chronologically continuous narrative.

22. *prince over Israel*: Abimelech's rule was a relatively local one; the idea that it encompassed Israel as a whole is the contribution of the Deuteronomist.

23f. Here we have the theological contribution of the Deuteronomist who envisages the death of Abimelech and the destruction of Shechem as the working out of God's judge-ment on them for the murderous way in which Abimelech gained his position. The idea that *the citizens of Shechem* are equally guilty with Abimelech has already been put forward in the interpretation of the plant fable earlier in the chapter. The Abimelech story from this point on is, indeed, seen in terms of a working-out of the 'curse of Jotham' (verse 57), though the story does not exactly fit the terms of the curse as expressed in verse 20. *God sent an evil spirit*: cp., e.g., 1 Sam. 16: 14. In early Israelite thinking God was believed to be the source of both the good and the evil that came to man. Only in later times was the evil thought of as originating from a figure who was completely independent of God and to whom the name 'Satan' ('adversary') was given (cp. 2 Sam. 24: 1 with 1 Chron. 21: 1).

25. The situation envisaged by this verse seems to be as follows: The Shechemites begin to engage in highway robbery. Shechem stood at a crossing of north–south and east–west roads, and much of the caravan trade must have passed through territory over which the city had control. Those who were posted *on the hill-tops* would warn those who were lying *in wait* of the approach of particularly lucrative caravans. *for him*: better understood as 'to his detriment'. One could reach one of two conclusions. Either Abimelech himself engaged in commerce, and his caravans were being robbed. Or, more probably, he exacted taxes from passing caravans in return for safe conduct through the territory,

including Shechem, over which he had control, and in this way the Shechemites were rendering his promised security ineffective and were depriving him of a source of revenue. *so the news reached Abimelech*: this particular narrative breaks off at this point. There follows the Gaal episode, and the narrative is resumed by a repetition of the almost identical words in verse 42 ('this was reported to Abimelech').

26. A new theme begins here. The revolt against Abimelech, in this instance, takes the form of a transference of allegiance to a newcomer, *Gaal son of Ebed*. The name is peculiar and the Hebrew manuscripts and the early translations of the Old Testament are not agreed as to its correct form. By a very slight change in the first element of the name, it could be translated as 'Loathing, son of a slave'. This may well be a parody of his real name, whatever that was. *his kinsmen*: literally 'his brothers'. Evidence from the fifteenth century B.C. would tend to suggest, however, that the term does not denote kinship but refers, rather, to a body of personal warriors. If this is correct then Gaal was not dependent on mercenaries, as was Abimelech, but on his own personal troops.

27. *held festival*: this is clearly a festival connected with the grape harvest. That it was not simply a drinking festival, but was of a religious nature as well, is indicated by the fact that it was held in *the temple of their god. reviled Abimelech*: it may be that local feelings, released by the feasting and drinking, found expression in words on this occasion. In this case, Gaal would be building upon an already existing feeling of discontent.

28f. The meaning of verse 28, in particular, is not very clear. Gaal seems to be identifying himself with the Shechemites (*that we should be his subjects*) and asking why he and they should be subject to Abimelech. Both Abimelech and Zebul are really, in a sense, merely the employees of *the men of Hamor*. According to Gen. 34, Hamor was the father of Shechem who, in turn, gave his name to the city. Transposing that genealogical terminology into tribal terms, one can say that the Hamorites are the original inhabitants of Shechem. They no doubt formed a kind of aristocracy in a city which, by now, probably contained a mixture of races. Gaal then offers to *get rid of Abimelech*, on condition that the Shechemites transfer their full allegiance to him (*If only this people were in my charge*).

30. *the governor of the city*: this is the correct, official title of Zebul; there is an element of disparagement in Gaal's reference to him as Abimelech's 'lieutenant' (verse 28).

31. *He resorted to a ruse*: this was presumably necessary since it would be unlikely that Gaal would permit him to send messengers to Abimelech informing him of the situation of rebellion in the city. The text at this point, however, is uncertain. By a slight emendation one can arrive at the following translation: 'He sent messengers to Abimelech at Arumah' (so the Revised Standard Version). According to verse 41, Abimelech had his residence at Arumah, which probably lay about 8 miles (13 km) south-east of Shechem.

37. *the central ridge of the hills*: literally 'the navel of the earth'. Opinions are varied as to the precise meaning of the phrase. Some think that the reference is to a local sanctuary on a hill-top, while others see it as referring to the main north–south/east–west crossroads not far from the city. *the Soothsayers' Terebinth*: another local landmark which can no longer be identified with certainty. There is no justification for equating it with 'the old propped-up terebinth' of verse 6; there may, however, be grounds for associating it with 'the terebinth-tree of Moreh' mentioned in Gen. 12: 6, especially since 'Moreh' means 'oracle-giver'.

38. *'Where are your brave words now?'*: literally 'where is your mouth', probably no more than a reference to Gaal's undoubted gift of oratory, as evidenced by his earlier ability to talk the Shechemites into accepting his leadership (verses 28–9).

39. *Abimelech routed him*: there is no indication of the means by which Abimelech won his victory. One would have

expected some reference to a stratagem in view of the fact that Abimelech's troops were divided into 'four companies' (verse 34). There may have been some telescoping of the original account when the narrative of Gaal's revolt was joined with that of the more general revolt in verses 43–9 where a stratagem involving three companies is, in fact, employed.

41. *Abimelech established himself in Arumah*: the N.E.B. rendering here definitely implies that Abimelech had not previously lived at Arumah. Verse 31, which, by emendation, can be made to refer to Arumah, still implies, nevertheless, that Abimelech did not live in Shechem. By very slight emendation, this phrase in verse 41 could read 'Abimelech returned to Arumah' and this might be the simplest solution to the difficulty. *Zebul drove away Gaal*: Abimelech leaves the mopping-up operations to the governor of the city. It is Zebul who restores order in Shechem.

42. *Next day the people came out into the open*: this is an editorial half-verse which links two unconnected narratives by placing them in a chronological sequence. *this was reported to Abimelech*: these are similar to the closing words of verse 25. The narrative which broke off at this point is now resumed.

43f. There is a degree of similarity between the preparations for the attack as described here and those outlined in verses 32–4. Here, however, unlike the previous description, the stratagem makes use of the division *into three companies*. *Abimelech and the company with him* cut off the retreat of the Shechemites back into the city, while *the other two companies* mounted the actual attack.

45. Having destroyed those forces who had ventured out of the city into 'the open country', Abimelech then turns his attention to the city itself. He succeeds in capturing it and destroys both it and the inhabitants. *sowed the site with salt*: this practice is unknown elsewhere in the Old Testament, and opinions differ as to its precise significance. Some believe that it was intended to neutralize the effect of the blood and avert

the vengeance of the shades of the slaughtered Shechemites; others are of the opinion that the procedure was intended to purify the site preparatory to rebuilding. There is, however, very little archaeological evidence of a town on the site of Shechem in the period after the destruction of the city by Abimelech (twelfth century B.C.). An apparently lively town stood there in the tenth century B.C., but the most that we could speak of would be a very slow recovery of importance over these 200 years. The reference in 1 Kings 12: 25 to the 'rebuilding' of Shechem by Jeroboam I about 900 B.C. refers to the strengthening of fortifications which were already in existence. It would be difficult, then, to say whether or not the city was rebuilt immediately after the destruction described in this verse.

46. As the narrative now stands it looks as if verses 46–9 are describing an incident which happened *after* the destruction of the city of Shechem. The difficulty about such a view is the impossibility of finding a satisfactory location for *the castle of Shechem* on a site somewhere other than the city. A better solution is to regard verses 46–9 as the narration of events which took place *during* the final siege of the city. *When the occupants of the castle of Shechem heard of this*: what they heard of was not, then, the final destruction of the city, but the defeat of the troops in the open country (verse 44). *the great hall of the temple of El-berith*: the alternative translation 'vault' is an impossible one, since no such feature has been discovered in the temple at Shechem. The verse describes a last-ditch stand in the temple-fortress by, perhaps, an upper class of Shechemite society (cp. above on verses 3f. for the temple structure and on verse 6 for the possibility of two strata of society in Shechem).

48. *Mount Zalmon*: literally 'shady', a particularly appropriate name if, as appears likely, the hill was thickly wooded. It is not certain which of the hills in the neighbourhood of Shechem is meant.

49. *burnt it over their heads*: this is no doubt intended as a

fulfilment of the curse expressed in verse 20, 'May fire come out of Abimelech and burn up the citizens of Shechem.' The judgement on Abimelech is still to come. ✶

THE DEATH OF ABIMELECH

50 Abimelech then went to Thebez, besieged it and took it.
51 There was a strong castle in the middle of the city, and all the citizens, men and women, took refuge there. They
52 shut themselves in and went on to the roof. Abimelech came up to the castle and attacked it. As he approached
53 the entrance to the castle to set fire to it, a woman threw
54 a millstone down on his head and fractured his skull. He called hurriedly to his young armour-bearer and said, 'Draw your sword and dispatch me, or men will say of me: A woman killed him.' So the young man ran him
55 through and he died. When the Israelites saw that Abimelech was dead, they all went back to their homes.
56 It was thus that God requited the crime which Abimelech had committed against his father by the murder of his
57 seventy brothers, and brought all the wickedness of the men of Shechem on their own heads. The curse of Jotham son of Jerubbaal came home to them.

✶ 50. The final section of the Abimelech story contains the account of a stratagem, similar to that employed successfully against Shechem, directed this time against Thebez, a place about 10 miles (16 km) north-east of Shechem.

51–4. A number of features are common to both narratives. Not only are the cities taken (verse 50; cp. verse 45), but both have the architectural feature of a *castle* (cp. verse 46) *in the middle of the city*. The citizens of Thebez also *took refuge* in the central fortified building. Here, too, Abimelech attempts *to set fire to* the stronghold (cp. verse 49), but on this occasion the plan is frustrated by the bold action of a woman. The motif of the slaying of the enemy by a woman has already featured in the Sisera story in chs. 4–5. The details of Abimelech's death are still remembered in the time of David; cp. 2 Sam. 11: 21.

55. *Israelites*: see above on verse 1.

56f. These two verses conclude the Abimelech narrative with further theological reflection on the part of the Deuteronomist. They are in the same vein as verses 23–4 (see above). Here, too, emphasis is placed not only on the 'requital' of Abimelech but also on the idea that the Shechemites are punished for their share in the criminal activities by which Abimelech gained his position as ruler of Shechem. The whole chain of events is seen as the working out of *The curse of Jotham*. There is, however, nothing in the story which corresponds, in any kind of literal sense, to the second part of that curse: 'may fire also come out from the citizens of Shechem and Beth-millo and burn up Abimelech' (verse 20). *

LIST OF MINOR JUDGES – I

After Abimelech, Tola son of Pua, son of Dodo, a man **10** of Issachar who lived in Shamir in the hill-country of Ephraim, came in his turn to deliver Israel. He was judge 2 over Israel for twenty-three years, and when he died he was buried in Shamir.

After him came Jair the Gileadite; he was judge over 3 Israel for twenty-two years. He had thirty sons, who rode 4 thirty asses; they had thirty towns in the land of Gilead, which to this day are called Havvoth-jair.[a] When Jair 5 died, he was buried in Kamon.

* 1f. *After Abimelech*: it is likely that the idea of succession within the 'minor judges' list is secondary (see p. 12). Also

[a] *That is* Tent-villages of Jair.

Miles
0   5   10   15
0   10   20
Kilometres

N

●Bethlehem in Galilee
Z e b u l u n
I s s a c h a r   Kamon   *LAND*
OF
H a v v o t h - j a i r   *TOB*

M a n a s s e h

●Zaphon
River Jabbok
Pirathon ●   ●Shechem

●Shamir?   ●Mizpah?

E p h r a i m

Abel-keramin?
●
●Minnith?
B e n j a m i n   ●
Heshbon

Bethlehem in Judah ●

River Arnon ●Aroer

4. Jephthah and the 'minor judges' (chs. 10-12)

secondary is the notion that these individuals were *judge over Israel*; rather, they exercised a purely local function, as is indicated by the fact that they are each associated with a very specific locality. According to the genealogical lists in the Old Testament (e.g. Gen. 46: 13), *Tola* and *Pua* are names of two clans of the tribe of Issachar; there is no reason why clan names, usually derived from a supposed ancestor, could not be borne by individuals within the clan. *Dodo* could mean 'his uncle', but it is more likely, however, that a proper name is intended of which an element containing a divine name has fallen away; the full name would have signified 'God is kinsman' or the like. *a man of Issachar who lived in Shamir in the hill-country of Ephraim*: Tola was an Issacharite who lived outside his tribal territory. The location of Shamir is uncertain, but the designation *the hill-country of Ephraim* points to an area south of Shechem. A specific site about 7 miles (11 km) south of Shechem has been suggested. *to deliver Israel*: the expression suggests that at some stage in the transmission of this material the period of Abimelech came to be regarded as one of oppression from which deliverance was needed. *twenty-three years*: the period of influence of each of the 'major judges' was the round figure of 'forty years' (see on 3: 8f.). In the case of the 'minor judges' the figure is always specific. In the case of the first two here in ch. 10, the numbers are relatively high; in the case of those listed in 12: 8-15 the numbers are low (seven to ten years; six to ten if we include Jephthah). These figures are often used in working out the chronology of the history of Israel; they can be so used only on the assumption that the element of succession in these lists is original. *he was buried in Shamir*: each of the notes about the 'minor judges' includes the location of his tomb, presumably at the place where he was most active. This information is also given in the case of Gideon; see above on 8: 32.

3–5. *Jair the Gileadite*: the genealogical lists (cp., e.g., Deut. 3: 14 where a different explanation is given for the place-name Havvoth-jair) suggest that Jair was a son of Manasseh. Gilead was the name given to the region to the east of the Jordan valley, and it is with that region, where part of the tribe of Manasseh lived, that Jair is to be associated. Kamon was probably located about 12 miles (19 km) south-east of the Sea of Chinnereth. The fact that Jair had *thirty sons* would suggest that he had a fairly large harem, a sign, too, of his

importance and standing. The *thirty asses* indicate the dignity
of each son, the *thirty towns* something of their wealth and
prosperity. The fact that there is a word-play here between
asses (Hebrew *'ayārīm*) and *towns* (Hebrew *'ārīm*) might suggest
that we need not treat this kind of information too seriously.
Indeed, the reference to the *towns* may be simply an attempt
to explain the origin of the name Havvoth-jair (see the
N.E.B. footnote). It may be doubted whether Havvoth-jair
originally had any connection with the 'judge' Jair. ✶

JEPHTHAH

✶ The Jephthah narrative runs from 10: 6 to 12: 7, and the
suggestion that Jephthah figured in the tradition both as a
deliverer of Israel from foreign oppression and as a 'minor
judge' has already been discussed (see above, p. 6). ✶

AMMONITE OPPRESSION

6 Once more the Israelites did what was wrong in the
eyes of the LORD, worshipping the Baalim and the
Ashtaroth, the deities of Aram and of Sidon and of Moab,
of the Ammonites and of the Philistines. They forsook the
7 LORD and did not worship him. The LORD was angry with
Israel, and he sold them to the Philistines and the Am-
8 monites, who[a] for eighteen years harassed and oppressed
the Israelites who lived beyond the Jordan in the Amorite
9 country in Gilead. Then the Ammonites crossed the
Jordan to attack Judah, Benjamin, and Ephraim, so that
10 Israel was in great distress. The Israelites cried to the
LORD for help and said, 'We have sinned against thee; we
have forsaken our God and worshipped the Baalim.'
11 And the LORD said to the Israelites, 'The Egyptians, the

[a] *Prob. rdg.; Heb. adds* in that year.

Amorites, the Ammonites, the Philistines; the Sidonians 12 too and the Amalekites and the Midianites[a] – all these oppressed you and you cried to me for help; and did not I deliver you? But you forsook me and worshipped other 13 gods; therefore I will deliver you no more. Go and cry 14 for help to the gods you have chosen, and let them save you in the day of your distress.' But the Israelites said to 15 the LORD, 'We have sinned. Deal with us as thou wilt; only save us this day, we implore thee.' They banished 16 the foreign gods and worshipped the LORD; and he could endure no longer to see the plight of Israel.

Then the Ammonites were called to arms, and they 17 encamped in Gilead, while the Israelites assembled and encamped in Mizpah. The people of Gilead and their 18 chief men said to one another, 'If any man will strike the first blow at the Ammonites, he shall be lord over the inhabitants of Gilead.'

✶ The section 10: 6–16 is a deuteronomistic sermon on the general theme of apostasy and repentance, now used to introduce the Jephthah story. Because of the general nature of this sermon, some of the details in it (e.g. the reference to the Philistines in verse 7) do not accord with the narrative which follows. Other details, however (e.g. the reference to Ammonite oppression in verse 9), pick out a theme of the ensuing narrative and use it within the context of the general sermon. Verses 17f. mark the beginning of the Jephthah story proper, though Jephthah himself is not mentioned in the narrative until 11: 1.

6. The apostasy of Israel is again described in terms of their *worshipping the Baalim and the Ashtaroth*; on these see the note on 2: 11–13. On this occasion the description is amplified by

[a] *So Sept.; Heb.* Maon.

the inclusion of *the deities* of various nations surrounding Israel. *Aram*: the reference is to the Aramaean tribes whose original home was in the northern part of the Arabian peninsula and who, about this time, were settling in Syria. They may have brought some kind of star worship with them but seem to have adopted Canaanite religion on their settlement. The gods of Sidon were also the regular Canaanite ones. The only Moabite deity known to the Old Testament was Kemosh; see 11: 24 and cp. 1 Kings 11: 33, a verse which refers also to 'Ashtoreth goddess of the Sidonians' and to 'Milcom god of the Ammonites'. The Philistines also seem to have adopted Canaanite deities when they settled in Palestine (e.g. Dagon; cp. 1 Sam. 5: 1–7). This amplified description of the apostasy reveals the sermon-like nature of this section.

7f. The divine anger takes the form of subjection to oppression from *the Philistines and the Ammonites*; on the former see above on 3: 3, on the latter see above on 3: 12–14. Double pressure, from the Philistines in the south-west and from the Ammonites in the east, is not in itself unlikely in this general period. However, the Philistines do not feature in the following narrative, and the oppression is at first, we are told, confined to the territory *beyond* [i.e. east of] *the Jordan*. The reference to the Philistines is part of the general nature of the sermon (see introductory note to the section).

9f. It is only when the Ammonite oppression extends to the territory west of the Jordan, that the *distress* of the Israelites elicits some kind of reaction from the people. They cry *to the LORD for help* and make confession of their sin of apostasy. The terms are familiar from earlier examples.

11–14. In the Gideon story (6: 8–10), God's response to the Israelites' cry for help was to send them a prophet whose task was to point out to them that their distress was a punishment for their disobedience. Here a similar reprimand is delivered, but on this occasion it is put into the mouth of *the LORD*. On the theme of God's contention with his people, see above on 6: 8–10. The sermon is slightly anachro-

nistic in this context, in that of the nations listed as having
already *oppressed* the Israelites and from whom God claims to
have delivered them, *the Philistines* were still a major threat
and were to continue to be so through the periods of Samson
and Saul, until they were finally defeated by David. In the
earlier sermon the divine accusation was that the people had
refused to obey God. Here it is the more specific one of having
forsaken him and having *worshipped other gods. the gods you
have chosen*: a reference back, in the context, to 'the deities'
enumerated in verse 6.

15f. The people renew their confession and their appeal for
help. On this occasion these are accompanied by the positive
action of the banishment of *the foreign gods* and of a rededica-
tion to the worship of *the LORD*. God's eventual yielding to
the Israelites' call for help anticipates the emergence, in this
situation too, of a leader who will deliver them from this
particular oppression.

17f. Before the actual emergence of the leader, we have in
these two verses the confrontation of the opposing forces and
the expression of the Israelite need for a leader. The term
Gilead is usually used to refer to the larger territory east of the
Jordan, but the contrast with Mizpah here suggests that
specific places are envisaged. The Mizpah mentioned here is
obviously east of the Jordan, but it cannot otherwise be identified with certainty; in so far as the name itself could mean
'watch-tower' (cp. the N.E.B. footnote to Gen. 31: 49), it
probably occupied a commanding position in the east-Jordan
mountains. *The people of Gilead* must refer to those Israelites
who lived east of the Jordan in Gilead, as must also the
expression *the inhabitants of Gilead*. The N.E.B. has rendered
the words of the Gileadites by an 'if' sentence. More literally
(cp. the Revised Standard Version), it is a direct question,
'Who will strike the first blow at the Ammonites?' This
looks as if they are seeking an oracle by way of an answer to
their question; cp. the comment on 1: 1. This in turn would
suggest that Mizpah was an Israelite–Gileadite sanctuary.

What is promised to the person designated by the oracle is worked out in terms of Jephthah in 11: 8–11. In the present context, however, there is no answer to the request for an oracle. The narrative breaks off at this point to fill in the background to Jephthah's emergence as leader. When it resumes at 11: 4, it does so from a slightly different point of view. One could perhaps say that the actual oracle has been lost or been replaced by 11: 1–3 and that the narrative from 11: 4 onwards presupposes that Jephthah, now resident in Tob, has in fact been designated leader. ✳

JEPHTHAH BECOMES LEADER

11 Jephthah the Gileadite was a great warrior; he was the
2 son of Gilead by a prostitute. But Gilead had a wife who bore him several sons, and when they grew up they drove Jephthah away; they said to him, 'You have no inheritance in our father's house; you are another woman's son.'
3 So Jephthah, to escape his brothers, went away and settled in the land of Tob, and swept up a number of idle men who followed him.

4 The time came when the Ammonites made war on
5 Israel, and when the fighting began, the elders of Gilead
6 went to fetch Jephthah from the land of Tob. They said to him, 'Come and be our commander so that we can
7 fight the Ammonites.' But Jephthah said to the elders of Gilead, 'You drove me from my father's house in hatred.
8 Why come to me now when you are in trouble?' 'It is because of that', they replied, 'that we have turned to you now. Come with us and fight the Ammonites, and
9 become lord over all the inhabitants of Gilead.' Jephthah said to them, 'If you ask me back to fight the Ammonites and if the LORD delivers them into my hands, then I will

be your lord.' The elders of Gilead said again to Jephthah, 10
'We swear by the LORD, who shall be witness between
us, that we will do what you say.' Jephthah then went 11
with the elders of Gilead, and the people made him their
lord and commander. And at Mizpah, in the presence of
the LORD, Jephthah repeated all that he had said.

* 1f. The similarities between the circumstances of Jephthah's birth and those of Abimelech's (cp. 8: 31) have often
been noted. There is also a similarity in the type of followers
which each had; cp. verse 3, below, with 9: 4. But the tenor
of the narrative is different; the reader's sympathies are with
Jephthah but not with Abimelech. *Jephthah*: the name means
'he opens'. Here again, the divine-name element in this name
is missing; cp. on 'Dodo' in 10: 1. The full form of the name
was probably 'God opens (the womb)'. *the son of Gilead*:
whereas Gilead is usually considered as a place-name, here it
is thought of as the name of an individual. It occurs as a tribal
name here (*the Gileadite*) and in 5: 17. The area to which the
geographical name Gilead is given was occupied by the tribe
of Gad. *a prostitute*: Jephthah's mother was a common
prostitute, so he himself had no legal standing, as he would
have had if she had been a concubine and had belonged to an
official, legally recognized harem. As it is, he can have *no
inheritance* in his father's estate. The sons of Gilead's legal wife
alone have the right of inheritance. This motif of strife with
his brothers is yet another element common both to the
Jephthah and to the Abimelech stories.

3. *the land of Tob* lay in the north-eastern part of the
territory east of the Jordan. The Ammonites were later to
use men from Tob as mercenary troops in their war against
David (2 Sam. 10: 6), so it is possible that Jephthah may have
come into contact with the Ammonites already in Tob and
thus have been ideally suited to conduct the diplomatic
negotiations described in verses 12–28. *a number of idle men*:

these may have been part of the Habiru class; see above on 9: 3f. It is possible that Jephthah and his followers indulged in brigandage and highway robbery.

4f. Jephthah has apparently already been designated as leader of the Israelite forces; see the comment on 10: 17f.

7. *the elders of Gilead*: an action which was originally ascribed to Jephthah's brothers (verse 2) is now ascribed to the leaders of the community. This transference could be explained in terms of corporate responsibility; the whole community is ultimately responsible for the actions of its individual members.

8. '*It is because of that*': this may well refer to the military expertise which Jephthah acquired at the head of his band of robbers. *become lord over all the inhabitants of Gilead*: what was offered in general terms in 10: 18 to the person who accepted the leadership against the Ammonites is now expressed in specific terms with regard to Jephthah.

9. Jephthah agrees to accept their offer of military leadership on the conditions which they themselves have laid down. If he is victorious against the Ammonites he will become their civilian leader.

10f. The offer is confirmed by *The elders of Gilead*, and the whole transaction is ratified *in the presence of the LORD* at the sanctuary at Mizpah. *the LORD* is *witness* to the agreement. It would seem that this is the appointment of Jephthah to an official position, at least among those Israelite tribes settled east of the Jordan. His charismatic designation as deliverer from this specific foreign oppression is not mentioned until later, at the actual commencement of hostilities (verse 29). Jephthah is careful to ensure that the Gileadites are fully aware of what is involved in having him as military commander (verse 9) and that the agreement is properly ratified and witnessed (verses 10–11). The official installation takes place, presumably, at Mizpah. Jephthah is installed as both civilian leader (*lord*) and military *commander*, even though accession to the former post is supposedly dependent on success in the latter. ✶

DIPLOMATIC NEGOTIATIONS

Jephthah sent a mission to the king of Ammon to ask 12 what quarrel he had with them that made him invade their country. The king gave Jephthah's men this answer: 13 'When the Israelites came up from Egypt, they took our land from the Arnon as far as the Jabbok and the Jordan. Give us back these lands in peace.' Jephthah sent a second 14 mission to the king of Ammon, and they said, 'This is 15 Jephthah's answer: Israel did not take either the Moabite country or the Ammonite country. When they came up 16 from Egypt, the Israelites passed through the wilderness to the Red Sea*a* and came to Kadesh. They then sent 17 envoys to the king of Edom asking him to grant them passage through his country, but the king of Edom would not hear of it. They sent also to the king of Moab, but he was not willing; so Israel remained in Kadesh. They 18 then passed through the wilderness, skirting Edom and Moab, and kept to the east of Moab. They encamped beside the Arnon, but they did not enter Moabite territory, because the Arnon is the frontier of Moab. Israel 19 then sent envoys to the king of the Amorites, Sihon king of Heshbon, asking him to give them free passage through his country to their destination. But Sihon would not 20 grant Israel free passage through his territory; he mustered all his people, encamped in Jahaz and fought Israel. But 21 the LORD the God of Israel delivered Sihon and all his people into the hands of Israel; they defeated them and occupied all the territory of the Amorites in that region. They took all the Amorite territory from the Arnon to 22

[a] *Or* the Sea of Reeds.

23 the Jabbok and from the wilderness to the Jordan. The
   LORD the God of Israel drove out the Amorites for the
   benefit of his people Israel. And do you now propose to
24 take their place? It is for you to possess whatever Kemosh
   your god gives you; and all that the LORD our God gave
25 us as we advanced is ours. For that matter, are you any
   better than Balak son of Zippor, king of Moab? Did he
26 ever quarrel with Israel or attack them? For three hundred
   years Israelites have lived in Heshbon and its dependent
   villages, in Aroer and its villages, and in all the towns by
   the Arnon. Why did you not oust[a] them during all that
27 time? We have done you no wrong; it is you who are
   doing us wrong by attacking us. The LORD who is judge
   will judge this day between the Israelites and the Ammon-
28 ites.' But the king of the Ammonites would not listen
   to the message which Jephthah had sent him.

✻ 12. *Jephthah sent a mission*: Jephthah first engages in
diplomatic activity to try to resolve the differences between
the Ammonites and the Israelites. *the king of Ammon*: although
Jephthah is here said to be treating with the Ammonites, the
territory to which reference is made is normally thought of as
Moabite territory, and 'Kemosh' (verse 24) is certainly a
Moabite god. Two main suggestions have been put forward
in an attempt to solve this apparent contradiction. One theory
is that there were originally two separate accounts, one telling
of Jephthah's dealings with the Ammonites and the other of
his dealings with the Moabites. But it is difficult to carry
through an analysis of the whole Jephthah story in terms of two
strands, originally separate but now fused together. A more
likely solution is that the territory which is described here,
and which is normally thought of as Moabite, was from time

[a] *Or* recover.

to time occupied also, perhaps even jointly, by the Ammonites. The Israelites certainly thought of the Moabites and the Ammonites as two closely related peoples. This is clear from the story of their origins as related in Gen. 19: 30–8. It may well be that at this period the population of the region was predominantly Ammonite.

13. The Ammonite complaint is that the Israelites occupied and settled in Ammonite territory, in particular between *the Arnon* and *the Jabbok*, immediately prior to their settlement in the area to the west of the Jordan. They now wish to have these lands returned to them. It looks as if something might be missing from this verse. *from the Arnon as far as the Jabbok* describes the south–north extent of it; the east–west extent is more accurately described by the phrase in verse 22 'from the wilderness to the Jordan'.

15–23. In this section Jephthah gives an account of the Israelite exodus and wilderness wanderings. In it he is careful to stress that they made no inroads on Moabite territory, of which, he says, *the Arnon is the* [northern?] *frontier*. The territory with which the present negotiations are concerned was occupied, says Jephthah, neither by the Moabites nor by the Ammonites, but by *the Amorites* under their king Sihon, whose capital was at Heshbon, about half-way between the Arnon and the Jabbok. Jephthah is very firm in his assertion that the territory under discussion was *Amorite territory*. It was won by the Israelites by right of conquest, and the Ammonites have no rightful claim to it (verse 23). The story of the defeat of Sihon and the Amorites is in Num. 21: 21–31. There, the region 'from the Arnon to the Jabbok' is described as 'the territory of the Ammonites' (verse 24). One could conclude that the territory where Sihon established his Amorite kingdom had formerly been Ammonite. What Jephthah is saying here, then, would be that the Ammonites had already lost their territory before ever the Israelites came on the scene.

24. This verse acknowledges the right of a nation to the territory which its particular god gives to it. The Ammonites

(Moabites?) are every bit as entitled to the land given to them by their god Kemosh as are the Israelites to the land given to them by their God. A later idea, expressed in Deut. 2 (see especially verses 5, 9, 19), is that it is Israel's God who allocates land to individual nations. On Kemosh, the god of the Moabites, see above on 10: 6.

25. The story of *Balak son of Zippor, king of Moab* is in Num. 22–4. Balak attempted to have Israel cursed by the powerful seer Balaam, but Balaam could pronounce nothing but blessings upon Israel. Balak therefore refrained from challenging an Israel which was stationed on his borders. Is the king of Ammon, then, any braver than Balak that he should dare to challenge Israel's right to this territory?

26. Jephthah makes the further point that the Israelite settlements in Heshbon and Aroer and *all the towns by the Arnon* are of long standing. It strikes him as odd that the Ammonites should have waited such a long time before pressing their claims to the territory. Aroer lay on the Arnon and was probably the most south-easterly boundary point of the whole region; cp. Josh. 13: 16. The figure *three hundred years* corresponds so closely to the present arithmetic of the preceding chapters of the book that it was very probably added at a late stage in the transmission of the book.

27. Jephthah ends his diplomatic message by claiming that Israel has done no wrong to the Ammonites and that the situation is rather the reverse. It is the Ammonites who are unjustified in their actions. *The LORD* is invoked as *judge* or arbitrator between the Israelites and the Ammonites. This is the only place in the book where a legal sense is definitely demanded for the title 'judge'. The sole exception to this is in 4: 5 which, as we have noted above, is probably secondary. The title 'judge' in this passage has, of course, nothing to do with the various holders of that office, since here it is applied to God.

28. The diplomatic activity has failed. Only hostilities can now resolve the difficulties. ☆

JEPHTHAH'S DAUGHTER

✻ Although this section of the Jephthah story does deal with the hostilities between the Israelites and the Ammonites, these occupy a minor place in the narrative as a whole. The main interest is in Jephthah's vow and in the working out of that vow in terms of his daughter and her fate. ✻

Then the spirit of the LORD came upon Jephthah and he 29
passed through Gilead and Manasseh, by Mizpeh of
Gilead, and from Mizpeh over to the Ammonites.
Jephthah made this vow to the LORD: 'If thou wilt deliver 30
the Ammonites into my hands, then the first creature that 31
comes out of the door of my house to meet me when I
return from them in peace shall be the LORD's; I will
offer that as a whole-offering.' So Jephthah crossed over 32
to attack the Ammonites, and the LORD delivered them
into his hands. He routed them with great slaughter all the 33
way from Aroer to Minnith, taking twenty towns, and
as far as Abel-keramim. Thus Israel crushed Ammon.
But when Jephthah came to his house in Mizpah, who 34
should come out to meet him with tambourines and
dances but his daughter, and she his only child; he had
no other, neither son nor daughter. When he saw her. 35
he rent his clothes and said, 'Alas, my daughter, you
have broken my heart, such trouble you have brought
upon me. I have made a vow to the LORD and I cannot
go back.' She replied, 'Father, you have made a vow to 36
the LORD; do to me what you have solemnly vowed,
since the LORD has avenged you on the Ammonites,
your enemies. But, father, grant me this one favour. 37

For two months let me be, that I may roam*[a]* the hills
with my companions and mourn that I must die a virgin.'
38 'Go', he said, and he let her depart for two months. She
went with her companions and mourned her virginity
39 on the hills. At the end of two months she came back
to her father, and he fulfilled the vow he had made; she
40 died a virgin. It became a tradition that the daughters of
Israel should go year by year and commemorate the fate
of Jephthah's daughter, four days in every year.

✳ 29. *Then the spirit of the LORD came upon Jephthah*: we
have already noted how, in verses 10-11 above, Jephthah was
installed as both civil leader and military commander. Only
at this point, at the beginning of hostilities, is Jephthah
endowed with the spirit of the LORD in the way that other
judges were; cp., e.g., 3: 10; 6: 34. *he passed through Gilead
and Manasseh*: this journey seems to have been a recruiting
march. The tribe of Manasseh was established both west and
east of the Jordan. If *Manasseh* here refers to east-Jordan
Manasseh, then the route of the march would seem to be from
north to south, ending up facing the Ammonites, whose
territory lay to the east of the north end of the Dead Sea.
This in turn might suggest that after his appointment had
been validated at the sanctuary at Mizpah, Jephthah had
returned to his home in Tob in order to gather his mercenary
troops before returning west and then south to recruit his
forces. As a geographical term, however, Manasseh usually
refers to the territory occupied by that tribe *west* of the
Jordan. If this were the reference here, then this would explain
when Jephthah had issued his unsuccessful appeal to the
Ephraimites for help (12: 2, the translation given in the N.E.B.
footnote; see the commentary below on 12: 2). *Mizpeh of*

[a] *Or* that I may go down country to...

144

Gilead: the recruiting march would no doubt end at what, at this period, seems to have been the principal sanctuary east of the Jordan. It is there that the final muster would take place. Mizpeh is simply a variant spelling of the Mizpah mentioned earlier in the Jephthah story; see above on 10: 17f.

30f. *Jephthah made this vow to the LORD*: the vow would no doubt be made at the Mizpah sanctuary before hostilities against the Ammonites began. The phraseology of the vow (*If thou wilt deliver the Ammonites...*) underlines the fact that the subsequent victory is thought of as God's victory; cp. verse 32, 'the LORD delivered them into his hands'. *the first creature*: the N.E.B. renders the Hebrew text in an impersonal way (literally 'whatever comes out...'). Human sacrifice was forbidden by law; cp. Lev. 18: 21; 20: 2, where this is probably what is meant by the expression 'surrender/give children to Molech'. Sometimes we read of it happening, particularly in a state of anxiety occasioned by war, e.g. 2 Kings 16: 3, but it was not a normal practice in Israel. The reference here, however, cannot be simply to animal sacrifice, since that would not have been anything unusual. Jephthah must have envisaged human sacrifice, though not, presumably, his daughter. The Deuteronomist passes no judgement on the practice; he simply records it. But the whole story, as we shall see, is really told by way of explanation of the ritual practice described in verse 40.

32f. As already noted, the emphasis here is on the idea that the victory is due to God's participation. On Aroer see above on verse 26. The sites of Minnith and Abel-keramim are unknown; they probably lay somewhere on the frontier between the Israelite settlements east of the Jordan and the territory normally thought of as being Ammonite.

34. *tambourines* is probably a fairly accurate description of the instruments intended here. They were used primarily for cultic dances and processions, almost exclusively by women.

Considerable emphasis is laid on the fact that Jephthah's daughter was *his only child*. Cp. a similar emphasis in the story of the sacrifice of Isaac (Gen. 22: 2). In both instances, the effect is to heighten the tragedy.

35. *he rent his clothes*: the tearing of one's garments was a sign of mourning; it was usually followed by the putting on of sack-cloth.

37–40. *a virgin*: great stress is laid on the virginity of Jephthah's daughter; cp. also *mourned her virginity* (verse 38) and *she died a virgin* (verse 39). This factor probably has some connection with the ritual described in verse 40. *It became a tradition*: this is the point at which this section of the Jephthah narrative, with its emphasis on the fate of his virgin daughter, has been aiming. It is an attempt to explain, by means of a legend about the sacrifice of a virgin, an annual four-day festival in Israel. We have no other evidence for the practice of such a festival, and we can only hazard a guess as to its nature and significance. It was probably connected with a fertility religion. With its apparent emphasis on virginity, it may have had something to do with the bewailing of the impending loss of the virginity of girls on the threshold of marriage. In this way a religious ritual has been given a historical explanation. This is common in the Old Testament, the best-known example being the way in which the Passover ritual is explained in terms of the flight from Egypt; see Exod. 12: 1–36. ✲

THE COMPLAINT OF THE EPHRAIMITES

12 The Ephraimites mustered their forces and crossed over to Zaphon. They said to Jephthah, 'Why did you march against the Ammonites and not summon us to go with
2 you? We will burn your house over your head.' Jephthah answered, 'I and my people had a feud with the Ammonites, and had I appealed to you for help, you would not

have saved us*ᵃ* from them. When I saw that we were not 3
to look for help from you, I took my life in my hands
and marched against the Ammonites, and the LORD
delivered them into my power. Why then do you attack
me today?' Jephthah then mustered all the men of Gilead 4
and fought Ephraim, and the Gileadites defeated them.*ᵇ*
The Gileadites seized the fords of the Jordan and held 5
them against Ephraim. When any Ephraimite who had
escaped begged leave to cross, the men of Gilead asked
him, 'Are you an Ephraimite?', and if he said, 'No', they 6
would retort, 'Say Shibboleth.' He would say 'Sibbo-
leth', and because he could not pronounce the word
properly, they seized him and killed him at the fords of
the Jordan. At that time forty-two thousand men of
Ephraim lost their lives.

* We have already noted above (see on 8: 1–3) the similarity
between the incident recorded here and that recorded in the
Gideon story in 8: 1–3. Indeed, it has been suggested that the
incident here is simply a secondary, literary imitation of
the earlier episode. Both certainly involve a complaint by
the Ephraimites that they have been left out of a particular
incident. The two incidents, however, end in quite different
ways, and the 'Shibboleth' episode has a ring of authenticity
about it.

    1. *Zaphon* ('north') probably lay north of the Jabbok, but
it is not clear why the Ephraimites should have headed in that
direction if they were intending to attack Jephthah who was,
presumably, domiciled at Mizpah. The latter is probably to
be located a good 12 miles (19 km) south-east of Zaphon. The

[*a*] and had I...saved us: *or* I did appeal to you for help, but you would
not save us...
[*b*] *So some MSS. of Sept.; Heb. adds* for they said, 'You are fugitives
from Ephraim, Gilead, in the midst of Ephraim, in the midst of Manasseh.'

complaint of the Ephraimites is that they were not summoned to join the fight against the Ammonites. We have already suggested, in the context of the earlier incident, that the real reason may have been jealousy on the part of the Ephraimites at the success and achievement of any other tribe, in this case the tribes east of the Jordan. See again the comment on 8: 1–3.

2. *had I appealed to you*: this suggests that such an appeal was not, in fact, made. The translators have adopted this rendering since there is no explicit reference earlier in the narrative to such an appeal having been issued to the Ephraimites. The rendering in the N.E.B. footnote, however, is the more natural way to understand the Hebrew. We have already noted (see on 11: 29) the possibility that such an unsuccessful appeal was, in fact, issued.

4. In this verse the N.E.B. reproduces a shorter form than the one found in the Hebrew text. The Septuagint has the shorter text, but the fuller one is reproduced in the footnote. It provides a reason for the Ephraimite attitude to the Gileadites, suggesting that those living east of the Jordan were only an offshoot or a sub-clan ('fugitives') of the Joseph tribes, Ephraim and Manasseh. This reason may explain the rather patronizing attitude of the Ephraimites to the Gileadites, but it is not the same reason for the complaint as the one originally given in verse 1. On this account its authenticity has been questioned, not least by the translators of the Old Testament into Greek.

5f. The same technique of seizing *the fords of the Jordan* to cut off the retreat of the Ephraimites is used here as was used against the Moabites by Ehud in 3: 28. In this instance the retreat is back across the Jordan from east to west. *Shibboleth*: the word means 'ear of corn' or, possibly, 'stream'. In the difference in pronunciation we may detect a difference between two Hebrew dialects. We might compare the difficulty which English people have in pronouncing the guttural 'ch' in the Scottish word 'loch'. *forty-two thousand*: this is clearly a saga-like exaggeration. ✻

LIST OF MINOR JUDGES – II

Jephthah was judge over Israel for six years; when he 7
died he was buried in his own city in*[a]* Gilead. After him 8
Ibzan of Bethlehem was judge over Israel. He had thirty 9
sons and thirty daughters. He gave away the thirty
daughters in marriage and brought in thirty girls for his
sons. He was judge over Israel for seven years, and when 10
he died he was buried in Bethlehem.

After him Elon the Zebulunite was judge over Israel 11
for ten years. When he died, he was buried in Aijalon in 12
the land of Zebulun. Next Abdon son of Hillel the Pira- 13
thonite was judge over Israel. He had forty sons and 14
thirty grandsons, who rode each on his own ass. He was
judge over Israel for eight years; and when he died he was 15
buried in Pirathon in the land of Ephraim on the hill of
the Amalekite.

* 7. This verse is clearly the end of the Jephthah story, but
the N.E.B. paragraph division rightly includes it in the continuation of the 'minor judges' list, the first part of which
occurs in 10: 1–5. As we have already noted (see p. 6),
Jephthah probably figured both in the 'minor judges' list and
in the collection of hero sagas. As a result of this, the deuteronomistic historian was able to fuse his two sources and so
construct the book of Judges much as we know it. As with the
rest of the 'minor judges', the length of Jephthah's term of
office is given and his place of burial. The fact that Jephthah
was appointed 'judge' for life is in line with 11: 9–11, where
Jephthah was installed not just as military commander but
also as civilian chief, apparently to an office extending beyond
the immediate military need. *in his own city in Gilead*: as can

[a] in his own city in: *so Sept.; Heb.* in the cities of...

be seen from the N.E.B. footnote, this represents a correction of the Hebrew text in terms of the Septuagint. This is undoubtedly a necessary correction, since the Hebrew makes little sense in the context. The city in question was doubtless Mizpah, where Jephthah is said to have had his home (11: 34).

8–10. *Bethlehem*: there is no indication whether this is the well-known Bethlehem in Judah or the northern Bethlehem, west of Nazareth, mentioned in Josh. 19: 15 .Again, as was the case with Jair in 10: 3–5, the *thirty sons and thirty daughters* would indicate the size of his harem and thus be a pointer to his standing and importance.

11f. According to the genealogical lists in Gen. 46: 14 and Num. 26: 26, Elon was a Zebulunite clan. Again, the name of the supposed ancestor of the clan could be borne by individuals within the clan; cp. the note on Tola and Pua in 10: 1f. The place-name *Aijalon* is the same word as Elon, but differently vocalized. We can say, then, that the clan gave its name to the settlement. This Aijalon, the site of which is unknown, is not to be confused with the better-known place of the same name in the Ephraimite foot-hills, about 15 miles (24 km) south-west of Bethel.

13–15. *Abdon* is not identified by a tribal designation but simply by the name of the town from which he came. Pirathon is probably to be located about 7 miles (11 km) south-west of Shechem, *in the land of Ephraim*. The size of his family and their possession of riding-beasts are again signs of Abdon's personal prestige; cp. on 10: 3–5. The significance of the closing words of the chapter, *on the hill of the Amalekite*, is entirely obscure. On the Amalekites, see above on 3: 12–14. ✲

Israel oppressed by the Philistines

✻ This next section of the book of Judges is concerned with Philistine oppression in general terms and, more specifically, with the figure of Samson. It is, in fact, a cycle of Samson stories. The figure of Samson differs very markedly from that of the other deliverer figures in the book of Judges. Ch. 13 is concerned almost in its entirety with an elaborate birth story accompanied by an appearance of 'the angel of the LORD' to Samson's parents. We are not told that the 'spirit of the LORD' came upon Samson, but that it 'began to drive him hard', a very unusual expression (13: 25). Only at the end of the cycle is Samson said to have been 'judge over Israel' (16: 31). There, too, we are told that he had been judge for only 'twenty years', precisely half of the round figure usually given in the deuteronomistic framework (cp. also 15: 20). This is no doubt an indication in numerical terms that Samson's work against the Philistines was incomplete at his death. This fact is also stressed when the angel says to his mother that the child to be born to her 'will strike the *first* blow to deliver Israel from the power of the Philistines' (13: 5). Again the implication is that Samson's activity will be only the beginning of the movement to free Israel from Philistine oppression. Samson, too, does not engage in any concerted, full-scale military activity against his country's oppressors as did the other deliverer figures in the earlier part of the book. His activities are much more in the nature of frivolous escapades, and the individual stories in the Samson cycle are more in the nature of folk-tales or else of legends explaining place-names and natural phenomena.

Although the Samson cycle is set firmly within the book of Judges by means of the deuteronomistic introduction in 13: 1, Samson's behaviour sets him apart from the other figures in the book. These other figures have been conscious of their high calling, and their efforts have invariably reached a successful outcome. Sometimes commentators have found difficulty in explaining the presence of Samson in the Bible at all. They have been particularly offended by his constant association with Philistine women: the woman of Timnath (ch. 14); the prostitute from Gaza (16: 1–3); Delilah (16: 4–22). These commentators have tended to suggest that Samson is included as an example of the abuse of a high calling, but there is no hint of any such judgement being passed. The Deuteronomist presents his material in a completely neutral and objective manner.

Much has been made, especially in the older commentaries, of the supposedly mythological character of the Samson cycle. The very name Samson (Hebrew *shimshōn*) bears an obvious relation to the word for 'sun' (*shemesh*). The locality in which the Samson stories are centred is very close to the city of Beth-shemesh, 'the temple of the sun'. Samson is at his prime in the summer ('during the time of wheat harvest', 15: 1), while his life ends in the darkness of his blindness (16: 21), regarded as symbolic of winter. His death between the pillars of a Philistine temple is thought of as symbolic of the setting sun. Other elements of sun mythology have been noted, as well as parallels with similar mythological stories from Greece and Assyria. There are probably too many parallels between the Samson cycle and sun mythology for us to doubt that there is at least some connection between the two. But we must not forget that we have no specific evidence of sun-worship at Beth-shemesh. Nor can we fail to realize that these stories as we now have them are far from purely mythological; they read very much like stories rooted in a historical context. They may have been mythological in their origins, but their nature now is best described as that of the folk-tale or hero-legend. ✳

THE BIRTH OF SAMSON

ONCE MORE THE ISRAELITES did what was wrong in **13**
the eyes of the LORD, and he delivered them into the
hands of the Philistines for forty years.

There was a man from Zorah of the tribe of Dan whose 2
name was Manoah and whose wife was barren and childless. The angel of the LORD appeared to her and said, 3
'You are barren and have no child, but you shall conceive
and give birth to a son. Now you must do as I say: be 4
careful to drink no wine or strong drink, and to eat no
forbidden[a] food; you will conceive and give birth to a 5
son, and no razor shall touch his head, for the boy is to be
a Nazirite consecrated to God from the day of his birth.
He will strike the first blow to deliver Israel from the
power of the Philistines.' The woman went and told her 6
husband; she said to him, 'A man of God came to me;
his appearance was that of an[b] angel of God, most terrible
to see. I did not ask him where he came from nor did he
tell me his name. He said to me, "You shall conceive 7
and give birth to a son. From this time onwards drink no
wine or strong drink and eat no forbidden food, for the
boy is to be a Nazirite consecrated to God from his birth
to the day of his death."' Manoah prayed to the LORD, 8
'If it please thee, O LORD, let the man of God whom thou
didst send come again to tell us what we are to do with
the boy who is to be born.' God heard Manoah's prayer, 9
and the angel of God came again to the woman, who
was sitting in the fields; her husband was not with her.
The woman ran quickly and said to him, 'The man who 10

[a] *Lit.* unclean.   [b] *Or* the.

came to me the other day has appeared to me again.'

11 Manoah went with her at once and approached the man and said, 'Was it you who talked with my wife?' He

12 said, 'Yes, it was I.' 'Now when your words come true,' Manoah said, 'what kind of boy will he be and what will

13 he do?' The angel of the LORD answered him, 'Your wife

14 must be careful to do all that I told her: she*a* must not taste anything that comes from the vine. She*a* must drink no wine or strong drink, and she*a* must eat no forbidden

15 food. She*a* must do what I say.' Manoah said to the angel of the LORD, 'May we urge you to stay? Let us

16 prepare a kid for you.' The angel of the LORD replied, 'Though you urge me to stay, I will not eat your food; but prepare a whole-offering if you will, and offer that to the LORD.' Manoah did not perceive that he was the

17 angel of the LORD and said to him, 'What is your name? For we shall want to honour you when your words come

18 true.' The angel of the LORD said to him, 'How can you

19 ask my name? It is a name of wonder.' Manoah took a kid with the proper grain-offering, and offered it on the rock to the LORD, to him whose works are full of wonder.

20 And while Manoah and his wife were watching, the flame went up from the altar towards heaven, and the angel of the LORD went up in the flame; and seeing this,

21 Manoah and his wife fell on their faces. The angel of the LORD did not appear again to Manoah and his wife; and Manoah knew that he was the angel of the LORD.

22 He said to his wife, 'We are doomed to die, we have

23 seen God',*b* but she replied, 'If the LORD had wanted to kill us, he would not have accepted a whole-offering and

[*a*] *Sept. has* he.   [*b*] *Or* a god.

a grain-offering at our hands; he would not now have
let us see and hear all this.' The woman gave birth to a   24-25
son and named him Samson. The boy grew up in
Mahaneh-dan between Zorah and Eshtaol, and the LORD
blessed him, and the spirit of the LORD began to drive
him hard.

✻ 1. This is the usual deuteronomistic introduction involving
apostasy and divine judgement in terms of foreign domination.
The verse sets the Samson stories within the context of the
book of Judges as a whole, and it indicates how the whole
cycle is to be read. On the Philistines see above on 3: 3; see
also on 10: 6, 7f.

2. The birth of a hero from a *barren and childless* woman is a
common motif in folk-tales. Zorah lay in the foothills about
14 miles (22½ km) west of Jerusalem. It is assumed here that
the town is in Danite territory, and this is borne out by Josh.
19: 41. Josh. 15: 33, on the other hand, allocates the town
to Judah. This last passage no doubt reflects a period when the
Danites have abandoned any claims to the area west of Jerusalem and have migrated to the far north. The story of that
migration is told in Judg. 18. *the tribe of Dan*: the word
rendered 'tribe' here might be more accurately translated by
'clan'. It is possible that the Samson stories reflect a stage at
which only isolated Danite groups still remain in this area.
Philistine pressure has clearly reached a peak of some intensity,
and the bulk of the Danites may already have left to seek new
territory elsewhere. It has, indeed, been suggested that the
very existence of the cycle of Samson stories is due to the
desire to collect Danite traditions and local folk-tales before
they disappeared completely in the course of the tribal
migration.

3. *The angel of the LORD*: see on 2: 1. The angel is subsequently referred to by the woman as 'A man of God' whose
'appearance was that of an angel of God, most terrible to see'

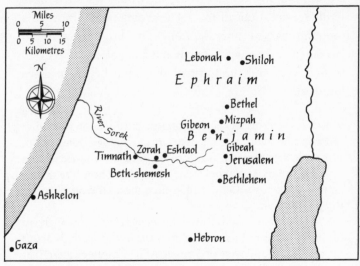

5. The Samson stories and the war against Benjamin (chs. 13–16, 19–21)

(verse 6). The expression 'man of God', which is used also by Manoah in verse 8, would usually be taken to refer to a prophetic figure. Only in verse 21 of the narrative do the human actors in the story become aware that the figure was a divine visitant.

4f. *the boy* who is promised to Manoah and his wife *is to be a Nazirite consecrated to God from the day of his birth*. The law about Nazirites is to be found in Num. 6: 1–21, a passage which is set within the context of a late collection of what are probably, nevertheless, very old laws. The only other reference to Nazirites in the period before the exile is in Amos 2: 11–12. The difference between these two references is that the Numbers passage envisages only a temporary vow, while the Amos passage thinks of a life-long vow and associates the Nazirites with the prophets. We can only conclude that both types of Nazirite were found. What is not clear is whether they were found at the same time or at different periods in history. One characteristic of the Nazirite was that his hair should remain uncut. This was one sign of his dedication, but this sign was not exclusive to the Nazirites; cp. on 5: 2 above. The other main Nazirite feature was that they were forbidden to drink wine, and in this respect there is a clear connection between them and the Rechabites (Jer. 35). The prohibition on the Nazirites was not simply with regard to wine but to any product of the vine (cp. Num. 6: 3–4). This is all that can be intended, in the Samson context, by the reference to *forbidden food*. Nothing, apart from the products of the vine, was specifically forbidden to the Nazirite. The vine was seen as the symbol of the culture of Canaan, contamination from which was regarded as the root cause of all Israel's apostasy and infidelity to her God. This attempt to turn their backs on the supposed evils of the settled agricultural and urban life is brought out clearly where the Rechabites are forbidden to live in houses and are ordered to 'remain tent-dwellers' all their lives (Jer. 35: 7). It is unusual that the prohibition with regard to wine in the Samson story is applied to the mother and not to Samson himself; this is emphasized again in verse 14 (see comment below). There are two possible explanations of this. One is that the prohibition applied to the mother before Samson's birth and that once the child was born the prohibition would then apply to him. To this the objection has been raised that Samson's frivolous activities during his life do not exactly suggest that he was a man *consecrated to God*. The alternative explanation then offered is this. The idea that Samson was a Nazirite was suggested to the compiler of the Samson stories by the motif of his long hair. This motif, however, is not to be explained on the grounds that Samson was a Nazirite but in terms of sun mythology. The sun's rays in primitive art and in ancient literature are always depicted as flowing locks of hair. Samson's hair is symbolic of his strength just as the rays of the sun are symbolic of its strength and life-giving power. When Samson's hair is cut he loses his strength, and this state is symbolic of winter when the sun's rays are lacking in power and effectiveness. We have already commented on the mythological features in the Samson stories (see above, p. 152). In this context we can say that the motif, if really present here, has been historicized in terms of the Israelite religious office of the Nazirite. *He will strike the first blow*: see above, p. 151. In the present context, this phrase suggests that the Samson stories are now part of the Deuteronomistic History which records also the activities of Saul and particularly of David against the Philistines.

6. *A man of God*: a term usually applied to a prophet or seer; see above on verse 3. *most terrible to see*: the reference is to the feeling of terror or awe in the human heart when confronted with the divine. The awareness of the true nature of the messenger is gradually dawning on the human participants in the story.

7. *from his birth to the day of his death*: only at this point in the narrative is the life-long nature of the office of Nazirite made specific in this instance.

8. It is just possible that the section of narrative contained in verses 9–23 was originally told in order to explain how the rock-altar at Zorah came to be a legitimate place of sacrifice and a cultic centre. In more technical language, it is an aetiology (or explanation of the origin) of the sanctuary at Zorah. Verse 8, in that case, is a transitional verse serving to link the narrative about the promised child and the narrative about the sacrifice on the rock-altar at Zorah. But even if this is a correct explanation of the original nature of verses 9–23, they have now become an integral part of Samson's birth narrative. *let the man of God...come again*: Manoah, in the present context, is asking for more information. The nature of his request here is spelled out in verse 12: 'what kind of boy will he be and what will he do?'

14. In this verse we meet again the difficulty of reconciling the prohibition addressed to the mother of the unborn child with what we know from elsewhere about the office of the Nazirite. As can be seen from the N.E.B. footnotes, the

Septuagint solves this problem simply by making all the pronouns masculine. For a discussion of this problem see above on verses 4f.

15. *Let us prepare a kid for you*: Manoah, at this point in the narrative, is still under the impression that he is entertaining a human, though prophetic, figure. This is emphasized in the closing words of verse 16, which some commentators wish to transfer to this point in verse 15. The *kid* mentioned here was intended as a normal meal.

16. *prepare a whole-offering*: the angel urges Manoah, rather, to *offer* a sacrifice *to the LORD*. In *a whole-offering*, the whole animal was consumed by fire on the altar.

18. The angel is unwilling to disclose his *name* to Manoah; to have done so would have given Manoah, according to primitive belief, power over the angel. It is usual, in an aetiology of an altar or a sanctuary, to find as part of the narrative the name of the god to whom the altar is dedicated (as, e.g., in Gen. 28: 10–19). Such a name is no longer clearly discernible in the present state of the text. It could have been either *Wonder* or 'The LORD who does wonders' (cp. verse 19).

19. *a kid with the proper grain-offering*: the kid is now being offered as the 'whole-offering'. The idea of there being a *proper grain-offering* to accompany each 'whole-offering' occurs only in the latest sacrificial rituals in the Old Testament. There is very specific legislation for it in Num. 15: 1–16 where the size of the grain-offering and the drink-offering rises in accordance with the size and importance of the sacrificial animal. *the rock:* the rock altar; see note on 6: 20 above. In this case, no drink-offering or libation is mentioned specifically, though the legislation in Num. 15 seems to demand one.

20f. *the flame went up from the altar*: as in the Gideon story, 6: 21, the fire, here too, is the sign of the divine acceptance of the offering. The fact that *the angel of the LORD* also *went up in the flame* is the sign for *Manoah and his wife* that the person who had appeared to them had indeed been *the angel of the LORD*. That the encounter ended in this way was a sign that it had been God, in the person of his angel or messenger, who had communicated with the couple.

22. It is a very basic idea that anyone who has *seen God* is *doomed to die*. Even Moses, the supreme mediator of God to Israel, was not permitted to see 'the face' of God; cp. Exod. 33: 18–23, especially the expression in verse 20, 'no mortal man may see me and live' (cp. also on 6: 22).

24f. *Mahaneh-dan*: the place-name means, literally, 'the camp of Dan'; cp. 18: 12 for the explanation of the name. The site indicated in 18: 12 lies about 8 miles (nearly 13 km) north-east of the site suggested by the present passage. Various explanations for this have been offered. It may be that they represent separate Danite settlements associated with the period when the tribe were still semi-nomads and practised seasonal migrations with their flocks. The two settlements with identical names would be occupied by the same people at different seasons in the year. On Zorah, see above on verse 2. Eshtaol lay in the same area as Zorah, about 2 miles (3 km) to the north-east. On the expression *the spirit of the LORD began to drive him hard* see p. 151. ✳

SAMSON CHOOSES A WIFE

14 Samson went down to Timnath, and there he saw a
2 woman, one of the Philistines. When he came back, he told his father and mother that he had seen a Philistine woman in Timnath and asked them to get her for him
3 as his wife. His father and mother said to him, 'Is there no woman among your cousins or in all our own people? Must you go and marry one of the uncircumcised Philistines?' But Samson said to his father, 'Get her for
4 me, because she pleases me.' His father and mother did not know that the LORD was at work in this, seeking an opportunity against the Philistines, who at that time were masters of Israel.

❉ 1. *Timnath* lay about 6 miles (about 9½ km) west of Zorah. It is identical with the Timnah mentioned in Josh. 15: 10 and 19: 43. The Timnah mentioned in Josh. 15: 57 lay south-east of Hebron; its site cannot be definitely located. On Timnath-serah/heres (Josh. 19: 50; 24: 30) see on 2: 9; this was Joshua's 'own property' and the site of his grave. The Timnath mentioned here in this verse was clearly in Philistine hands.

2. *he...asked them to get her for him as his wife*: although Samson seems to have selected the woman himself, it was clearly the task of his parents to arrange the marriage. This was the usual method of arranging a marriage; cp., e.g., Gen. 34 where Hamor discusses with Jacob his son's marriage to Jacob's daughter Dinah. By this arrangement the wife would leave her family and join her husband's family. As we shall see, this is not the type of marriage into which Samson eventually enters. It may be that his parents' attempted negotiations failed.

3. *the uncircumcised Philistines*: this is a common term of abuse directed against the Philistines by the Israelites. It occurs again in 15: 18 and commonly in the stories in 1 Samuel (e.g. 1 Sam. 14: 6). The Philistines seem to have been the main people known to the Israelites who did not practise the rite of circumcision. Circumcision was probably originally a puberty rite, but in Israel it became a rite of initiation into the religious community and thus a symbol of a man's membership of that community.

4. This verse is probably a late editorial addition to the story, an attempt to reconcile Samson's behaviour with the idea that he was a person dedicated to the service of *the LORD*. Like 13: 1, it again emphasizes the fact that all the Samson stories are to be read as part of that history which is, in its entirety, under God's control and guidance. *masters of Israel*: cp. 15: 11 for a similar idea. The reference is surely only to part of 'Israel', probably the area in the immediate vicinity of Zorah and Eshtaol, that is, in the region where the Danites originally attempted to settle. ❉

SAMSON'S WEDDING

5 Samson[a] went down to Timnath and, when he[b] reached the vineyards there, a young lion came at him growling.

6 The spirit of the LORD suddenly seized him and, having no weapon in his hand, he tore the lion in pieces as if it were a kid. He did not tell his parents what he had done.

7 Then he went down and spoke to the woman, and she

8 pleased him. After a time he went down again to take her to wife; he turned aside to look at the carcass of the

9 lion, and he saw a swarm of bees in it, and honey. He scraped the honey into his hands and went on, eating as he went. When he came to his father and mother, he gave them some and they ate it; but he did not tell them that he had scraped the honey out of the lion's carcass.

10 His father went down to see the woman, and Samson

11 gave a feast there as the custom of young men was. When the people saw him, they brought thirty young men to be

12 his escort. Samson said to them, 'Let me ask you a riddle. If you can guess it during the seven days of the feast, I will give you thirty lengths of linen and thirty changes of

13 clothing; but if you cannot guess the answer, then you shall give me thirty lengths of linen and thirty changes of clothing.' 'Tell us your riddle,' they said; 'let us hear it.'

14 So he said to them:

> Out of the eater came something to eat;
> out of the strong came something sweet.

At the end of three days they had failed to guess the riddle.

[a] *Prob. rdg.; Heb. adds* and his father and mother.
[b] *So Sept.; Heb.* they.

162

On the fourth[a] day they said to Samson's wife, 'Coax your 15
husband and make him tell you[b] the riddle, or we shall
burn you and your father's house. Did you invite us here[c]
to beggar us?' So Samson's wife wept over him and said, 16
'You do not love me, you only hate me. You have asked
my kinsfolk a riddle and you have not told it to me.' He
said to her, 'I have not told it even to my father and
mother; and am I to tell you?' But she wept over him 17
every day until the seven feast days were ended, and on
the seventh day, because she pestered him, he told her, and
she told the riddle to her kinsfolk. So that same day the 18
men of the city said to Samson before he entered the
bridal chamber:[d]

> What is sweeter than honey?
> What is stronger than a lion?

and he replied, 'If you had not ploughed with my heifer,
you would not have found out my riddle.' Then the 19
spirit of the LORD suddenly seized him. He went down to
Ashkelon and there he killed thirty men, took their belts
and gave their clothes to the men who had answered his
riddle; but he was very angry and went off to his father's
house. And Samson's wife was given in marriage to the 20
friend who had been his groomsman.

✻ The nature of Samson's marriage with the Philistine woman
of Timnath has often been discussed by commentators. The
usual type of marriage in ancient Israel was for the wife to
leave her family and take up residence with her husband's

[a] *So Sept.; Heb.* seventh.　[b] *So Sept.; Heb.* us.
[c] here: *so some MSS.; others* or not.
[d] he entered...chamber: *prob. rdg.; Heb.* the sun went down.

family. This is not the case with Samson. From the fact that
the wedding takes place in his wife's home town and that
she apparently continues to reside there (cp. 15: 1), it has been
suggested that this is a type of marriage known as a *beena*
marriage. These have been studied in Sri Lanka (where the word
beena comes from), and in them the husband leaves his family
and takes up residence with his wife's family. This is still not
the case, however, with Samson, who goes to visit his wife
(cp., again, 15: 1). Nor is the marriage accurately described
by the term *sadīqa* marriage (*sadīqa* is the Arabic word for
'lover'), in which the marriage is by use and wont and where
the woman is more of a concubine than a wife of full standing.
Samson's marriage is of yet another type, one which is still
practised among the bedouin Arabs, where there is true
marriage but not permanent cohabitation. In this type of
marriage, too, the wife is mistress in her own home. The
husband is a visiting husband who comes to her as a guest and
brings gifts (cp., again, 15:1).

5f. *Samson went down to Timnath*: as can be seen from the
footnotes to the N.E.B. text, two conjectural readings have
been adopted in this verse by the translators, one of them on the
basis of the Septuagint. The difficulty is that in its present
form this seems to be a composite narrative, a fusion of two
originally independent stories. In one he slays the lion, and it
would appear that his parents were not witnesses of this:
He did not tell his parents what he had done; cp. also 'When he
came to his father and mother' (verse 9). The other story
concerns the wedding feast at which his father and mother
would normally be present (cp. the Hebrew text of verse 5, as in
N.E.B. footnotes, and verse 10). The Septuagint has gone part
of the way towards harmonizing the two stories by reading
he reached in place of the Hebrew 'they reached'. The N.E.B.
translators have gone further by omitting the words 'and his
father and mother', but they have done this with no support
from either the early translations of the Old Testament such
as the Septuagint, Peshitta or Vulgate or from Hebrew

manuscripts. It is probably better to retain the original text and accept the fact that two stories have been fused here, though without complete logical consistency. *The spirit of the LORD suddenly seized him*: again, emphasis is placed on God's share in Samson's activities. This is not simply a strong-man act, but part of God's overall plan to free his people from Philistine oppression. This element was probably not present in the original story but has been imposed on it by the editor who fitted the cycle of Samson stories into their present context in the book of Judges.

7. *Then he went down and spoke to the woman*: this looks like the beginning of negotiations for the marriage. According to verse 2, Samson had only so far seen the woman. See the comment on verse 2 for the possible failure of earlier negotiations.

8. *to take her to wife*: the visit, on this occasion, is for the wedding ceremony itself. See above, pp. 163f., for a discussion of the nature of Samson's marriage.

9. *When he came to his father and mother*: it is not clear whether they are thought of as being in Timnath or, as is more probable, in Zorah. It is, in that event, uncertain how many visits to Timnath and with what purpose are envisaged in this section. There is one visit in verse 5, one in verse 7, another in verse 8 and possibly a fourth in verse 10. If the visit of verse 7 was for the betrothal and that in verse 8 for the marriage ceremony, it is not clear what the purpose of his father's visit is in verse 10. Again, the most that we can say is that in the present form of the narrative, at least two different stories have been woven together without their having been satisfactorily harmonized.

10f. *as the custom of young men was*: this kind of expression is usually used by an editor by way of explanation of something which would strike his readers as odd. In this instance, it could be their surprise that Samson, supposedly a Nazirite, should give *a feast* (Hebrew literally 'a drinking session'). It could equally be their surprise that the feast was *there*, in the

bride's place of residence. Again this has to do with the peculiar nature of Samson's marriage; see above, pp. 163f. *they
brought thirty young men*: normally this *escort* would be made
up of friends of the bridegroom. Here they are provided by
the inhabitants of Timnath; this, too, is no doubt to be seen
in the light of the peculiar nature of Samson's marriage.

12f. *a riddle*: the same word is used for the 'hard questions'
put to Solomon by the queen of Sheba (1 Kings 10: 1).
Normally at a wedding feast it would be the duty of the
bridegroom's 'friend', his 'groomsman' (see verse 20), to
compose and sing songs at the festivities. Here the only song
mentioned is composed, unusually, by the bridegroom. *thirty
lengths of linen and thirty changes of clothing*: the references are
to a large linen sheet which could serve either as an outer
garment or as a sleeping cover and to the best set of garments
worn on special, festive occasions. In the event of the young
men guessing the correct answer, each would receive one
linen sheet and one festal garment. If they fail to guess
correctly, each has to contribute one linen sheet and one
festal garment, and Samson would thus acquire thirty of each.

14. The riddle is in rhythmic form. The *eater*, the *strong*, is,
of course, the lion while the *something to eat*, the *something
sweet*, is the honey. The correct solution is obvious to the
reader who knows the full story. To the Philistines, *the strong*
might have been thought to refer to Samson's virility and
sexual prowess. In the event, however, this was a false clue, a
red herring.

15. There are difficulties of chronology here. Apparently
the Philistines tried for three days to guess the answer to the
riddle, but the Hebrew text (see footnote) states that they did
not enlist the aid of Samson's wife until the 'seventh day'.
The Septuagint has solved the problem by reading *On the
fourth day*, and the N.E.B. translators have adopted this
solution. *to beggar us*: by forcing them to pay the wager
through their failure to guess the answer to the riddle.

16. *my kinsfolk*: it is unlikely that all the thirty young men

of verse 11 were close relatives of the bride. 'My countrymen' (so the Revised Standard Version) might be a better rendering.

18. *before he entered the bridal chamber*: as can be seen from the N.E.B. footnotes, this is a conjectured reading. Although the Hebrew could be translated 'before the sun went down', it is not normal Hebrew, and the conjectured reading is a very probable one. If that reading is correct, it suggests that the marriage was not consummated until the end of the seven-day festival. In the only other similar passage in the Old Testament, Jacob consummates his marriage to Leah on the first night of the seven-day feast; Gen. 29: 21–8. The reply to the riddle is again rhythmic. It is also highly alliterative; the letter *m* occurs five times in six words in the Hebrew. Samson's response to their successful discovery sounds like a popular proverbial saying which has been secondarily applied to the situation. It, too, is rhythmic, and it is surprising that the N.E.B. has printed it as if it were prose.

19. *the spirit of the LORD suddenly seized him*: again, this is probably editorial emphasis on Samson's role as deliverer of his people from the Philistines. Ashkelon, on the coast about 12 miles (19 km) north of Gaza, was one of the five Philistine cities; see on 3: 3. *took their belts*: it is not quite clear what the significance of such an act would be. The word rendered 'belts' could be more literally translated as 'spoil' or perhaps even 'armour'. Whatever the precise sense of the verse, Samson pays the Philistines of Timnath the unfairly won wager at the expense of the Philistines of Ashkelon.

20. The giving of *Samson's wife* to the *groomsman* is no doubt to avoid the shame at having been abandoned by Samson apparently on the wedding night. It is difficult to give much credence to the closing events of this story as it now stands in view of the difficulty of knowing the chronological relationship to each other of the various events described. ✳

SAMSON'S REVENGE

15 After a while, during the time of wheat harvest, Samson went to visit his wife, taking a kid as a present for her. He said, 'I am going to my wife in our bridal chamber',
2 but her father would not let him in. He said, 'I was sure that you hated her, so I gave her in marriage to your groomsman. Her young sister is better than she – take her
3 instead.' But Samson said, 'This time I will settle my score with the Philistines; I will do them some real harm.'
4 So he went and caught three hundred jackals and got some torches; he tied the jackals tail to tail and fastened a
5 torch between each pair of tails. He then set the torches alight and turned the jackals loose in the standing corn of the Philistines. He burnt up standing corn and stooks
6 as well, vineyards and[a] olive groves. The Philistines said, 'Who has done this?' They were told that it was Samson, because the Timnite, his father-in-law, had taken his wife and given her to his groomsman. So the Philistines came
7 and burnt her and her father. Samson said, 'If you do things like this, I swear I will be revenged upon you
8 before I have done.' He smote them hip and thigh with great slaughter; and after that he went down to live in a cave in the Rock of Etam.

✶ 1. *during the time of wheat harvest*: in the region in which the Samson stories are set, this would be about the end of May. The season is summer, and this may be a reflection of the sun mythology which is discernible behind the Samson cycle; see p. 152. *Samson went to visit his wife*: on the character of

[a] and: *so Sept.; Heb. om.*

Samson's marriage see pp. 163f. *our bridal chamber*: the marriage had not yet been consummated; see on 14: 18 and 14: 20. The bridal chamber seems to have been in the wife's father's house.

3. Samson vows to revenge himself on the Philistines. The Hebrew is not entirely clear here, as can be seen from a comparison with other versions such as the Revised Standard Version, 'This time I shall be blameless in regard to the Philistines, when I do them mischief.'

4f. *three hundred jackals*: 'foxes' according to most versions, but foxes are solitary animals, not usually found in such large numbers. This strange incident has usually been explained in terms of sympathetic magic. The red 'foxes' symbolize the red-coloured rust-fungus which tends to attack the growing corn in Palestine about the middle of April. The rust-fungus was believed to be caused by the hot sun beating on corn stalks left wet by the dew. What, on this view, lies behind this incident is another aspect of sun mythology. Samson, the sun-god with his fiery heat, lets loose the destructive rust-fungus which destroys the growing corn of the Philistines. The Roman author Ovid tells of the ceremonial hunting of foxes with torches tied to their tails which takes place in the circus in Rome in mid-April. This Roman custom is probably of Semitic origin since the time in question is when the corn is susceptible to rust-fungus in Palestine. In Italy this would not happen until the end of June at the earliest.

6. The retaliation by the Philistines presumably involved *her and her father*'s house. This is made explicit in many Hebrew manuscripts and in several of the ancient versions.

7f. Samson's second act of revenge is not specified. All that we are told is that *He smote them hip and thigh*. The expression is apparently a proverbial one, possibly originating from the art of wrestling, though its precise significance is not entirely clear. The reference (cp. *with great slaughter*) is to some crushing defeat. The *Rock of Etam* can no longer be identified with certainty. It presumably lay in the same general area as that in which the Samson stories are set. ✱

THE PHILISTINES TRY TO CAPTURE SAMSON

9 The Philistines came up and pitched camp in Judah,
10 and overran Lehi. The men of Judah said, 'Why have you
attacked us?' They answered, 'We have come to take
11 Samson prisoner and serve him as he served us.' So three
thousand men from Judah went down to the cave in the
Rock of Etam. They said to Samson, 'Surely you know
that the Philistines are our masters? Now see what you
have brought upon us.' He answered, 'I only served them
12 as they had served me.' They said to him, 'We have come
down to bind you and hand you over to the Philistines.'
'Then you must swear to me', he said, 'that you will not
13 set upon me yourselves.' They answered, 'No; we will
only bind you and hand you over to them, we will not
kill you.' So they bound him with two new ropes and
14 brought him up from the cave in the Rock. He came to
Lehi, and when they met him, the Philistines shouted in
triumph; but the spirit of the LORD suddenly seized him,
the ropes on his arms became like burnt tow and his
15 bonds melted away. He found the jaw-bone of an ass, all
16 raw, and picked it up and slew a thousand men. He made
this saying:

> With the jaw-bone of an ass[a] I have flayed them like
> asses;[b]
>
> with the jaw-bone of an ass I have slain a thousand
> men.

17 When he had said his say, he threw away the jaw-bone;

[a] ass: *Heb.* hamor.
[b] I have...asses: *or* I have reddened them blood-red, *or* I have heaped
them in heaps; *Heb.* hamor himmartim.

and he called that place Ramath-lehi.[a] He began to feel 18
very thirsty and cried aloud to the LORD, 'Thou hast let
me, thy servant, win this great victory, and must I now
die of thirst and fall into the hands of the uncircumcised?'
God split open the Hollow[b] of Lehi and water came out 19
of it. Samson drank, his strength returned and he revived.
This is why the spring in Lehi is called En-hakkore[c] to
this day.

Samson was judge over Israel for twenty years in the 20
days of the Philistines.

* 9. *Lehi*: the place cannot be identified. Again, this is an
aetiological narrative; the explanation of the place-name
comes at the end in verse 17. Lehi is the Hebrew for 'jaw-
bone'.

10. The reason for this Philistine attack on Judah is osten-
sibly the Philistine desire to capture Samson in retaliation for
his latest exploit against them, presumably that referred to in
verses 7 and 8.

11. *three thousand men from Judah*: the large number indicates that we are in the realm of saga. The fact that it is *men
from Judah* who are involved here has been taken to be an
indication that the Danite migration to the north, described
in ch. 18, has already in the main taken place. *the Philistines
are our masters*: the Philistine superiority is clear from the way
in which they can stipulate precisely how Samson is to be
handed over and from the way in which the Israelites un-
protestingly comply with their demands.

13. *two new ropes*: not only would new ropes be particularly difficult to break, but new objects were particularly
sacred and therefore particularly effective (cp. 1 Sam. 6: 7).

[a] *That is* Jaw-bone Hill.
[b] *Lit.* Mortar.
[c] *That is* the Crier's Spring.

This serves to heighten the miraculous nature of Samson's feat of strength in breaking them.

14. *the spirit of the LORD suddenly seized him*: again we have this recurrent motif of the strengthening of Samson at particular moments in his story by the divine spirit. This incident, too, is to be regarded as part of God's plan of deliverance for his people from Philistine oppression.

15. *jaw-bone*: it is this element in the story which gives the name to the place. *all raw*: a fresh jaw-bone would be hard and less brittle than a dried one; in this respect it would stand up more easily to the use made of it by Samson. *a thousand men*: the number is again indicative of the legendary character of the story.

16. As can be seen from the N.E.B. footnotes, the couplet which Samson *made* contains some word-play. As can also be seen from these footnotes, the second half of the first line is obscure and various translations are possible. 'I have heaped them in heaps' is the more usual rendering. The Hebrew as given in the second footnote represents an emendation of the standard Hebrew text. More literally rendered it would run 'a heap, two heaps', i.e. 'heaps upon heaps' (so the Revised Standard Version).

17. *Ramath-lehi*: in the present narrative the word 'Ramath' has been wrongly connected with a verb meaning 'to throw'. The verse suggests that the name means 'the throwing of the jaw-bone'. But this derivation of 'Ramath' is wrong; the place-name can only mean 'hill of the jaw-bone'. Presumably the place would have been called something else prior to Samson's heroic deed, but the narrative does not tell us what the original name of the place was. Already in verse 9 it is simply called Lehi. In connection with this incident in the Samson story reference is often made to the defeat of the Philistines at Lehi by Shammah, one of 'David's heroes', in 2 Sam. 23: 11–12. There is a similarity between the names of the heroes, the incidents happen at the same place, and the heroes defeat the Philistines single-handed. But in the Sham-

mah incident there is no reference to the weapon used and there is, therefore, no aetiology of the place-name. The two stories may, in the long run, go back to the same source, but it is not clear how either of them could have influenced the other, as some commentators have claimed.

18f. These two verses contain a second aetiological narra-tive, this time an explanation of another place-name in the Lehi district, the name of *the spring...En-hakkore*. As the N.E.B. footnote explains, the name means 'Crier's Spring', and it is explained as due to Samson's having *cried aloud to the LORD* to save him from dying of thirst. This is a very unlikely origin for the name of the spring. The word 'crier' or 'caller' is used, in Hebrew, as a bird-name, that of the partridge. The name of the spring is much more likely to be 'the Spring of the Partridge' and to have quite a different origin from the one suggested here. In the present context, this story is connected to the immediately preceding one by the reference to *this great victory*, the victory at Ramath-lehi. On *the uncircumcised* see on 14: 3.

20. This looks like a concluding note to the Samson cycle. The gist of it is repeated at the end of 16: 31. It is not at all clear why it should have been inserted at this point when the Samson cycle obviously concludes only with the death of Samson in 16: 30. The narrator was aware that Philistine domination in Israel lasted for forty years (13: 1) and that Samson strikes only 'the first blow to deliver Israel from the power of the Philistines' (13: 5). He concludes, therefore, that Samson's term of office came to an end before the Philistine oppression did. *twenty years*: see p. 151. *

SAMSON AT GAZA

Samson went to Gaza, and there he saw a prostitute **16** and went in to spend the night with her. The people of 2 Gaza heard[a] that Samson had come, and they surrounded

[a] The...heard: *so Sept.; Heb.* To the people of Gaza.

him and lay in wait for him all that night at the city gate. During the night, however, they took no action, saying to themselves, 'When day breaks we shall kill him.' 3 Samson lay in bed till midnight; and when midnight came he rose, seized hold of the doors of the city gate and the two posts, pulled them out, bar and all, hoisted them on to his shoulders and carried them to the top of the hill east of Hebron.

✻ 1. *Gaza* was the most southerly of the five Philistine cities; see above on 3: 3. It lay a mile (1½ km) or so inland from the coast. *a prostitute*: the story is told as one of Samson's encounters with Philistine women.

2. The Philistines of Gaza are determined to seize this opportunity of killing Samson.

3. There are a number of factors in this verse which make this incident difficult to understand in historical terms. There is, in the first place, the question of how Samson could have carried the tremendous weight of the city gates of Gaza. Secondly, Hebron lay in the hills about 40 miles (64 km) east of Gaza; the *hill* in question lay *east of Hebron*, that is, on the far side of Hebron from Gaza. How could Samson have gone so far in the one night? Commentators have wondered whether the 'hill that is before Hebron' (so the Hebrew literally) was really near Hebron or whether it might not have been near Gaza itself, but on the Hebron road. It is, however, easier to remove this story completely from any geographical context and to regard it as yet another motif from sun mythology. In Babylonian art sunrise is often represented as the sun-god passing through open gates. In this narrative the following elements are possibly significant in this respect. The Philistines plan to kill Samson 'When day breaks'. Samson lies *in bed* in the night, a possible reference to where the sun goes during the hours of darkness. The hill is *east* of Hebron, the place of the sunrise. Samson spends the

night with a woman; cp. the comparison of the rising sun with 'a bridegroom' coming out 'from his wedding canopy' in Ps. 19: 5. These various elements in the narrative seem to suggest that we are in the realm of sun mythology. They have, in the present context, however, been connected to the historical situation existing between Samson and the Philistines. ✻

SAMSON AND DELILAH

After this Samson fell in love with a woman named 4 Delilah, who lived in the valley of Sorek. The lords of 5 the Philistines went up country to see her and said, 'Coax him and find out what gives him his great strength, and how we can master him, bind him and so hold him captive; then we will each give you eleven hundred pieces of silver.' So Delilah said to Samson, 'Tell me 6 what gives you your great strength, and how you can be bound and held captive.' Samson replied, 'If they bind 7 me with seven fresh bowstrings not yet dry, then I shall become as weak as any other man.' So the lords of the 8 Philistines brought her seven fresh bowstrings not yet dry, and she bound him with them. She had men already 9 hidden in the inner room, and she cried, 'The Philistines are upon you, Samson!' But he snapped the bowstrings as a strand of tow snaps when it feels the fire, and his strength was not tamed. Delilah said to Samson, 'I see 10 you have made a fool of me and told me lies. Tell me this time how you can be bound.' He said to her, 'If 11 you bind me tightly with new ropes that have never been used, then I shall become as weak as any other man.' So Delilah took new ropes and bound him with them. 12 Then she cried, 'The Philistines are upon you, Samson!',

while the men waited hidden in the inner room. He
13 snapped the ropes off his arms like pack-thread. Delilah
said to him, 'You are still making a fool of me and have
told me lies. Tell me: how can you be bound?' He said,
'Take the seven loose locks of my hair and weave them
into the warp, and then drive them tight with the beater;
and I shall become as weak as any other man.' So she
lulled him to sleep, wove the seven loose locks of his hair
14 into the warp,*a* and drove them tight with the beater,
and cried, 'The Philistines are upon you, Samson!' He
woke from sleep and pulled away the warp and the loom
15 with it.*b* She said to him, 'How can you say you love
me when you do not confide in me? This is the third
time you have made a fool of me and have not told me
16 what gives you your great strength.' She so pestered him
with these words day after day, pressing him hard and
17 wearying him to death, that he told her his secret. 'No
razor has touched my head,' he said, 'because I am a
Nazirite, consecrated to God from the day of my birth.
If my head were shaved, then my strength would leave
me, and I should become as weak as any other man.'
18 Delilah saw that he had told her his secret; so she sent to
the lords of the Philistines and said, 'Come up at once,
he has told me his secret.' So the lords of the Philistines
19 came up and brought the money with them. She lulled
him to sleep on her knees, summoned a man and he
shaved the seven locks of his hair for her. She began to
20 take him captive and his strength left him. Then she
cried, 'The Philistines are upon you, Samson!' He woke

[*a*] and then drive...warp: *so Sept.; Heb. om.*
[*b*] the warp...with it: *prob. rdg.; Heb. adds an unintelligible word.*

from his sleep and said, 'I will go out as usual and shake
myself'; he did not know that the LORD had left him.
The Philistines seized him, gouged out his eyes and brought 21
him down to Gaza. There they bound him with fetters
of bronze, and he was set to grinding corn in the prison.
But his hair, after it had been shaved, began to grow 22
again.

✻ 4. *Delilah*: the name could mean 'devotee' or 'wor-
shipper', and it has been thought that Delilah might have
been connected with the cult of the fertility goddess, possibly
as a sacred prostitute. It is not certain whether she was herself
a Philistine woman or possibly an Israelite woman in the pay
of the Philistines (cp. verse 5). *the valley of Sorek*: still the main
scene of the Samson stories; Zorah, Mahaneh-dan and
Timnath all lay in this valley, with Eshtaol only a little to the
north.

5. *The lords of the Philistines*: each of the five main Philistine
cities (see above on 3: 3) was ruled by a prince or 'lord'.
The Hebrew word for these Philistine rulers, *seranim*, is
probably related to the Greek word *tyrannos*. This would lend
support to the idea that the Philistines originally came from
the Aegean area. *went up country*: this could mean either
simply that they went north to the valley of Sorek or else
that they went up into the foothills from the plains where
their cities lay. *each*: presumably each of the five rulers of the
Philistine city-states.

7. *seven fresh bowstrings not yet dry*: the number 'seven' was
thought to be a magic number. It recurs in the Samson story
in verses 13 ('the seven loose locks of my hair') and 19 ('the
seven locks of his hair'). Like the jaw-bone in 15: 15, these
are *not yet dry* and therefore not brittle.

9. *he snapped the bowstrings*: Samson's reaction is presumably
in response to Delilah's cry. In view of the remainder of the
story, we must assume that the Philistines remained *hidden*

in the inner room. Had they revealed themselves at this point, Samson would have been suspicious of Delilah's motives on the subsequent occasions.

11. *new ropes*: cp. on the same device in 15: 13.

12. On this occasion we are specifically told that the men remained (*waited*) *hidden in the inner room*.

13f. In the third attempt to deprive Samson of his strength, Delilah weaves the long locks of his hair into *the warp* on the horizontal loom. She makes the resultant woven material tight by means of *the beater*. The latter was a flat piece of wood used to push the weaving tightly together.

17. *because I am a Nazirite*: this first sentence of verse 17 refers us back to ch. 13; see on 13: 4f.

18. Somehow, intuitively perhaps, Delilah is aware that this time Samson has told the truth and has revealed *his secret*.

19. *She began to take him captive*: presumably Delilah tied him up in some way. *his strength* leaves him not as a result of Delilah's tying up but because his head has been shaved. In the following verse he tries to 'shake' himself (? free of the bonds with which Delilah had presumably tied him).

20. *the LORD had left him*: the presence of the LORD was clearly connected with Samson's fidelity to the Nazirite vows. Once his hair was cut, once he had abandoned one at least of these vows, the spirit of God was no longer with him, and he was an easy prey to his enemies. In earlier parts of the Samson cycle, 'the spirit of the LORD' has been associated with Samson's superhuman strength; cp. 14: 6, 19; 15: 14.

21. *gouged out his eyes*: Samson's blindness is symbolic of the darkness of the night and of the winter, times when the earth is deprived of the sun. Here again, we have a motif possibly derived from sun mythology. *grinding corn*: this was degrading work, usually given to the lowest slaves. If the mill were large, the wheel was usually turned by an animal. The ceaseless round of grinding has been compared with the ceaseless round of the sun; again, this may be a motif from sun mythology.

22. The information that *his hair...began to grow again* is necessary for our understanding of the end of the story when Samson's strength returns with his growing hair. *

SAMSON'S FINAL REVENGE AND DEATH

The lords of the Philistines assembled together to offer 23 a great sacrifice to their god Dagon and to rejoice before him. They said, 'Our god has delivered Samson our enemy into our hands.' The people, when they saw him, 24 praised their god, chanting:

> Our god has delivered our enemy into our hands,
>   the scourge of our land who piled it with our dead.

When they grew merry, they said, 'Call Samson, and 25 let him fight to make sport for us.' So they summoned Samson from prison and he made sport before them all. They stood him between the pillars, and Samson said to 26 the boy who held his hand, 'Put me where I can feel the pillars which support the temple, so that I may lean against them.' The temple was full of men and women, 27 and all the lords of the Philistines were there, and there were about three thousand men and women on the roof watching Samson as he fought. Samson called on the 28 LORD and said, 'Remember me, O Lord GOD, remember me: give me strength only this once, O God, and let me at one stroke be avenged on the Philistines for my two eyes.' He put his arms round the two central pillars which 29 supported the temple, his right arm round one and his left round the other, and braced himself and said, 'Let 30 me die with the Philistines.' Then Samson leaned forward with all his might, and the temple fell on the lords and

on all the people who were in it. So the dead whom he killed at his death were more than those he had killed in
31 his life. His brothers and all his father's family came down, carried him up to the grave of his father Manoah between Zorah and Eshtaol and buried him there. He had been judge over Israel for twenty years.

✲ 23f. *to offer a great sacrifice to their god Dagon*: in spite of the taunt-song chanted by the people in verse 24, the real purpose of this feast cannot have been to rejoice at the eventual capture of Samson. Sufficient time has elapsed since his capture for his hair to grow again and his strength to return sufficiently for him to be able to pull the Philistine temple down about the ears of the worshippers. Samson, therefore, is incidental to the feast. An alternative explanation would be that the present form of the narrative has telescoped two originally fairly widely separated incidents. *Dagon* was a grain-god; his name is closely related to the Hebrew word for 'corn' (*dagan*). He was originally a Semitic god who was no doubt adopted by the Philistines when they settled in the rich agricultural area of south-west Palestine. It may be that the taunt-song should come after the arrival of Samson on the scene; it would certainly be more effective if the song were sung in his presence. There is also the fact that the phrase *when they saw him* is out of place before Samson's actual appearance in verse 25. Verses 24 and 25 should, then, perhaps be reversed. The couplet itself has a five-fold rhyme on the Hebrew equivalent of the word *our*. Hebrew poetry is usually based on rhythm and parallelism, and rhyme is rare. It is probably used deliberately in this taunt-song.

25f. *let him fight to make sport for us*: what seems to be envisaged is that Samson indulged in wrestling bouts for the amusement of the spectators. *They stood him between the pillars*: here again we may have a motif connected with sun mythology, the reference this time being to the setting sun.

Cp. a similar idea connected with the rising sun in 16: 3 above.

27–30. It is difficult to envisage the structure of the temple. It obviously had a flat roof, though the number of people supposedly *on the roof* is clearly a saga-like exaggeration. It was probably built round a central or perhaps a three-sided court-yard in the centre of which Samson *fought*. Samson eventually pulled down *the two central pillars which supported the temple*. How, precisely, he could have reached these two pillars, which presumably were some distance apart, is not made clear.

31. The note about where Samson was *buried* may be an attempt on the part of the narrator to bring Samson into line with the 'minor judges' whose burial places are always noted (cp. above on 10: 1–5 and 12: 7–15). That the length of his term of office is repeated at this point (cp. on 15: 20) would support that suggestion. There may, of course, in addition, have been a local tradition about Samson's tomb. Mahaneh-dan is described in 13: 25 as being *between Zorah and Eshtaol*; it may have been there that Samson was buried. ✷

Years of lawlessness

✷ This final section of the book of Judges consists of two appendices, one dealing with the tribe of Dan (chs. 17–18), the other with the tribe of Benjamin (chs. 19–21). They can be described as appendices to the book since neither of them refers to a 'judge'; to this extent they stand outside the deuteronomistic framework of the book. They do, however, have the odd fact in common that both refer to a Levite who is connected with Bethlehem (cp. 17: 7 and 19: 1). A recurring emphasis is laid, in these two sections, on the fact that there was as yet 'no king in Israel' (18: 1; cp. 19: 1) and that this was, for that reason, a time when 'every man did what was

right in his own eyes' (17: 6; 21: 25). The fact that they are
set in the period before the emergence of the monarchy
explains why these two sections have been inserted at this
point in the story of Israel's history. The fact that they pre-
suppose no strong central authority has led to the description
of the period in which they are set as 'Years of lawlessness'. *

THE DANITE MIGRATION TO THE NORTH

* The section on Dan (chs. 17–18) describes how a new home
was found for this small tribe. The original allotment of
territory to Dan in the western foothills and on the coastal
plain is described in Josh. 19: 40–6. Josh. 19: 47 suggests
that the Danites 'lost this territory'. Judg. 1: 34–5 suggests
that it was Amorite pressure which prevented the Danites
from ever settling in their territory at all (see on 1: 34f.).
The context of the Samson stories would suggest that the
presence of the Philistines in the region to the south of the
area of supposed Danite settlement had something to do with
the migration of the Danites. It was, at any rate, in this area
that the confrontation between Israelites and Philistines prin-
cipally took place. Both the Samson stories and the Song of
Deborah (5: 17) seem to suggest that the Danites had already
left the territory originally allocated to them and had settled
in the far north. One can assume, then, that the Danite migration to the north probably happened at a fairly early stage in
the process of the Israelite settlement in Palestine. Thus,
though chs. 17–18 occur towards the end of the book of
Judges, the events which they describe probably happened at
an early point in the period of time covered by the book.
But perhaps the main point of this section is not the migration
of the tribe of Dan but the foundation of the sanctuary at Dan
in the north. This sanctuary can only be the one which,
according to 1 Kings 12: 28–33, was set up by Jeroboam I and
which was particularly dedicated to bull worship. As might
be expected, the story is told from an anti-Dan point of view.

Fun is poked at this sanctuary which is centred round a stolen idol and is served by a runaway priest. It may be that it was this tribal sanctuary which was given the status of a royal sanctuary by Jeroboam. *

MICAH'S IDOL

THERE WAS ONCE A MAN named Micah from the **17** hill-country of Ephraim. He said to his mother, 'You 2 remember the eleven hundred pieces of silver which were taken from you, and how you called down a curse on the thief in my hearing? I have the money; I took it and now I will give it back to you.'[a] His mother said, 'May the LORD bless you, my son.' So he gave the eleven hundred 3 pieces of silver back to his mother, and she said, 'I now solemnly dedicate this money of mine to the LORD for the benefit of my son, to make a carved idol and a cast image.' He returned the money to his mother, and she 4 took two hundred pieces of silver and handed them to a silversmith, who made them into an idol and an image, which stood in Micah's house.

* 1. *Micah*: the name means 'Who is like Yahweh'. It is spelled in two different ways within chs. 17–18 as a whole, in one way in 17: 1–4 and in a shorter form in the rest of the narrative. This, along with other variations which we shall note in due course, has sometimes been taken as evidence that within these two chapters we have two different literary sources which have subsequently been worked together. But such a theory is difficult to pursue with consistency, and it is probably nearer the truth to consider that the two chapters are basically a literary unity. This is not, of course, to deny

[a] and now...you: *transposed from verse 3.*

that such an original unity has been distorted to some extent by subsequent additions and alterations. *the hill-country of Ephraim* is a very vague description of where Micah resides.

2. *eleven hundred pieces of silver*: this was the sum paid by each of the Philistine lords to Delilah for her betrayal of the secret of Samson's strength. In that context it was traitor's money; here it is cursed money. It is probable that the Samson context has influenced the use of the same sum here. *you called down a curse on the thief*: Micah's mother clearly did not expect this particular thief and has unwittingly cursed her own son. *I took it*: 18: 14 seems to suggest that Micah owned more than one house, and the narrative tells us that he could afford to maintain a priest. Both of these factors would suggest a man of considerable wealth and standing, but this does not prevent him from appropriating what was no doubt by any standards a considerable sum of money. *and now I will give it back to you*: as can be seen from the N.E.B. footnote, these words belong to the end of verse 3. In that context they are spoken by Micah's mother. We shall consider them in that context. In their present context in the N.E.B. they are superfluous, since Micah's restoring of the money to his mother is specifically mentioned at the beginning of verse 3. The closing words of verse 2 are an attempt on the part of the mother to change her curse into a blessing.

3. Micah returns the money to his mother who, in pursuit of her attempt to change her curse into a blessing, dedicates it to a sacred purpose in such a way that her son has the use and benefit of it. As a symbolic token of this she expresses her intention of giving the money back to her son. She does so in the words which the N.E.B. translators have transferred to verse 2: 'and now I will give it back to you'. The text does not explicitly state that she did so, but the words of her intention are so definite that it was perhaps hardly necessary to spell out the completion of the action.

4. Micah now solemnly returns the money to his mother for her to carry out her intention of dedicating it to the LORD and

making an idol. There is a certain irony in the fact that no discrepancy is felt by Micah or his mother in the association of 'the LORD' with 'an idol and an image'. Only *two hundred pieces of silver* of the original eleven hundred are *handed* to the *silversmith* for the making of the idol. It may be that this is poking additional fun at the whole business; in the end the god was deprived of the bulk of the money. It may, on the other hand, be that the remainder of the sum was to be used for the maintenance of the sanctuary. The N.E.B. translation implies that two cult objects were manufactured, *an idol and an image*, but the verb *stood* is singular in the Hebrew, and this seems to imply that there was only one object, possibly a carved wooden image covered with a metal overlay (cp. the Revised Standard Version 'a graven image and a molten image'). The description of this single cult object has been misunderstood by some parts of ch. 18 as referring to two distinct objects (cp. verses 17f.), though other parts of ch. 18 (cp. verses 30f.) definitely envisage only one object ('the idol'). ✶

MICAH'S PRIEST

This man Micah had a shrine, and he made an ephod 5 and teraphim*a* and installed one of his sons to be his priest. In those days there was no king in Israel and every 6 man did what was right in his own eyes. Now there was 7 a young man from Bethlehem in Judah, from the clan of Judah, a Levite named Ben-gershom.*b* He had left the 8 city of Bethlehem to go and find somewhere to live. On his way he came to Micah's house in the hill-country of Ephraim. Micah said to him, 'Where have you come 9 from?' He replied, 'I am a Levite from Bethlehem in Judah, and I am looking for somewhere to live.' Micah 10

[a] *Or* household gods.
[b] named Ben-gershom: *prob. rdg.*, *cp. 18: 30; Heb.* he lodged there.

said to him, 'Stay with me and be priest and father to me.
I will give you ten pieces of silver a year, and provide
11 you with food and clothes.'[a] The Levite agreed to stay
12 with the man and was treated as one of his own sons. Micah
installed the Levite, and the young man became his priest
13 and a member of his household. Micah said, 'Now I
know that the LORD will make me prosper, because I have
a Levite for my priest.'

✳ 5f. Micah's *shrine* was clearly some kind of domestic
chapel (literally 'house of God') and it was no doubt there
that the idol was housed. But other cult objects were felt to
be necessary, so Micah *made an ephod and teraphim*. On *ephod*
see above on 8: 27. Here it is clearly a cult object, possibly
used as a means of divination. The *teraphim* (a Hebrew plural
form) may also have been used for divination, but they are
more usually thought of as 'household gods' (cp. Gen. 31:
17–35). According to Gen. 31: 34, these were small enough
to be hidden in a camel-bag and sat upon; according to 1 Sam.
19: 13, they appear to have been life-size, though the Hebrew
there could perhaps more probably be translated to suggest
that Michal placed the household gods 'beside' (N.E.B. 'on')
the bed. The expression rendered in N.E.B. as *installed* is the
technical Hebrew term for ordination. *one of his sons to be his
priest*: according to 2 Sam. 8: 18 David's sons were priests,
but gradually a preference for a special priestly class came to
be felt. Although, then, there is nothing very unusual about
the installation of a layman as priest, the practice is being
criticized in this narrative. The general observation of verse 6,
the recurrence of which we have already noted (see pp. 181f.),
is obviously applied here to the cultic sphere. The practice of
having a 'lay' priest is seen as an irregularity due to the general
'lawlessness' of the period in which these events take place.

[a] *So Vulg.; Heb. adds* and the Levite went.

Expression is also given, in this narrative, to the preference for having a Levite as a priest (cp. verse 13).

7. The *young man* in question here comes from the Judaean town of Bethlehem, but it is also emphasized that he is himself a Judahite. It is clear, then, that the term *Levite* tells us not his tribal origin but the class of people to which he belongs. By the time of the narrator, the term *Levite* has lost any tribal identity it may have had and has become a term descriptive of the priestly class. The terms 'priest' and 'Levite' are virtually synonyms during the period of the monarchy. It is not until the period after the exile that they begin to be differentiated and that the Levites become merely a class of minor clergy. *Ben-gershom* (literally 'son of Gershom'; cp. 18: 30): the occurrence of the name here depends on a textual emendation. The priest's full name and genealogy are given in 18: 30, but it would have been strange if his name had been given only at the very end of the narrative.

8. *to go and find somewhere to live*: that is, to live as a 'resident alien'. The 'resident alien' (Revised Standard Version 'sojourner') was a member of Israelite society who, along with the widow and the orphan, was particularly cared for in Israelite legislation (cp., e.g., Deut. 14: 29). The fact that here we have an itinerant Levite who is on the look-out for a job wherever he can pick one up is again fun being poked at the origins of the Danite priesthood.

10. *be priest and father to me*: cp. Gen. 45: 8 where Joseph refers to himself as 'father' or, as in the N.E.B. footnote, 'counsellor', to Pharaoh. The words omitted at the end of the verse by the N.E.B. (see footnote), 'and the Levite went', are probably an erroneous repetition of the opening words of verse 11, 'The Levite agreed.'

11. *as one of his own sons*: the Levite is treated as a full member of Micah's household; so, too, verse 12.

12. *installed*: see on verse 5 above.

13. The emerging preference for a Levitical priesthood is

clear here. Micah can now be the recipient of the LORD's blessing; the Levite is the guarantee of it. ✳

THE DANITE RECONNAISSANCE PARTY

18 In those days there was no king in Israel and the tribe of the Danites was looking for territory to occupy, because they had not so far come into possession of the territory*a* allotted to them among the tribes of Israel.

2 The Danites therefore sent out five fighting men of their clan from Zorah and Eshtaol to prospect, with instructions to go and explore the land. They came to Micah's house in the hill-country of Ephraim and spent the night there.

3 While they were there, they recognized the speech of the young Levite; they turned there and then and said to him, 'Who brought you here? What are you doing?

4 What is your business here?' He said, 'This is all Micah's doing: he has hired me and I have become his priest.'

5 They said to him, 'Then inquire of God on our behalf

6 whether our mission will be successful.' The priest replied,

7 'Go in peace. Your mission is in the LORD's hands.' The five men went on their way and came to Laish. There they found the inhabitants living a carefree life, in the same way as the Sidonians, a quiet carefree folk, with no hereditary king to keep the country under his thumb.*b* They were a long way from the Sidonians, and had no

8 contact with the Aramaeans.*c* So the five men went back to Zorah and Eshtaol, and when their kinsmen asked their

[a] they had...territory: *so Sept.; Heb. obscure.*
[b] with no...thumb: *prob. rdg.; Heb.* and none humiliating anything in the land with inherited authority.
[c] *So some MSS. of Sept.; Heb.* men.

news, they said, 'Come and attack them. It is an excellent   9
country that we have seen. Will you hang back and do
nothing about it? Start off now and take possession of the
land. When you get there, you will find a people living   10
a carefree life in a wide expanse of open country. God
has delivered it into your hands, a place where there is no
lack of anything on earth.'

* 1. Again, the opening phrase refers to the lawlessness and
generally unsettled state of the country, though this is not
made explicit as it is in 17: 6 and 21: 25 with the additional
phrase 'every man did what was right in his own eyes'. The
inability of the Danites to settle in *the territory allotted to them*
has already been discussed above, p. 182.

2. The sending out of spies to reconnoitre a given region is
not without parallel in Israelite tradition; cp. the sending out
of a similar expedition into southern Judah from the wilderness of Paran in Num. 13–14. Like the Samson stories, this
narrative too is aware that there was at least a remnant of
Danite settlement in the region of *Zorah and Eshtaol*. On the
place-names see on 13: 2 (Zorah) and 13: 24f. (Eshtaol). The
'six hundred armed men' who eventually set out to conquer
the recommended territory (verse 11) can have been only a
part of the population, so the settlement must have been a
fairly extensive one.

3. *they recognized the speech of the young Levite*: the N.E.B.
translation implies, probably correctly, that it was the Levite's
accent or dialect which they recognized. The Hebrew literally
has 'the voice of the young Levite', but it is extremely unlikely that the Danites knew him personally. It is equally
unlikely that they heard him performing the cult and realized
from what he was saying that he was a priest. If this were the
meaning, there would have been then no need for them to ask
What is your business here? This encounter between the Danite
spies and the young Levite indicates that the whole of ch. 17

has been simply a prelude to the events now described in ch. 18, the migration of the Danites and the establishment of the sanctuary in their new place of settlement.

5f. *inquire of God on our behalf*: they ask him for an oracle on the outcome of their mission. On the asking of oracles see above on 1: 1. In this instance the Levite probably had the means of securing an oracle in the ephod and possibly also in the teraphim; see on 17: 5f. We are not told how the oracle was obtained, but it is a favourable one.

7. *Laish*: only here is the city called by this name. In Josh. 19: 47 it is called Leshem, a form very similar to Laish. Elsewhere in the Old Testament the city is always called Dan, even, anachronistically, in Gen. 14: 14. It probably lay on one of the sources of the Jordan in the foothills of Mt Hermon. *the inhabitants* of Laish are compared to *the Sidonians* who, here, seem to be regarded as a peaceable, unwarlike people. Sidon was a Phoenician settlement on the coast about 20 miles (32 km) north of Tyre and almost due west of Damascus. It is probable that at this period the Sidonians had been confined to the coastal region by *the Aramaeans* who were settled in inland Syria, with Damascus as the principal Aramaean kingdom. Sidon was primarily a trading and commercial settlement, and this verse suggests that this was true of pre-Danite Laish as well. Laish lay only about 30 miles (48 km) south-east of Sidon but was cut off from it by the Lebanon mountains. Damascus lay about 40 miles (nearly 64½ km) to the north-east, but again access was rendered difficult by the Hermon mountain range. The implication of the final sentence of verse 7 is that the inhabitants of Laish had no allies who would come quickly and easily to their aid if they were attacked. This is made explicit in verse 28, below. *Aramaeans* is a conjectured reading, but a very likely one. There is little difference between the Hebrew words for 'Aramaeans' (*'aram*) and 'men' (*'adam*). The end of the previous sentence, however, is more difficult. The N.E.B. version implies a rather negative judgement on the institution of kingship, one which

is at variance with the recurring motif of these two appendices
to the book (17: 6; 18: 1; 19: 1; 21: 25). There the implication
is that kingship is a desirable institution which would put
an end to the state of anarchy in the country. The more usual
rendering of the phrase is along the lines of the Revised
Standard Version 'lacking nothing that is in the earth, and
possessing wealth'; cp. the closing words of verse 10.

8–10. The report of the reconnaissance party is in very
favourable terms. *a wide expanse of open country* lies at the
disposal of the land-hungry Danites, *a place where there is no
lack of anything on earth*. They encourage their fellows to *take
possession of the land* without delay. *

THE DANITES TAKE MICAH'S PRIEST AND IDOL

And so six hundred armed men from the clan of the 11
Danites set out from Zorah and Eshtaol. They went up 12
country and encamped in Kiriath-jearim in Judah: this
is why that place to this day is called Mahaneh-dan;[a] it
lies west of Kiriath-jearim. From there they passed on to 13
the hill-country of Ephraim and came to Micah's house.
The five men who had been to explore the country round 14
Laish spoke up and said to their kinsmen, 'Do you know
that in one of these houses there are now an ephod and
teraphim, an idol and an image? Now consider what
you had best do.' So they turned aside to[b] Micah's house 15
and greeted him. The six hundred armed Danites took 16
their stand at the entrance of the gate, and the five men 17
who had gone to explore the country went indoors to take
the idol and the image, ephod and teraphim, while the
priest was standing at the entrance with the six hundred

[a] *That is* the Camp of Dan.
[b] *So Luc. Sept.; Heb. adds* the house of the young Levite.

18 armed men. The five men entered Micah's house and
took the idol and the image, ephod and teraphim.[a] The
19 priest asked them what they were doing, but they said
to him, 'Be quiet; not a word. Come with us and be our
priest and father. Which is better, to be priest in the
household of one man or to be priest to a whole tribe
20 and clan in Israel?' This pleased the priest; so he took the
ephod and teraphim, the idol and the image,[b] and joined
21 the company. They turned and went off, putting the
22 dependants, the herds, and the valuables in front. The
Danites had gone some distance from Micah's house,
when his neighbours were called out in pursuit and
23 caught up with them. They shouted after them, and the
Danites turned round and said to Micah, 'What is the
24 matter with you? Why have you come after us?' He said,
'You have taken my gods which I made for myself, you
have taken the priest, and you have gone off and left me
nothing. How dare you say, "What is the matter with
25 you?"' The Danites said to him, 'Do not shout at us.
We are desperate men and if we fall upon you it will be
26 the death of yourself and your family.' With that the
Danites went on their way and Micah, seeing that they
were too strong for him, turned and went home.

✳ 11. *six hundred armed men*: see on 18: 2.

12. *Kiriath-jearim* (literally 'village of the woods') lay about
7 miles (11 km) north-west of Jerusalem, further into the hills
than, that is *up country* from, Zorah and Eshtaol. Kiriath-
jearim was where the Ark was installed when it was recovered
from the Philistines who had captured it; 1 Sam. 6: 21 – 7: 2.

[a] *Prob. rdg.; Heb.* the idol of the ephod, and teraphim and image.
[b] and the image: *so Sept.; Heb. om.*

We are here provided with an explanation of the place-name *Mahaneh-dan*; cp. on 13: 24f. for the problems of location and for a more likely explanation of the name. The fact that we are given an explanation for the name of a comparatively obscure Judaean place might lend support to the suggestion that the story of the founding of the Danite sanctuary is told from an anti-Danite, indeed Judaean, point of view.

15-17. As verse 15 stands in the N.E.B. translation, it is *Micah* who is *greeted* by the Danites. However, as can be seen from the N.E.B. footnote, the Hebrew text is fuller, and it suggests, more plausibly, that it was 'the young Levite' whose attention was thus diverted while the *five men...went indoors* to take possession of the various cult objects. The words *Micah's house* have been added as a gloss by some editor of the text to let us understand that 'the house of the young Levite' was in reality the house of his employer. The fact that it was the Levite who was engaged in what is, in the East, the fairly elaborate ritual of greeting, is brought out explicitly by the closing words of verse 17, *while the priest was standing at the entrance with the six hundred armed men*.

18. The N.E.B. footnote indicates that the text is not entirely clear. In every other place where the words *idol* and *image* occur in these two chapters they occur together and probably refer, as we have already noted (cp. on 17: 4), to a single cult object, a carved wooden image overlaid with metal. Only in verse 18 are they separated from each other, and it seems obvious that whoever wrote verse 18 thought of them as two separate objects. The Hebrew of verse 18 could be more accurately rendered 'the idol and the ephod, the teraphim and the image'. There is no real justification for rearranging the word order as the N.E.B. has done.

19. The Danites' invitation to the Levite is in terms similar to those used by Micah, *be our priest and father* (cp. 17: 10).

20. *This pleased the priest*: the prospect of functioning on a much grander scale is obviously more attractive to the Levite than remaining in Micah's establishment, so he connives at

the theft of the cult objects. Again, the footnote indicates that the N.E.B. translators have altered the Hebrew text, though this time with the support of the Septuagint. The Hebrew text refers simply to *the idol*, again a single cult object; this is surely correct and is in line with verses 30-1 below.

21. The military strategy described in this verse was no doubt to protect *the dependants...and the valuables* from attack from the rear in case of eventual pursuit.

22-6. Micah, with the help of *his neighbours*, attempts to recover his stolen cult objects. But the determination (*We are desperate men*) and superior strength (*they were too strong for him*) of the Danites discourage him, and he abandons the attempt. ✶

THE DANITES SETTLE IN LAISH

27 Thus they carried off the priest and the things Micah had made for himself, and attacked Laish, whose people were quiet and carefree. They put them to the sword and
28 set fire to their city. There was no one to save them, for the city was a long way from Sidon and they had no contact with the Aramaeans,[a] although the city was in the vale near Beth-rehob. They rebuilt the city and settled
29 in it, naming it Dan after the name of their forefather Dan,
30 a son of Israel; but its original name was Laish. The Danites set up the idol, and Jonathan son of Gershom, son of Moses,[b] and his sons were priests to the tribe of
31 Dan until the people went into exile. (They set up for themselves the idol which Micah had made, and it was there as long as the house of God was at Shiloh.)

✶ 27f. The emphasis in the first part of verse 27 is on the fact that the stolen cult objects were *made* by human hands.

[a] *Prob. rdg., cp. verse 7; Heb.* men.
[b] *So some MSS.; others* Manasseh (*altered from* Moses).

On Laish and the character of its inhabitants see above on
verse 7. The fact that the *people were quiet and carefree* and that
There was no one to save them brings out the brutality of the
Danite attack on this unsuspecting community. This is the
very antithesis of the heroic deeds of the earlier figures in the
book of Judges. On the geographical position of Laish as
described in verse 28 see also on verse 7. This time the significance of their isolated position is made explicit (*for*). *in the
vale near Beth-rehob*: in the time of David, Beth-rehob was
inhabited by Aramaeans (2 Sam. 10: 6), and it is probable
that this is also implied by the present passage. The *vale* is
the valley lying between the two Lebanon mountain ranges,
but the precise location in it of Beth-rehob is unknown. In
spite, then, of the close proximity of the Aramaeans of Beth-
rehob, Laish was still unable to resist the Danite onslaught.

29. *their forefather Dan, a son of Israel*: the reference is to
the genealogical scheme in which the supposed ancestors of
the Israelite tribes are presented as the sons of the same father,
Jacob/Israel. The birth and naming of Dan are recorded in
Gen. 30: 5–6.

30. *the idol*: there is no reference here to the ephod and the
teraphim. Also, what has appeared, in the N.E.B. translation
at least, as two objects ('an idol and an image'), now appears
only as one. But see the notes on 17: 4 and 18: 18. *Jonathan
son of Gershom*: here for the first time in the narrative the
name of the priest is given. It is possible that part of his
name occurs in 17: 7, though the text there is uncertain.
son of Moses: Gershom was the name of Moses' eldest son
(Exod. 2: 22; 18: 3f.). There is too long a time-gap for the
individual referred to here to have been the actual grandson
of Moses. What the passage is claiming is that the Danite
priesthood was of Mosaic origin through the line of Moses'
eldest son. As the N.E.B. footnote states, in the bulk of the
Hebrew manuscript tradition the name of Moses has been
deliberately changed to that of Manasseh. Jewish scholars
clearly felt that it was blasphemous to attribute to Moses a

grandson who was the priest of an idolatrous cult. The Manasseh referred to is not the ancestor of the tribe which bears that name but the king of Judah whose name was a byword for idolatrous worship; cp. 2 Kings 21: 1–9. The difference between the names Moses and Manasseh in Hebrew script is only the letter *n*. We know that the alteration of names has been deliberate in this instance since the scribes have written the *n* at a higher level than the rest of the letters (m^nsh).

until the people went into exile: the reference here would seem to be to the deportation of the bulk of the population of the northern kingdom of Israel in 734 B.C. or else to the final end of Israel in 722 B.C. One or other of these two dates is suggested as the terminal point of the Danite priesthood.

31. Verse 31, however, suggests a different terminal point, though this time what seems to be being said is that *the idol* did not survive as long as the priesthood. Shiloh probably lay about 12 miles (19 km) south-east of Shechem, in Ephraimite territory. For a time it housed the Ark; see Josh. 18: 1, though the reference there to Shiloh may not be original. It was originally thought that Shiloh was destroyed following the battle described in 1 Sam. 4, but recent excavations have suggested a much later destruction, possibly by the Babylonians in the time of Jeremiah (cp. Jer. 7: 12–15; 26: 6). It is difficult to know how to relate these two time references in verses 30 and 31. Are we dealing with two different traditions concerning the end of the sanctuary at Dan, or have two sources been put side by side with no attempt at harmonization? It has been suggested that both refer to the same event and that 'Shiloh' is a deliberate alteration of 'Laish'. It is not clear, however, why such an alteration should have been made. ✶

THE OUTRAGE AT GIBEAH

✶ The second of these two appendices to the book of Judges consists of the final three chapters of the book, 19–21. It tells how the Benjamites of Gibeah commit a terrible breach of hospitality, how they are punished for such an act and how attempts are nevertheless made to ensure their survival as an Israelite tribe. The narrative itself, however, seems to have a complex history. There are a number of fairly obvious doublets. For example, there seem to be two accounts of the defeat of the Benjamites and the conquest of Gibeah, one in 20: 30–6*a*, the other in 20: 36*b*–46. Again there are two ways in which wives are provided for the Benjamite survivors; one tradition suggests that these came from Jabesh-gilead (21: 7–14), another suggests that they came from Shiloh (21: 15–23). It is possible to carry through a division of the narrative into two separate sources, especially in chs. 20–1, and to suggest that one was probably handed down at Mizpah and the other at Bethel. A number of elements in the narrative are clearly editorial attempts to fuse the two narratives together. It is not so easy to think of two narratives in connection with ch. 19, but here there are clear links with the story of the outrage at Sodom in Gen. 19 as well as lesser links with part of the narrative of 1 Sam. 11.

The narrative in these three chapters is presented as an action on the part of 'all Israel' against the Benjamites, and this presupposes the existence of a tribal organization in Israel of a fairly developed kind. We have noted, however, that in the rest of the book this all-Israel stamp has been given to the various stories by the deuteronomistic editor. Generally speaking, the stories involved only one or two tribes. It may be that here, too, the idea that all Israel waged war against Benjamin has been imposed on the narrative at a later stage in its transmission. In that case, possibly only the Benjamites on the one hand and the Ephraimites on the other were involved in this incident. It has even been suggested that the historical kernel from which this narrative grew was the successful attempt on the part of some elements in Ephraim to form themselves into a separate political entity. In this way, so the suggestion goes, the tribe of Benjamin came into being. This movement for political independence was resisted by the Ephraimites, and it is that conflict between Ephraimites and emergent Benjamites which is reflected in the present narrative. If the real historical germ of these chapters is the origin of the Benjamites, then, like the first appendix, these chapters refer to a time early in the period of the judges. *

THE LEVITE AND HIS CONCUBINE

19 In those days when no king ruled in Israel, a Levite was living in the heart of the hill-country of Ephraim. He had taken himself a concubine from Bethlehem in Judah. 2 In a fit of anger she had left him and had gone to her father's house in Bethlehem in Judah. When she had 3 been there four months, her husband set out after her with his servant and two asses to appeal to her and bring her back. She brought him in to the house of her father, 4 who welcomed him when he saw him. His father-in-law, the girl's father, pressed him and he stayed with him three days, and they were well entertained during their visit. 5 On the fourth day, they rose early in the morning, and he prepared to leave, but the girl's father said to his son-in-law, 'Have something to eat first, before you go.' 6 So the two of them sat down and ate and drank together. The girl's father said to the man, 'Why not spend the 7 night and enjoy yourself?' When he rose to go, his father-in-law urged him to stay, and again he stayed for 8 the night. He rose early in the morning on the fifth day to depart, but the girl's father said, 'Have something to eat first.' So they lingered till late afternoon, eating and 9 drinking*a* together. Then the man stood up to go with his concubine and servant, but his father-in-law said, 'See

[a] and drinking: *so some MSS. of Sept.; Heb. om.*

how the day wears on towards sunset.[a] Spend the night
here and enjoy yourself, and then rise early tomorrow
and set out for home.' But the man would not stay the 10
night; he rose and left. He had reached a point opposite
Jebus, that is Jerusalem, with his two laden asses and his
concubine, and when they were close to Jebus, the weather 11
grew wild and stormy, and the young man said to his
master, 'Come now, let us turn into this Jebusite town
and spend the night there.' But his master said to him, 12
'No, not into a strange town where the people are not
Israelites; let us go on to Gibeah. Come, we will go and 13
find some other place, and spend the night in Gibeah or
Ramah.' So they went on until sunset overtook them; 14
they were then near Gibeah which belongs to Benjamin.
They turned in to spend the night there, and went and 15
sat down in the open street of the town; but nobody
took them into his house for the night.

⁂ 1. The expression *In those days* refers not to the period of
the Danite migration to the north, but to the period of the
judges generally. Here again the absence of a central mon-
archical system is used to explain the generally anarchic state
of the country. The fuller form of this note appears at the end
of the appendix in 21: 25. As in chs. 17-18, *a Levite* figures in
this narrative. Here, however, the reference is not to the kind
of person he is (i.e. a priest) but to his racial origins. This also
explains how he is regarded as a 'resident alien' (N.E.B. *was
living*) in Ephraimite territory. *the heart*: more literally, 'the
furthermost parts', possibly the most northerly part of the
Ephraimite tribal area. The fact that the Levite has *a concubine*
would suggest that he is a man of considerable wealth and
position. A concubine had a legal marital status, as is shown

[a] *So Sept.; Heb. adds* Spend the night: behold the camping of the day.

by the fact that the man is referred to as 'her husband' (verse 3). In addition, the concubine's father is called the Levite's 'father-in-law' (verse 4) while the Levite is referred to as 'his son-in-law' (verse 5).

2. *In a fit of anger*: the reason for her departure seems to have been some passing quarrel which was fairly easily resolved. The fact that the husband goes after her to bring her back suggests that he might have been in the wrong. He leaves a considerable time to elapse (*four months*) before making an attempt at reconciliation. This particular time-span may simply be a round figure referring to a considerable length of time. It occurs again in 20: 47.

4f. The fact that the word *father-in-law* is defined by the following phrase (*the girl's father*) has been taken as an indication of the fusion of two independent sources, but it is more likely that the latter is a necessary definition of the former which could designate any male relative of the wife. *three days* would be the normal length of a visit of this kind. The reckoning is inclusive: the first day is the day of arrival; the second and third days are devoted to the purpose of the visit; *the fourth day* is the day of departure. The delay in departure is partly indicative of the harmonious relations which exist between the parties and is partly also, no doubt, a literary device to explain why, when they did eventually leave, they were able to reach only Gibeah, about 8 miles (nearly 13 km) north of Bethlehem, by nightfall. The lavish hospitality of his father-in-law is in sharp contrast to the churlish treatment which he receives at Gibeah.

8f. In these two verses three different expressions are used to indicate different points of time between noon and nightfall. The second and third of them have been regarded as variants. In agreement with this view, the N.E.B. has relegated the third one, the Hebrew of which is unusual, to a footnote.

10. *a point opposite Jebus, that is Jerusalem*: the main road north does not pass through Jerusalem, but a mile or so (about 1½ km) to the west. The present passage seems to

suggest that Jebus was the older, pre-Davidic name of Jerusalem. The name Jerusalem, however, occurs in texts from as early as the nineteenth century B.C., and it is probable that Jebus is a name artificially constructed from the name of the inhabitants of Jerusalem, 'Jebusites'. There is another theory, namely that Jebus was the name of an independent village slightly to the north of Jerusalem; for a discussion of this theory see the commentary on *Joshua* in this series, pp. 121, 128 and 144. The Joshua passages (15: 8; 18: 16, 28) all refer to Jerusalem as 'the Jebusite(s)'. The N.E.B. has followed the Septuagint in the third of these and has translated 'Jebus'. Only otherwise in 1 Chron. 11: 4f. is the name 'Jebus' used of Jerusalem. This is the first of a number of affinities between Judg. 19–21 and the late literature of the Old Testament.

11. *the weather grew wild and stormy*: the Hebrew text is obscure at this point, but the N.E.B. is a not unlikely rendering of it. Most commentators emend it and produce a translation along the lines of the Revised Standard Version 'the day was far spent'. The point would then be that it would have been sensible to stop there for the night since it was now almost sunset.

12f. The irony of the master's objection is that in the Israelite town where he expects to be treated hospitably he is subjected to the most indecent outrage. Gibeah lay about 3 miles (nearly 5 km) north of Jerusalem and Ramah just over 2 miles (3 km) further north still. Gibeah means 'hill' and Ramah 'height'; both lay in the hills just to the east of the main road north.

14. *until sunset overtook them*: it was important at this stage to find lodging for the night at once, since the city gates would be closed at sunset, and total darkness would follow very soon. *which belongs to Benjamin*: the Gibeah referred to in this narrative is usually defined in some way such as this, possibly in order to distinguish it from Gibeah in Judah which lay south-east of Hebron. Since it was Saul's home town, it is sometimes called 'Gibeah of Saul' (e.g. 1 Sam. 11: 4). The designation here that it *belongs to Benjamin* is, of course,

necessary for the ensuing story. The action of the inhabitants of Gibeah brings the punishment on the whole tribe of Benjamin.

15. *in the open street of the town*: towns in ancient Israel did not usually have wide streets. The 'open place' was usually in the town gate, and it was there that business, both legal and commercial, was transacted. A typical city gate with its 'open place' can be seen in the reconstruction of the city of Lachish in *Old Testament Illustrations* in this series, p. 81. This is probably what is referred to in the present passage. It was 'in the gateway of the city' that Lot was sitting when he met the two angels who came to Sodom and offered them hospitality (Gen. 19: 1-2). This is the first of a number of very close parallels between Gen. 19 and Judg. 19. The closing words of verse 15 indicate the attitude of the inhabitants of Gibeah to strangers. This attitude is worked out in the specific incident described in the next section of the narrative.   ✶

HOSPITALITY IN GIBEAH

16 Meanwhile an old man was coming home in the evening from his work in the fields. He was from the hill-country of Ephraim, but he lived in Gibeah, where the people 17 were Benjamites. He looked up, saw the traveller in the open street of the town, and asked him where he was 18 going and where he came from. He answered, 'We are travelling from Bethlehem in Judah to the heart of the hill-country of Ephraim. I come from there; I have been to Bethlehem in Judah and I am going home,[a] but nobody 19 has taken me into his house. I have straw and provender for the asses, food and wine for myself, the girl, and the 20 young man; we have all we need, sir.' The old man said, 'You are welcome, I will supply all your wants; you

[a] home: *so Sept.; Heb.* to the house of the LORD.

must not spend the night in the street.' So he took him 21
inside and provided fodder for the asses; they washed
their feet, and ate and drank. While they were enjoying 22
themselves, some of the worst scoundrels in the town
surrounded the house, hurling themselves against the
door and shouting to the old man who owned the house,
'Bring out the man who has gone into your house, for us
to have intercourse with him.' The owner of the house 23
went outside to them and said, 'No, my friends, do nothing
so wicked. This man is my guest; do not commit this
outrage. Here is my daughter, a virgin;*a* let me bring 24
her*b* out to you. Rape her*b* and do to her*b* what you please;
but you shall not commit such an outrage against this
man.' But the men refused to listen to him, so the Levite 25
took hold of his concubine and thrust her outside for
them. They assaulted her and abused her all night till the
morning, and when dawn broke, they let her go. The 26
girl came at daybreak and fell down at the entrance of
the man's house where her master was, and lay there until
it was light. Her master rose in the morning and opened 27
the door of the house to set out on his journey, and there
was his concubine lying at the door with her hands on the
threshold. He said to her, 'Get up and let us be off'; 28
but there was no answer. So he lifted her on to his ass and
set off for home. When he arrived there, he picked up a 29
knife, and he took hold of his concubine and cut her up
limb by limb into twelve pieces; and he sent them
through the length and breadth of Israel. He told the 30
men he sent with them to say to every Israelite, 'Has

[a] *Prob. rdg.; Heb. adds* and his concubine.
[b] *Prob. rdg.; Heb.* them.

the like of this happened or been seen[a] from the time the
Israelites came up from Egypt till today? Consider this
among yourselves and speak your minds.' So everyone
who saw them said, 'No such thing has ever happened
or been seen before.'

✱ 16. The *old man* is an Ephraimite but he lives in Benjamite
Gibeah. He is, therefore, technically a 'resident alien'; this
was the status of Lot in Sodom (cp. Gen. 19: 9).

17. If the travellers were waiting in the town gate, then
the old man would naturally encounter them as he entered
the town on his way home from the fields.

18. On the expression *the heart of the hill-country of Ephraim*
see above on verse 1. *I am going home*: the presumed Hebrew
original was 'my home'. The possessive adjective 'my' in
English is represented by a *y* in Hebrew added to the end of
the word. At some stage in the transmission of the Hebrew
text this *y* was misunderstood as an abbreviation for the divine
name Yahweh, and the text was expanded accordingly:
'I am going to the house of Yahweh.' This no doubt happened
the more easily because the term 'Levite' was thought to
indicate that the man was of the priestly class; see, however,
on verse 1. The sanctuary envisaged was no doubt that at
Bethel, about 8 miles (nearly 13 km) north of Gibeah.

19. The man makes it plain that all he is needing is a roof over
his head; he will not be a burden on whoever takes him in.

20f. The old man insists that he will provide full hospitality.
Anything less would have been a reflection on his generosity.
The remarkable generosity of this 'resident alien' is in marked
contrast to the total lack of hospitality on the part of the
local inhabitants. *they washed their feet*: this detail is not
mentioned in Gen. 19, but it does feature in the previous
chapter in the story of Abraham's reception of the three men
at Mamre (Gen. 18: 4).

[a] He told...been seen: *prob. rdg., cp. Sept.; Heb. om.*

22. *some of the worst scoundrels in the town*: here only part of the populace is involved in the incident. Gen. 19: 4 indicates that all the male inhabitants of Sodom were involved there. *hurling themselves against the door*: a similar detail in the Lot story, 'pressed close to smash in the door' (Gen. 19: 9), is not mentioned until after Lot has gone outside to attempt to appease the Sodomites. *to have intercourse with him*: this demand, too, is a feature of the Lot story, Gen. 19: 5.

23. Compliance with the request of the men of Gibeah would have been a terrible breach of the laws of hospitality.

24f. The Hebrew text introduces the man's concubine already in verse 24, but the context suggests that the provision of the concubine happened only when an earlier offer had been rejected. The initial offer of the host's *daughter, a virgin* is paralleled by Lot's offer of his 'two daughters, both virgins' (Gen. 19: 8). It may indicate two originally separate traditions that the host's virgin daughter is offered on the one hand and the Levite's *concubine* on the other. If so, these have been skilfully fused by a later editor by the device of allowing the first offer to be rejected. Again, if we are dealing with two separate traditions, then only one of them is paralleled in Gen. 19. The refusal of Lot's virgin daughters ends in disaster for the Sodomites. Here, the acceptance of the Levite's concubine as an acceptable substitute for the stranger leads the story along a different path towards a different conclusion. The actions described in verses 24–5 seem highly offensive to us, but there is no hint of condemnation in the way in which the story is told.

27. *with her hands on the threshold*: obviously a final, desperate attempt on the part of the dying woman to reach safety.

28. Again, there is no condemnation of the apparent brutality of the man's attitude. Medieval Jewish commentators tried to excuse the Levite's apparent harshness by saying

that he thought she was only asleep. *but there was no answer*: it is a sign of the amazing reticence of the narrative that nowhere does it say that the woman was dead.

29. The action described in this verse is paralleled by that taken by Saul to summon the Israelites to war against the Ammonites in 1 Sam. 11: 7. In the incident in 1 Samuel the act is explained; the same fate of being cut up will befall the cattle of all who fail to obey the summons to battle. Here, the action is clearly intended to arouse the horror and indignation of all against those who had perpetrated such an outrage. *twelve pieces*: the number is obviously suggested by the idea that there were twelve Israelite tribes. It is, however, doubtful whether such a concept corresponded to any kind of reality at this period. The tradition here may have been influenced by the tradition of Saul's action in the Samuel story.

30. The Hebrew text (see N.E.B. footnote) contains no message from the Levite to the Israelites, but the N.E.B. reproduces the longer Septuagint text which may well be correct.

The possibility has already been suggested that Judg. 19 is a composite narrative (see especially on verses 24f.). It is always difficult in such cases to say where the priority lies. It would seem, however, that in this case Judg. 19 is a skilful fusion of two separate traditions, one of which has been influenced by the narrative of Gen. 19, the other of which has borrowed at least one element (verse 29) from 1 Sam. 11. The use of Jebus as a supposedly archaic name for Jerusalem (verse 10) may well be the sign of a late editor. It is probable, then, that these two independent narratives, each influenced to a greater or lesser extent by earlier written narratives, have been fused together at a fairly late stage in Israelite literary history. We shall see in the next two chapters further evidence of the fusion of sources and of late editorial activity. As was the case in chs. 17–18, ch. 19 here serves primarily as the prologue to the main narrative of chs. 20–1, the defeat and survival of the tribe of Benjamin. ⁎

VENGEANCE ON BENJAMIN

All the Israelites, the whole community from Dan to **20**
Beersheba and out of Gilead also, left their homes as one
man and assembled before the LORD at Mizpah. The 2
leaders of the people and*ᵃ* all the tribes of Israel presented
themselves in the general assembly of the people of God,
four hundred thousand foot-soldiers armed with swords;
and the Benjamites heard that the Israelites had gone up 3
to Mizpah. The Israelites asked how this wicked thing
had come about, and the Levite, to whom the murdered 4
woman belonged, answered, 'I and my concubine came
to Gibeah in Benjamin to spend the night there. The 5
citizens of Gibeah rose against me that night and surrounded the house where I was, intending to kill me; and
they raped my concubine and she died. I took her and 6
cut her in pieces, and sent them through the length and
breadth of Israel, because of the filthy outrage they had
committed in Israel. Now it is for you, the whole of Israel, 7
to say here and now what you think ought to be done.'
All the people rose to their feet as one man and said, 8
'Not one of us shall go back to his tent, not one shall
return home. This is what we will now do to Gibeah. 9
We will draw lots for the attack:*ᵇ* and we will take ten 10
men out of every hundred in all the tribes of Israel, a
hundred out of every thousand, and a thousand out of
every ten thousand, to collect provisions from the people
for those who have taken the field against Gibeah in

[a] and: *so Sept.; Heb. om.*
[b] We will…attack: *so Sept.; Heb.* Against it by lot.

Benjamin to avenge[a] the outrage committed in Israel.'
11   Thus all the Israelites to a man were massed against the
town.

✻ 1f. *All the Israelites*: there are a number of indications that
the 'all-Israel' character of this narrative has been imposed
upon it at a fairly late stage in its development. The expressions
the whole community and *the general assembly* as well as the verb
assembled are all characteristic of late usage after the exile and
ring strangely in a pre-monarchic context. Here again are
indications of late editorial activity. *from Dan to Beersheba*:
this phrase is commonly used to refer to the whole extent ot
Israelite territory from Dan in the north to Beersheba in the
south. It is a particularly common designation of the united
kingdom prior to the death of Solomon. *Gilead*, in this
context, seems to refer to the territory east of the Jordan
occupied by the Israelites. *assembled before the LORD at
Mizpah*: Mizpah is here thought of as an important sanctuary,
a role which it has elsewhere in Israelite history (cp. 1 Sam.
7: 5; 10: 17). The name means 'watch-tower', and several
different places seem to have borne that name. The place
referred to here lay about 4 miles (nearly 6½ km) north-north-
west of Gibeah. *four hundred thousand*: the numbers here and
elsewhere in the narrative are obvious exaggerations and bear
no relationship to reality.

4–7. These verses contain an account by the Levite of events
leading up to the tribal gathering. This résumé of events is
probably editorial. The phrase translated as *the length and
breadth of Israel* is found only otherwise after the exile. The
same is true of one of the two nouns which have been rendered by the N.E.B. as *filthy outrage*. The expression *intending
to kill me* does not correspond to the facts as we know them
from ch. 19. The phrase could betray a variant tradition or
represent a summary description of the dangerous situation in

[a] who have...to avenge: *prob. rdg., cp. Sept.; Heb.* to do when they
come to Geba in Benjamin.

which the Levite had found himself. But it could equally well represent a deliberate toning-down of the rather crude description of events in ch. 19 by a later editor for a more refined public.

8f. *go back to his tent*: the expression is an anachronism, a remnant of speech from Israel's nomadic origins. It corresponds to *return home* in the second part of the sentence. *We will draw lots for the attack*: no immediate designation is made, but cp. verse 18 where the procedure is the seeking of an oracle with the specific designation of Judah. The N.E.B. rendering here is a very probable emendation on the basis of the Septuagint.

10. Ten per cent of the forces are designated to see to the provisioning of the army. *to avenge the outrage*: the decision to seek vengeance is taken on the strength of the Levite's eye-witness account of the events which took place. The Hebrew text is corrupt at this point (see N.E.B. footnote) and has confused Gibeah with Geba. The latter lay about 3 miles (nearly 5 km) to the north-east of Gibeah. The name Geba is a masculine form of the word for 'hill', of which Gibeah is a feminine form; the two names, therefore, mean the same and are easily confused.

11. The Israelites now seem poised for immediate attack. This conflicts with the following section of the narrative where an attempt is made to come to terms with the Benjamites without resorting to hostilities. Again this probably betrays conflicting narrative traditions. ✲

ATTACK ON GIBEAH

The tribes of Israel sent men all through the tribe of 12 Benjamin saying, 'What is this wicked thing which has happened in your midst? Hand over to us those scoundrels 13 in Gibeah, and we will put them to death and purge Israel of this wickedness.' But the Benjamites refused to

14 listen to their fellow-Israelites. They flocked from their
15 cities to Gibeah to go to war with the Israelites, and that
day they mustered out of their cities twenty-six thousand
men armed with swords. There were also seven hundred
16 picked men from Gibeah,^{*a*} left-handed men, who could
17 sling a stone and not miss by a hair's breadth. The Israelites,
without Benjamin, numbered four hundred thousand
18 men armed with swords, every one a fighting man. The
Israelites at once moved on to Bethel, and there they
sought an oracle from God, asking, 'Which of us shall
attack Benjamin first?', and the LORD's answer was,
19 'Judah shall attack first.' So the Israelites set out at dawn
20 and encamped opposite Gibeah. They advanced to do
battle with Benjamin and drew up their forces before the
21 town. The Benjamites made a sally from Gibeah and
left twenty-two thousand of Israel dead on the field that
23^{*b*} day. The Israelites went up to Bethel,^{*c*} lamented before
the LORD until evening and inquired whether they should
again attack their brother Benjamin. The LORD said, 'Yes,
22 attack him.' Then the Israelites took fresh courage and
24 again formed up on the same ground as the first day. So
the second day they advanced against the Benjamites,
25 who sallied out from Gibeah to meet them and laid an-
26 other eighteen thousand armed men low. The Israelites,
the whole people, went back to Bethel, where they sat
before the LORD lamenting and fasting until evening, and
they offered whole-offerings and shared-offerings before
27 the LORD. In those days the Ark of the Covenant of God

[*a*] *So Sept.; Heb. adds* out of all this army there were seven hundred
picked men.   [*b*] *Verses 22 and 23 transposed.*
[*c*] to Bethel: *prob. rdg., cp. verses 18, 26; Heb. om.*

was there, and Phinehas son of Eleazar, son of Aaron, 28
served before the LORD.[a] The Israelites inquired of the
LORD and said, 'Shall we again march out to battle
against Benjamin our brother or shall we desist?' The
LORD answered, 'Attack him: tomorrow I will deliver
him into your hands.' Israel then posted men in ambush 29
all round Gibeah.

✻ 12f. Before hostilities commence, the Israelites make an
attempt to avert full-scale warfare by asking that the Benjamites hand over the actual perpetrators of the outrage for
punishment. The Benjamites, however, give expression to
tribal solidarity by refusing to hand over the guilty.

14–17. The Benjamite muster of troops would more naturally follow directly on verse 3a, and many commentators have
suggested that this was the order in the basic narrative and that
the intervening material is secondary, editorial material. Again,
the numbers of troops (*twenty-six thousand*) are obvious exaggerations. At the end of verse 15 and the beginning of verse 16,
the Hebrew text refers to two lots of *seven hundred picked men*,
one lot *from Gibeah*, the other *left-handed* slingers. It seems
likely that this represents erroneous repetition. The Septuagint
form of the text, reproduced by the N.E.B., is more probable.
Already in Ehud (3: 12–30) we have encountered a 'left-
handed' Benjamite; see note on 3: 15.

18. *Bethel*, like Mizpah, was an important religious centre
about 8 miles (nearly 13 km) north of Gibeah. It has already
featured in 2: 1–5, where the Septuagint, at any rate, suggests
that the place referred to by the otherwise unknown name
Bokim was in fact Bethel. The explanation of the name
(literally 'house of God') is given in Gen. 28: 10–19. Later,
under Jeroboam I, it became a royal and national sanctuary
for the northern kingdom of Israel (1 Kings 12: 25–33).
According to the late note in verses 27–8 below, Bethel was a

[a] *Or* before the Ark.

religious centre at this time because of the location there of the Ark served by a priesthood descended from Aaron. On this occasion, the seeking of oracular guidance on the proper procedure for the beginning of hostilities is exactly parallel to 1: 1–2. It may well be that the reference to the seeking of an oracle here is modelled on that passage and that the present form of chs. 19–21 presupposes the existence of the earlier part of the book with the preface of 1: 1 – 2: 5 already attached to it. This, again, would suggest a late date for the present form of chs. 19–21. It should be noted that the divine oracle is extremely brief and contains no promise of a successful outcome to the attack. This is in contrast to the form of the oracle in 1: 2 ('I hereby deliver the country into his power'). In this context, there is no divine assurance until the third time of asking; see verse 28 and cp. the form at the end of verse 23: 'Yes, attack him.'

19–21. The Israelite attack is launched but proves unsuccessful. The number of Israelite slain again passes the bounds of credibility. It is unthinkable that, had this corresponded to reality, the Benjamites would not have followed up such a success.

22f. The N.E.B. has made the narrative much more logical in placing verse 23 before verse 22. The lamenting at Bethel must have taken place before the oracle was consulted as to the wisdom of re-engaging in battle. The Hebrew text does not contain the place-name *Bethel* at this point, but since the oracle was consulted there on the two other occasions, it is more than likely that they repaired to Bethel after their initial defeat. *lamented before the LORD*: some kind of ritual lamentation is envisaged. The earlier reference to Bethel in 2: 1–5 also thought of the sanctuary as the location of ritual mourning; cp. the place-name 'Bokim' ('weepers') in 2: 1, 5. We have already referred to the brevity of the oracular answer; see on verse 18.

24f. The employment of similar tactics results in a similar defeat.

26. On this occasion *fasting* is also mentioned in addition to the ritual lamentation. In *whole-offerings* the whole beast was consumed upon the altar and thus offered to God. The exact significance of the term rendered *shared-offerings* here is uncertain, but it does seem to lie along the lines suggested by the N.E.B. rendering. Only parts of the sacrificial animal were consumed, the fat parts; the meat was shared between priest and worshippers in some kind of communal meal, the aim of which was presumably to strengthen the link between God and his people.

27f. The N.E.B. has tidied up the Hebrew here. The words *The Israelites inquired of the LORD* actually precede the sentence beginning *In those days the Ark*... Thus, in the Hebrew text, the whole sentence about the Ark and Phinehas is clearly seen to be parenthetical, coming between *LORD* and *and said*. In the narratives about the Ark in the books of Samuel, it is usually referred to simply as 'the Ark' or 'the Ark of the LORD'. It is usually thought of as the symbol of God's presence with the armies of Israel (cp. Num. 10: 35–6). The concept of the Ark as the receptacle for the tablets on which the Ten Commandments were inscribed is a peculiarly deuteronomistic one (cp. Deut. 10: 1–5). It is this concept which is expressed in the phrase *the Ark of the Covenant of God*, and the occurrence of the expression here suggests that this is a late deuteronomistic or post-deuteronomistic addition which was never part of the original narrative. *Phinehas* was Aaron's grandson; cp. Exod. 6: 25. We have already noted in connection with ch. 17 (see especially on verses 5f. and 13) that in the period of the judges the preference for a Levitical priesthood was only beginning to emerge. It was not, however, until the period late after the exile that the question of an Aaronic priesthood became a burning issue. This parenthetical note, then, is yet another sign of late editorial work in these three chapters. *served before the LORD*: the Hebrew text has 'before it (i.e. the Ark)', which could also be understood as 'before him (i.e. God)'. The N.E.B. text and footnote reflect the two possibilities. On this third occasion, the divine oracle is accompanied by a word of promise, assuring the Israelites of victory.

29. *ambush*: a more sophisticated military tactic is suggested here than had been employed hitherto. ✻

THE FINAL ATTACK

30 On the third day the Israelites advanced against the Benjamites and drew up their forces at Gibeah as they
31 had before; and the Benjamites sallied out to meet the army. They were drawn away from the town and began the attack as before by killing a few Israelites, about thirty,[a] on the highways which led across open country, one to
32 Bethel and the other to Gibeah. They thought they were defeating them once again, but the Israelites had planned a retreat to draw them away from the town out on to the
33 highways. Meanwhile the main body of Israelites left their positions and re-formed in Baal-tamar, while those in ambush, ten thousand picked men all told, burst out
34 from their position in the neighbourhood of Gibeah[b] and came in on the east of the town. There was soon heavy fighting; yet the Benjamites did not suspect the disaster
35 that was threatening them. So the LORD put Benjamin to flight before Israel, and on that day the Israelites killed twenty-five thousand one hundred Benjamites, all armed men.

✻ As the narrative of ch. 20 now stands, the third day's fighting is depicted as having taken place in two stages. The final conquest of the town and the defeat of the Benjamites

[a] *Or* about thirty wounded men.
[b] *Prob. rdg., cp. Sept.; Heb.* Geba.

are described in verses 36–48. However, a number of features
in the narrative suggest that verses 30–6a on the one hand and
verses 36b–46 on the other are really alternative accounts of
the same incident. Here the editorial process, instead of fusing
these two accounts together, has laid them side by side and
presented them as if they were successive incidents. It is
possible that the details of this final stratagem have been
influenced by similar details, particularly the pretended flight,
the ambush and the smoke signal, in the story of the capture
of Ai in Josh. 8.

30f. The Israelite ambush mentioned in verse 29 is not, of
course, apparent to the Benjamites. To them the Israelites
seem to be employing the same technique as on their two
previous attacks. Accordingly, the Benjamites react as on
the previous occasions and emerge to slaughter a number of
Israelite troops. On this occasion the number of the Israelite
dead (*about thirty*) is in marked contrast to the numbers found
elsewhere in this narrative and may well reflect more sober
historical reality. *the highways*: just north of Gibeah the road
forked. One road led on northwards to *Bethel*; the other
branched to the north-west towards Gibeon and eventually
the coastal plain. The Hebrew text with *Gibeah* here as the
direction of one branch of the road is surely wrong; 'Gibeon',
about 4 miles (nearly 6½ km) north-west of Gibeah, should be
read instead. A 'highway' was a properly made road, some
kind of raised causeway, as opposed to the usual beaten dust-
track.

32. The Israelite *retreat* is *planned* as a ruse to lure the
Benjamites out into the open country. The latter imagined
that *they were defeating* the Israelites *once again*, but the reality
is soon to prove otherwise.

33. The site of *Baal-tamar* is unknown. It must have been
somewhere in fairly close proximity to Gibeah. *in the neighbourhood of Gibeah*: this is the most likely rendering of a
difficult Hebrew text. It involves reading *Gibeah* in place
of the Hebrew 'Geba'. The Revised Standard Version's

approach ('west of Geba') involves reading a word for 'west' in place of the rather obscure Hebrew word rendered by N.E.B. as *neighbourhood*. Geba lay about 3 miles (nearly 5 km) north-east of Gibeah, and the sense would then be that the ambush was laid in the area between Geba and Gibeah. The N.E.B. is less precise than that, with its vague reference to *the neighbourhood of Gibeah*.

34. In spite of the *heavy fighting*, the Benjamites still seem to be unaware of the impending *disaster*.

35. The Benjamite losses, out of a total force of 26,700 (so verse 15), are 25,100 according to this note. ✷

DEFEAT OF THE BENJAMITES

36 The men of Benjamin now saw that they had been defeated, for all that the Israelites, trusting in the ambush which they had set by Gibeah, had given way before
37 them. The men in ambush made a sudden dash on Gibeah, fell on the town from all sides and put all the inhabitants
38 to the sword. The agreed signal between the Israelites and those in ambush*a* was to be a column of smoke sent
39 up from the town. The Israelites then faced about in the battle; and Benjamin began to cut down the Israelites, killed about thirty of them,*b* in the belief that they were defeating them as they had done in the first encounter.
40 As the column of smoke began to go up from the town, the Benjamites looked back and thought the whole town
41 was going up in flames. When the Israelites faced about, the Benjamites saw that disaster had overtaken them and
42 were seized with panic. They turned and fled before the

[a] *Prob. rdg.; Heb. adds an unintelligible word.*
[b] *to cut...them: or to kill about thirty wounded men among the* Israelites.

Israelites in the direction of the wilderness, but the fighting caught up with them and soon those from the town[a] were among them, cutting them down. They hemmed in the 43 Benjamites, pursuing them without respite,[b] and overtook them at a point to the east of Gibeah. Eighteen 44 thousand of the Benjamites fell, all of them fighting men. The survivors turned and fled into the wilderness towards 45 the Rock of Rimmon. The Israelites picked off the stragglers on the roads, five thousand of them, and chased them until they had cut down and killed two thousand more. Twenty-five thousand armed men of Benjamin 46 fell in battle that day, all fighting men. The six hundred 47 who survived turned and fled into the wilderness as far as the Rock of Rimmon, and there they remained for four months. The Israelites then turned back to deal with 48 the Benjamites, and put to the sword the people in the towns and the cattle, every creature that they found; they also set fire to every town within their reach.

* 36. The first part of verse 36 really rounds off the previous section and is the concluding sentence of the first account of the final Benjamite defeat. The second part of verse 36 again refers to the false retreat of the Israelites with the intention of drawing the Benjamites out of Gibeah; cp. verses 31–2 for the first account of this retreat.

37. The action described in this verse corresponds to that described in verses 33–4.

38f. *The agreed signal* was to let those Israelites who were drawing the Benjamites away from Gibeah know that the ambush party had occupied the town. On seeing the signal, the Israelites *faced about* and launched an attack on the

[a] So *Vulg.*; *Heb.* towns.
[b] without respite: *or* from Nohah.

Benjamites who were pursuing them. The N.E.B. faithfully renders the Hebrew text at the beginning of verse 39 (*The Israelites then faced about in the battle*), but this is a rather strange anticipation of verse 41. It may be that verse 39 should be more closely connected with verse 38 and that the sense is that at the *agreed signal* the Israelites '*should* face about in the battle'. This involves a slight emendation in the Hebrew text. The remainder of verse 39 is parallel to the second part of verse 31.

40f. The combination of the signal from the town and the sudden turning of the supposedly fleeing Israelites brings home to the Benjamites the full force of the predicament in which they find themselves. Only now do the Israelites turn round; only now do the Benjamites become aware of the *disaster*.

42. *in the direction of the wilderness*: this must have been eastwards. The country east of Gibeah was on the other side of the watershed, and the eastern side of the mountain range lay in the rain-shadow. *those from the town*: the ambush party, having taken the town, were then in a position to join in the pursuit of the Benjamites.

43. *without respite*: the N.E.B. text here is closer to the Hebrew text. The Septuagint seems to have read what is, perhaps, a not very clear Hebrew expression, as a place name, 'Nohah'; so the N.E.B. footnote. Nohah is listed as a clan or settlement of Benjamin in 1 Chron. 8: 2, but its location is uncertain.

44–7. According to the first account of the Benjamite defeat, 25,100 Benjamites were killed (verse 35). According to the second, the casualties numbered only *Eighteen thousand* (verse 44). Verse 45 is an editorial attempt to harmonize these two figures by accounting for another 7000 dead. But this brings the total of the second account to only *Twenty-five thousand* (verse 46). By neither reckoning, however, are there *six hundred* survivors (verse 47), since the total Benjamite force was given as 26,700 (verse 15). *the Rock of Rimmon* is probably to be located about 4 miles (nearly 6½ km) east of Bethel,

that is, north-east of Gibeah. *for four months:* there appears to
be no significance in the length of time; but see on 19: 2.
Here it presumably serves as a suitable interlude before the
events of ch. 21.

48. *put to the sword:* the concept of the total annihilation of
an enemy and of the total destruction of all the enemy's
property was part of Israel's idea of a holy war. Israel's enemies
were her God's enemies too. When they were defeated they
had to be totally destroyed; none of the enemy property
could be allowed to contaminate God's people, so it too had
to be destroyed. The technical term for this operation was the
'ban'; enemy and enemy property alike were 'put under the
ban'. An example of what happened to someone who defied
the ban may be found in the story of Achan in Josh. 7. ✲

THE PROBLEM OF BENJAMITE SURVIVAL

In Mizpah the Israelites had bound themselves by oath **21**
that none of them would marry his daughter to a Benjamite. The people now came to Bethel and remained 2
there in God's presence till sunset, raising their voices in
loud lamentation. They said, 'O LORD God of Israel, why 3
has it happened in Israel that one tribe should this day be
lost to Israel?' Next day the people rose early, built an 4
altar there and offered whole-offerings and shared-
offerings. At that the Israelites asked themselves whether 5
among all the tribes of Israel there was anyone who did
not go up to the assembly before the LORD; for under
the terms of the great oath anyone who had not gone up
to the LORD at Mizpah was to be put to death. And the 6
Israelites felt remorse over their brother Benjamin,
because, as they said, 'This day Israel has lost one whole
tribe.' So they asked, 'What shall we do for wives for 7

those who are left? We have sworn to the LORD not to
8a give any of our daughters to them in marriage. Is there
anyone in all the tribes of Israel who did not go up to the
LORD at Mizpah?'

✻ 1. Two facts seem to lie behind this chapter. One is the
connection between Benjamin and Jabesh-gilead. This emerges
in the story of Saul, when Saul saves Jabesh-gilead from the
Ammonites (1 Sam. 11: 1–11) and again when the men of
Jabesh-gilead bury Saul and his sons after the battle of Mount
Gilboa (1 Sam. 31: 11–13). Here it is expressed in terms of
inter-marriage between the Jabesh-gileadites and the Benjamites. The other fact seems to be connected with some kind
of festivities practised at the time of the grape harvest in
Shiloh. These festivities provide the occasion for the kidnap-
ping of the girls of Shiloh by Benjamites. These two traditions
are fitted into this story of the punishment of the Benjamites
and are depicted as two ways whereby the decimated tribe
of Benjamin was able to survive. They are probably variants,
to be associated with the two differing traditions which we
have observed in the two preceding chapters. There is no
earlier reference to the making of an oath in the terms
mentioned here, but it may have been part of the Jabesh-gilead
tradition. Its connection with the Shiloh tradition is less clear;
see below on verse 12.

2f. Again the public *lamentation* takes place at Bethel (see
above on 20: 22f.). The cause of the lamentation on this
occasion is the loss of one tribe, Benjamin, to Israel.

4. *built an altar there*: it is not clear why this was necessary.
Earlier in the narrative, the Israelites had already offered these
same offerings at Bethel, of necessity on an altar. This note
may be due to the fact that perhaps some specific altar at
Bethel was particularly associated with this incident. On
whole-offerings and *shared-offerings* see on 20: 26.

5. The specific purpose of the assembly on this occasion is

now said to be the punishment of those who did not rally to
the call to wage a war of revenge on Benjamin. The first part
of the verse is really asking, 'Is there anyone exempt from the
oath who could, therefore, provide wives for the Benjamites?'
The second part of the verse provides the explanation for the
massacre inflicted on the inhabitants of Jabesh-gilead. They
are punishable by death for having failed to attend the tribal
assembly. The following verses work out the problem specifically in terms of the Benjamite survivors ('those who are
left', verse 7). ✻

WIVES FROM JABESH-GILEAD

Now it happened that no one from Jabesh-gilead had 8*b*
come to the camp for the assembly; so when they held a 9
roll-call of the people, they found that no inhabitant of
Jabesh-gilead was present. Thereupon the community 10
sent off twelve thousand fighting men with orders to go
and put the inhabitants of Jabesh-gilead to the sword,
men, women, and dependants. 'This is what you shall do,' 11
they said: 'put to death every male person, and every
woman who has had intercourse with a man, but spare
any who are virgins.' This they did.[a] Among the inhabi- 12
tants of Jabesh-gilead they found four hundred young
women who were virgins and had not had intercourse
with a man, and they brought them to the camp at Shiloh
in Canaan. Then the whole community sent messengers 13
to the Benjamites at the Rock of Rimmon to parley
with them, and peace was proclaimed. At this the 14
Benjamites came back, and were given those of the women
of Jabesh-gilead who had been spared; but these were
not enough.

[a] but spare…they did: *so Sept.; Heb. om.*

✻ 8f. The question of verse 8a is answered with reference to the inhabitants of *Jabesh-gilead*. The 'gilead' element in the name locates it east of the Jordan. The site of the town Jabesh is uncertain, but it probably lay about 14 miles (22½ km) north of the Jabbok. *the assembly*: again a word characteristic of late writings after the exile; see on 20: 1f.

10. *twelve thousand fighting men*: the number is again unrealistically high.

11. *put to death*: literally 'put under the ban'. On the 'ban' see on 20: 48. The justification for this has already been given in verse 5b. The sparing of the *virgins* is a necessary element for the sequel of the story. The second half of verse 11 is not explicit in the Hebrew text. It is found in the Septuagint and has probably accidentally fallen out of the Hebrew. It is doubtful how much historical credibility can be attached to this aspect of the story. Jabesh-gilead is a flourishing community of sufficient significance to be desired by the Ammonites in the days before Saul became king (1 Sam. 11).

12. *to the camp at Shiloh in Canaan*: it is not clear why Shiloh should be introduced into the narrative at this point. The final section of the chapter is set there, but the very nature of that story assumes that the Israelites are not in fact *at* Shiloh. The vague description of the location of Shiloh as being *in Canaan* is probably intended to suggest that Shiloh was a Canaanite, not an Israelite, settlement. If this were the case, then the inhabitants of Shiloh would clearly not have taken part in the tribal assembly of ch. 20 and, more importantly, would not have bound themselves by the oath referred to in 21: 1. This may well be the real reason why the women of Shiloh feature in the parallel tradition in verses 15–24. It is not, however, the explanation provided by that narrative itself why the Benjamites are able to marry wives from Shiloh. On the more precise location of Shiloh see on verse 19.

13. The Benjamite survivors, 600 of them according to 20: 47, are still at *the Rock of Rimmon*. On this location see on 20: 44–7.

14. *but these were not enough*: this provides the link between the Jabesh-gilead tradition and the Shiloh tradition. According to verse 12, there were 400 virgins found at Jabesh-gilead; this left 200 Benjamites still without wives. The numbers may be late artificial additions in order to explain precisely why more women had to be found. ✻

WIVES FROM SHILOH

The people were still full of remorse over Benjamin 15 because the LORD had made this gap in the tribes of Israel, and the elders of the community said, 'What shall we do 16 for wives for the rest? All the women in Benjamin have been massacred.' They said, 'Heirs there must be for the 17 remnant of Benjamin who have escaped! Then Israel will not see one of its tribes blotted out. We cannot give 18 them our own daughters in marriage because we have sworn that there shall be a curse on the man who gives a wife to a Benjamite.' Then they bethought themselves 19 of the pilgrimage in honour of the LORD, made every year to Shiloh, the place which lies to the north of Bethel, on the east side of the highway from Bethel to Shechem and to the south of Lebonah. They said to the Benjamites, 20 'Go and hide in the vineyards and keep watch. When 21 the girls of Shiloh come out to dance, sally out of the vineyards, and each of you seize one of them for his wife; then make your way home to the land of Benjamin. Then, if their fathers or brothers come and complain 22 to you, say[a] to them, "Let us keep them with your approval, for none of us has captured a wife in battle. Had you offered them to us, the guilt would be yours."'

[a] you, say: *lit.* us, we will say.

23 All this the Benjamites did. They carried off as many wives as they needed, snatching them as they danced; then they went their way and returned to their patrimony,

24 rebuilt their cities and settled in them. The Israelites also dispersed by tribes and families, and every man went back to his own patrimony.

* 15–18. These verses again go over ground covered in the earlier part of the narrative. It is clear from this that we are dealing not with two consecutive situations but with parallel accounts of the same situation. The *remorse* of verse 15 is parallel to the 'lamentation' of verse 2, and the subsequent discussion is recapitulated here. The expression *the rest* in verse 16 seems, from the context, to refer to those who were not accommodated by the women from Jabesh-gilead. The expression *the remnant of Benjamin who have escaped*, however, refers to the 600 survivors at the Rock of Rimmon. The oath referred to in verse 1 is referred to again in verse 18.

19. The idea that the festivities in the vineyards of Shiloh are part of a *pilgrimage in honour of the LORD* is surely a late editorial idea. If this had been a well-known annual pilgrimage it would scarcely have been necessary to give such a precise geographical location for Shiloh. The latter here is not a well-known centre of a long-established annual pilgrimage but a place which is entering Israelite history for the first time. The next part of the Deuteronomistic History is located there (1 Sam. 1–4). Lebonah was about half-way between Bethel and Shechem and lay just to the west of the *highway*. Shiloh lay just to the east of it at a point just south of Lebonah. On Shiloh see also on 18: 31.

21. *the girls of Shiloh come out to dance*: this dancing in the vineyards is most probably some kind of vintage festival celebrated at the end of the agricultural year. Such agricultural festivals were usually of Canaanite origin and were adopted by the Israelites when they entered Canaan and took

up the life of settled farmers. Usually they related these festivals to events in their own sacred history. In the case of the autumn festival, they called it the Feast of Booths and recalled on that occasion how their God had brought them out of Egypt (cp. Lev. 23: 39–43). In this way, these festivals became festivals 'in honour of the LORD' (verse 19). But in this narrative, the Shiloh festival is still primarily agricultural and still Canaanite.

22. This verse envisages that the inhabitants would be guilty if they actually gave their daughters in marriage to the Benjamites. The narrator tries to suggest, however, that since the Benjamites themselves take the girls, the inhabitants of Shiloh are absolved from the curse implicit in the oath (cp. verse 18). This is hardly a very convincing explanation. The real explanation may be that the inhabitants of Shiloh, being Canaanites, had not taken part in the Israelite tribal assembly nor in the oath. See on verse 12. *you, say*: the change in the text is partly based on the Septuagint and partly demanded by the sense.

23f. The Benjamites return home and re-establish themselves in their original territory (*their patrimony*). So, too, do the rest of the Israelites, and life returns to normal. ✵

POSTSCRIPT

In those days there was no king in Israel and every man   25
did what was right in his own eyes.

✵ We have already noted the occurrences of this idea within the larger context of chs. 17–21 of the book of Judges (17: 6; 18: 1; 19: 1). One of the aims of the writer(s) of these two appendices to the book has been to show how the absence of a stable, central government has been one of the causes of the state of anarchy in Israel at this period. This is one view of the period between the settlement of the Israelites in Canaan and the establishment of the monarchy in the person of Saul. The

other view, expressed in the main central section of the book
(3: 6 – 12: 15), was that this period was characterized by a
cycle of apostasy on the part of the Israelites, punishment of
his people by God and the deliverance of his people from that
punishment through the intermediacy of a 'judge'. These
deliverer figures were 'raised up' by God in answer to his
people's cry for help. In this view, history, in spite of the
people's repeated apostasy, is controlled and guided by God.
This postscript to the book of Judges is not, however, one of
pessimism. It is clearly from the hand of a monarchist, and
it looks forward with hope and anticipation to the establishment of the monarchy in Israel. This is where 1 Sam. 1 takes
up the story. The book of Ruth does not stand in the Hebrew
Bible where it stands in ours. It follows Judges in the English
Bible only because it is set 'in the time of the Judges' (Ruth
1: 1). The true sequel to Judges is 1 Samuel, and this was the
order in the Deuteronomistic History. The latter probably
did not originally contain these two appendices in Judg. 17–21,
but 1 Samuel is equally appropriate as a sequel to them too.
The king, like the judge before him, is God's chosen instru-
ment to care for the welfare of his people.

The office of judge never became a permanent feature of
Israelite society. In the long run it did not prove to be an
effective form of government in the changing historical
situations of the time. Something more permanent was
needed, and so the institution of monarchy emerged. It was
an idealistic dream that kingship would prove the solution to
Israel's social and religious ills. The reality was to prove very
different. But the book of Judges ends with this note of hope
for the future. The assurance from the experience of the past
is that God will always hear and respond to his people's cry
for help. Their history in the most recent past has been shaped
and guided by him. The assurance for the future is that this
will continue to prove true. ✳

A NOTE ON FURTHER READING

The only large-scale modern commentary on Judges in English is that by John Gray in the New Century Bible, a volume which covers also the books of Joshua and Ruth (Oliphants, 1967). A much older and fuller commentary which is still of great value is that by C. F. Burney, 2nd ed. (1920; reprinted by the Ktav Publishing House, New York, 1970). For the historical background to the period reference may be made to G. W. Anderson, *The History and Religion of Israel*, New Clarendon Bible, vol. 1 (Oxford University Press, 1966) and, more fully, to Martin Noth, *History of Israel: Biblical History*, 2nd ed. (A. and C. Black, 1960) and John Bright, *A History of Israel*, 2nd ed. (S.C.M. Press, 1972). On the institutions of ancient Israel, the best reference book is that by R. de Vaux, *Ancient Israel: Its Life and Institutions*, 2nd ed. (Darton, Longman and Todd, 1965; paperback 1973). Those who wish to pursue geographical and topographical questions are recommended to consult Y. Aharoni, *The Land of the Bible* (Burns and Oates, 1967) and *The Macmillan Bible Atlas* (The Macmillan Company, 1968).

A recent monograph by A. D. H. Mayes, *Israel in the Period of the Judges*, Studies in Biblical Theology, Second Series, 29 (S.C.M. Press, 1974), is particularly concerned with criticizing the amphictyony theory (see pp. 9–11). A recent German work has just been translated into English: S. Herrmann, *A History of Israel in the Old Testament Period* (S.C.M. Press, 1975).

INDEX

229

INDEX

Ephraim (tribe) 26, 50, 69, 70, 100; territory of 29, 71, 150
Ephraimite hill-country 34, 131, 150, 184, 204
Ephraimite territory 27, 50, 196, 199
Ephraimite tradition 100
Ephraimites: and Benjamites 197, 198; and Gideon 97, 99, 100, 101, 103, 108; and Jephthah 144, 147, 148
Eshtaol 160, 161, 177, 181, 189, 192
Etam, Rock of 169
Euphrates 11, 42
Exodus, book of 40

fertility religion 35, 37, 83, 146, 177

Gaal 122, 124, 125, 126
Gaash, Mount 34
Gad 71, 137
Galilee, Galilean 28, 54, 70, 72
Galud 94
Gaza 81, 152, 167, 174
Geba 209, 215, 216
Gerizim, Mount 118
Gershom 195; see also Ben-gershom
Gezer 27
Gibeah 2, 196-7, 200-4, 208-9, 211, 215-19
Gibeon 215
Gideon 32, 37, 38, 77-111, 131
Gideon story 50, 77-111, 115, 119, 134, 147, 159
Gilboa, Mount 93, 94, 220
Gilead (geographical term) 71, 94, 131, 135, 137, 144, 149, 208
Gilead (tribal name) 69, 137
Gileadites 138, 148; see also Jephthah; Jair
Gilgal 10, 30, 48
Girgashites 41

Habiru 114-15, 138
Hamath 27
Hamor 124-5, 161
Harosheth-of-the-Gentiles 55, 59, 60
Havvoth-jair 131-2
Hazor 52, 54, 57

Heber the Kenite 57, 60, 75
Hebrew: meaning of words/terms 18, 20, 22, 30, 46, 55, 86, 88, 89, 132, 152, 173, 177, 180, 186, 190, 204; more correct translation of 58, 91
Hebrew dialects 148
Hebrew manuscripts 124, 195-6
Hebrew text: alternative rendering of 61, 74, 167; clearly wrong 94, 209; difficulty of 62, 215; emended 116, 124, 125, 150, 172, 194, 201, 212, 215, 222; more literal rendering of 31, 50, 64, 81, 119, 145, 148, 165, 166, 172, 174, 189, 193; original form of 74, 164, 204, 205, 218; probably wrong 29, 51, 150, 166; rearranged 212, 213; uncertain 61, 94, 100, 105, 106, 115, 125, 169, 200, 201, 216, 218
Hebron 18, 21, 22, 24, 57, 174, 201
Helbah 28
Heres, ascent of 105
Heres, Mount 28
Hermon, Mount 190
Heshbon 141, 142
Hittite(s) 26, 27, 40
Hivites 40
Hobab 57
holy war 60, 67, 93, 99, 219
Horeb 65
Huleh, Lake 56, 71
Hurrians 40

Ibzan 110
Iron Age 23
Isaac 31, 146
Ishmaelites 109
Issachar 56, 69, 70, 71, 130, 131

Jabbok 104, 105, 141, 147, 222
Jabesh-gilead 197, 220, 221, 222, 223, 224
Jabin, king of Hazor 52, 54, 55, 57, 60, 61, 76
Jacob 31, 161, 167, 195
Jael 51, 57, 60, 61, 65, 75

231

INDEX

Jair 110, 131-2, 150
Jebel Musa 65
Jebus 201, 206
Jebusite(s) 21, 40, 201
Jephthah 10, 32, 37, 101, 131, 132-50; daughter of 76; followers of 114-15
Jephthah story 2, 6, 32
Jeremiah 84, 196
Jericho 22, 30, 46, 48, 50
Jeroboam I 127, 182, 183, 211
Jerubbaal 77, 78, 88, 89, 93, 110, 111, 113, 119
Jerusalem 21, 26, 28, 40, 115, 155, 192, 200, 201, 206
Jether 106
Jethro/Reuel 58, 106
Jezreel, Plain of 4, 23, 27, 28, 55, 56, 70, 73, 91, 93
Jezreel (town) 94
Joash 77, 83, 88, 89, 110
Jogbehah 105
Jonathan 195
Jordan 48, 91; crossings 100; east of 20, 30, 46, 50, 51, 71, 77, 99, 100, 103, 104, 131, 134, 135, 137, 138, 144, 145, 148, 222; upper reaches of 28; valley 99; west of 20, 46, 50, 51, 79, 104, 134, 141, 144, 148
Joseph 23, 26, 29, 109, 148, 187
Joshua 8, 9, 16, 18, 34, 40, 54
Joshua, book of 1, 5, 8, 9, 14, 18, 27, 34, 40, 227
Josiah 23
Jotham 112, 117, 118, 123, 129
Judaean hill-country 23
Judaean point of view 8, 193
Judah (geographical term) 155, 171, 189, 201
Judah (kingdom) 16, 23, 24, 26, 76
Judah (tribe) 18, 20, 21, 22, 23, 24, 26, 29, 70, 71, 209
Judges, book of 1-15, 32, 35, 36, 39, 149, 151, 155, 165, 181, 182, 196, 212, 225-7
judges: 'major' 2, 6, 9-13, 32, 110, 131; 'minor' 2, 6, 9-13, 32, 51, 110, 129-32, 149-50, 181; period

of 3, 36, 52, 69, 182, 198, 199, 213, 227; role of in ancient Israel 3, 9-13, 36, 37, 44, 226

Kadesh 29, 65
Kamon 131
Karkor 104
Kattath 28
Kedesh 56, 57
Kemosh 134, 140, 142
Kenaz, Kenizzite(s) 18, 42
Kenite(s) 22, 23, 57, 58, 60
Kings, book(s) of 5, 14, 76
kingship 103, 190-1, 226; of Abimelech 78, 111; of Gideon 106-8, 110; in Jotham's fable 112, 117-18
Kiriath-jearim 192
Kiriath-sepher see Debir
Kishon, River 54, 56, 60, 72, 74
Kitron 28

Lab'ayu 114
Lachish 202
Laish 190, 195
Lappidoth 55
Leah 167
Lebanon mountains 190
Lebo-hamath 40
Lebonah 224
Lehi 171, 172, 173
Leshem 190
Levite 181, 187-90, 193, 199-200, 204-5, 208-9
Lot 202, 204, 205
Luz 27

Machir 69, 70
Mahaneh-dan 160, 177, 181, 193
Mamre 204
Manasseh, king of Judah 195-6
Manasseh (tribe) 26, 69, 70, 77, 83, 91, 131, 144, 148
Manoah 156, 158, 159
Mari 11, 12
Merom, waters of 54
Meroz 74, 75, 104
Mesopotamia 26, 42
Micah 183-8, 193, 194